After the Firs

After the First Urban Christians

The Social-Scientific Study of Pauline Christianity Twenty-Five Years Later

Edited by

Todd D. Still

David G. Horrell

t&t clark

Published by T&T Clark International
A Continuum Imprint
The Tower Building, 11 York Road, London SE1 7NX
80 Maiden Lane, Suite 704, New York, NY 10038

www.continuumbooks.com

British Library Cataloguing-in-Publication Data
A catalogue record for this book is available from the British Library

ISBN: 978-0-567-42774-8 (Hardback)
 978-0-567-21967-1 (Paperback)

Typeset by Newgen Imaging Systems Pvt Ltd, Chennai, India
Printed in the United States of America

To our students—past, present, and future

CONTENTS

CONTRIBUTORS

EDWARD ADAMS	Senior Lecturer in New Testament Studies, King's College London, UK
DAVID G. HORRELL	Professor of New Testament Studies, University of Exeter, UK
LOUISE J. LAWRENCE	Lecturer in New Testament Studies, University of Exeter, UK
BRUCE W. LONGENECKER	Professor of Religion (New Testament) and W. W. Melton Chair, Baylor University, Waco, Texas, USA
DALE B. MARTIN	Woolsey Professor of Religious Studies, Yale University, New Haven, Connecticut, USA
WAYNE A. MEEKS	Woolsey Professor of Religious Studies Emeritus, Yale University, New Haven, Connecticut, USA
PETER OAKES	Greenwood Lecturer in New Testament Studies, University of Manchester, UK
TODD D. STILL	Associate Professor of Christian Scriptures (New Testament), George W. Truett Theological Seminary, Baylor University, Waco, Texas, USA

PREFACE

In September 2008 a small group of participants, each of whom had previously prepared and circulated a draft essay, met for a two-day symposium in the city of Durham, UK, prior to the annual British New Testament Conference, which was being held at Durham University. The idea, which originated with Todd Still, was to reassess the contribution of Wayne Meeks's landmark volume, *The First Urban Christians,* twenty-five years after its appearance in 1983. The essays which follow, revised and reworked in the light of our discussion at the symposium, begin by appraising the material presented by Meeks, and then offer a survey of subsequent developments in this field of study, presenting their authors' own arguments as to what our current level of knowledge suggests and where future research might proceed. We hope that this work will serve not only to introduce a new generation of students to Meeks's book but also to provide an outline of current discussion and debate in the various areas addressed in *The First Urban Christians.* This is not an honorific volume, though it will be clear that the authors all find much to appreciate (as well as things to criticize) in Meeks's benchmark work. We are thankful for and indebted to all the contributors for their willingness to participate in this project, and are especially grateful to Wayne Meeks himself, for agreeing to read and respond to the essays.

We would also like to thank most sincerely a number of institutions and individuals who made the project possible: Baylor University, for a research grant which covered the costs of the symposium and of Todd Still's visit to the University of Exeter, where a good deal of the initial editorial work was done; the University of Exeter, for allowing Todd Still to visit the Centre for Biblical Studies, in the Department of Theology, as an Honorary University Fellow during December 2008; Burke Gerstenschlager and the staff of T&T Clark/Continuum New York, for eagerly agreeing to publish the book and for providing a generous stipend to defray travel costs for some participants at the symposium; Brad Arnold, for skillfully preparing the indices; and last, but by no means least, our families, who generously encourage and support our work.

Todd D. Still
Truett Seminary, Baylor University, Waco, Texas

David G. Horrell
Department of Theology and Religion,
University of Exeter, Exeter, England, UK

ABBREVIATIONS

AB	Anchor Bible
AGJU	Arbeiten zur Geschichte des antiken Judentums und des Urchristentums
ANTC	Abingdon New Testament Commentaries
BCHSup	Bulletin de correspondance hellénique Supplement
BK	*Bibel und Kirche*
BNTC	Black's New Testament Commentaries
BJRL	*Bulletin of the John Rylands University Library of Manchester*
CBR	*Currents in Biblical Research*
ConBNT	Coniectanea biblica: New Testament Series
ECC	Early Christianity in Context
ExpT	*Expository Times*
FFNT	Foundation and Facets: New Testament
HTR	*Harvard Theological Review*
HTS	Harvard Theological Studies
Int	*Interpretation*
JAAR	*Journal of the American Academy of Religion*
JBL	*Journal of Biblical Literature*
JRH	*Journal of Religious History*
JSJ	Journal for the Study of Judaism in the Persian, Hellenistic, and Roman Periods
JR	*Journal of Religion*
JTS	*Journal of Theological Studies*
LNTS	Library of New Testament Studies
JRASup	Journal of Roman Archaeology Supplement
JSNT	*Journal for the Study of the New Testament*
JSNTSup	Journal for the Study of the New Testament Supplement Series
NIGTC	New International Greek Testament Commentary
NovT	*Novum Testamentum*
NTOA	Novum Testamentum et Orbis Antiquus
NTS	*New Testament Studies*
RelSRev	*Religious Studies Review*
ResQ	*Restoration Quarterly*
RevExp	*Review and Expositor*

SBL	Society of Biblical Literature
SBLDS	Society of Biblical Literature Dissertation Series
SBLSBS	Society of Biblical Literature Sources for Biblical Study
SBS	Stuttgarter Bibelstudien
SemeiaSt	Semeia Studies
SNTSMS	Society for New Testament Studies Monograph Series
SNTW	Studies in the New Testament and its World
SR	*Studies in Religion*
TS	*Theological Studies*
VC	*Vigiliae christianae*
WUNT	Wissenschaftliche Untersuchungen zum Neuen Testament

INTRODUCTION

David G. Horrell and Todd D. Still

Nineteen-eighty-three was an auspicious year for New Testament studies in general and Pauline studies in particular. In 1983, James Dunn's essay "The New Perspective on Paul," originally given as the T. W. Manson Memorial Lecture in 1982, appeared in the *Bulletin of the John Rylands Library*. This article introduced to the world of Pauline studies a phrase that continues to stand at the storm center of discussion and debate concerning Paul's theology and its relationship to Judaism. In 1983, Elisabeth Schüssler Fiorenza's book *In Memory of Her: A Feminist Reconstruction of Christian Origins* was published, challenging the androcentric presuppositions of much "malestream" scholarship, stimulating a wide range of feminist treatments of early Christian texts and topics and changing for many their view of the participation of women in earliest Christianity, not least in relation to the Pauline material. Also published in 1983, of course, was Wayne Meeks's *The First Urban Christians*, a groundbreaking work on the social world of the churches founded and addressed by Paul.

In none of these cases, however, did 1983 mark the beginning of a new phase of study. Dunn's work on Paul was stimulated by the changed view of first-century Judaism presented in E. P. Sanders's *Paul and Palestinian Judaism*, published in 1977—a massively influential study, still being vigorously discussed and debated (see, e.g., Carson, O'Brien, and Seifrid 2001, 2004). Schüssler Fiorenza's work in many ways marked the consolidation and further development of a feminist approach to the New Testament which had been explored in previous essays, not least by Schüssler Fiorenza herself.[1] Similarly, Meeks's *The First Urban Christians* did not initiate social-scientific study of the Pauline churches, but rather brought to mature and substantial fruition an approach to New Testament study which had been developing, with Meeks's early involvement, since the early 1970s (see the opening of Horrell's essay below).

Meeks's book not only consolidated and synthesized much of the innovative early work on the Pauline communities (such as Theissen's work on the social status of the Corinthian Christians), but it also covered new areas (such as the

---

1 See Fiorenza 1998: 1–7, where Fiorenza describes the origins of feminist theology in meetings convened in the early 1970s and four articles that she herself wrote between 1972 and 1975 (precisely the period in which social-scientific approaches were also developing). For further development of her approach and methods, see Fiorenza 1984, 1992.

study of early Christian rituals) and introduced new proposals and hypotheses (such as the importance of status inconsistency in making Christianity attractive to potential converts). A wide-ranging treatment of various key aspects of the social world of earliest Christianity, it was rapidly recognized as a landmark study which hugely influenced and inspired subsequent studies, as will become clear from the essays below.

In the following decades, however, research and debate have continued and, twenty-five years on, it is timely to reassess the contribution of *The First Urban Christians* and to offer critical and suggestive surveys of developments in the social-scientific study of Pauline Christianity since that time. The following essays engage with various aspects of Meeks's study. With the exception of the initial essay by David Horrell and the response by Wayne Meeks, each of the contributors discusses one of the chapters in *The First Urban Christians*, following the order of Meeks's book. The shape of Meeks's book, then, determines the scope of this volume and the areas of research and debate that are pertinent. As a result, many potentially worthy subjects are not addressed here.

In the first essay, Horrell discusses the methodological stance of Meeks's book, its use of social-scientific resources, and the subsequent developments and debates concerning appropriate methodology (cf. Meeks 1983: 1–8). He argues against Bruce Malina's view that only a particular kind of model-based approach counts as genuinely social-scientific. He does so in part by examining the methods employed in some recent sociological and anthropological studies. In concluding his essay, Horrell sketches some directions for ongoing future development in social-scientific study of the New Testament in light of what he sees as a (necessarily) methodologically broad and increasingly unbounded field of enquiry.

The chapter by Peter Oakes considers "the urban environment of Pauline Christianity" (see Meeks 1983: 9–50). While appreciative of Meeks's work on the subject and its abiding relevance, Oakes maintains that what Meeks does not offer in either physical or social terms is a sustained general description of the urban environment of Pauline congregations. To remedy this perceived shortcoming, Oakes proposes using the well-documented, first-century Roman city of Pompeii as a model. After offering a "thick description" of Pompeii's physical features and social structures, Oakes proceeds to discuss Philippi, Thessalonica, and Corinth against a Pompeian backdrop. By doing so, Oakes helps readers to discover similarities and differences between these cities while sharpening and deepening our knowledge of these intrinsically interesting ancient locales.

The essay authored by Bruce Longenecker coincides with Meeks's chapter on the social level of the Pauline Christians (pp. 51–73). Longenecker commences his chapter by considering Meeks's well-known proposal that not a few Pauline converts were subject to "status inconsistency" prior to joining a Christian group. While finding this hypothesis lacking in full explanatory power, Longenecker is no less critical of scholars who, unlike Meeks, employ binary economic categories (i.e., a few elite versus a massive number of "poor") in their analysis of

Paul's converts. Positively, Longenecker continues his essay by reworking Steven Friesen's economic model of Greco-Roman urbanism and applying it to individuals named by Paul in 1 Corinthians, Romans, and Philemon. Longenecker then considers Paul's "rhetorical construal" of his converts' economic levels, as well as what might have drawn them to and kept them in Pauline fellowships. In conclusion, Longenecker stresses the importance of reference groups for understanding the growth of early Christianity. Since adherence to Christian groups might not have enhanced the social prestige of people at certain economic levels (and might have even put their social prestige in question), groups of Jesus followers must have had significant counter-balancing attractions.

At the outset of his chapter, which relates to chapter 3 in *The First Urban Christians* (pp. 74–110), Edward Adams summarizes Meeks's discussion of four possible comparative models from the first-century environment for the Pauline churches, namely, the household, the voluntary association, the synagogue, and the philosophical or rhetorical school. Adams then carefully and insightfully sifts through subsequent scholarly work relative to these particular groups and organizations. Having done so, he draws attention to Richard Horsley's contention that Paul intended his congregations to serve as alternative societies within the Roman Empire. By way of conclusion, Adams suggests that scholars should make more careful distinctions when comparing "Pauline Christianity" to other ancient groups. Moreover, he maintains that the overlapping nature of these "models" may call into question the "quest" for *the* most appropriate analogue, given the "generic" features of the most telling points of comparison. As an alternative, Adams suggests that future research focus upon group practices rather than social institutions.

Todd Still's essay treats Meeks's chapter on governance (pp. 111–39). After a summary and analysis of this chapter in *The First Urban Christians*, Still notes three particular areas where Pauline scholars have conducted related research since 1983: Paul's use of metaphors to describe relations between and among himself, his coworkers, and his churches; institutionalization within Pauline congregations; and Paul's perception and exercise of authority and power. Thereafter, Still furthers Meeks's work on Pauline church governance by adducing and interpreting relevant texts from Romans, Philippians, Philemon, and 2 Thessalonians. As Still draws his chapter to a close, he posits that Pauline congregations were characterized by: conflict and community; mutuality and authority; structure and spontaneity. Furthermore, he suggests that such dialectical relational dynamics are not unrelated to the paradoxical pairings Paul employs in his letters to explain his ministry and to explicate his theology.

Louise Lawrence begins her essay by outlining Meeks's treatment of ritual, particularly his classification of rituals into major, minor, and unknown and controverted (Meeks 1983: 140–63). She notes some criticisms of this treatment, especially of the separation of the major rituals (baptism and Lord's Supper) from other aspects of the ritual complex of early Christianity, but also emphasizes the importance of Meeks's focus on what rituals *do*, anticipating the recent shift to a practice-based approach to ritual. Lawrence then proceeds to summarize some key developments in the study of ritual, some of which build on the directions outlined in Meeks's study. These are: ethnographic studies of the relationship between social action and literary texts; the study of ritual as formative of Christian morality; the importance of ritual in constructing social memory; and the role of ritual in relation to imperial/colonial powers. Finally, she draws attention to the extent to which early Christian ritual, like ritual in many other cultural contexts, is focused on the boundary between life and death. With its focus on the death and resurrection of Christ, and the believer's ritualized dying, early Christianity, she suggests, de-emphasized the actual event of physical death.

In the final essay engaging with chapters of Meeks's book, Dale Martin considers the correlations Meeks draws between "patterns of belief and patterns of life"—the title of the sixth chapter of *The First Urban Christians* (pp. 164–92)—noting Meeks's caution about implying any causal relation between the two. Using his own work, influenced at the start by Meeks, as an initial example, Martin shows how deeply the attempt to find such correlations between social situations ("patterns of life") and symbolic systems ("patterns of belief") runs. While Martin's work is more informed by critical and Marxist theory than is Meeks's, nonetheless, Martin argues, Meeks's work too employs a certain form of structuralism. The interest is not so much in finding specific parallels or identifying the origins of beliefs or practices but rather in comparing systems of belief and action and analyzing the social function of patterns of belief. Martin then proceeds to show how three different types of work, subsequent to Meeks's volume, also reflect and imply some kind of interest in discovering correlations between patterns of life and patterns of belief. First, there are studies that follow the approach and agenda set out by Meeks; second, there is work by members of the Context Group; and third, there is work by those whose stance is primarily informed by liberation theology or feminism. Despite some criticism of Meeks's search for correlations, notably by Stanley Stowers and Bengt Holmberg, Martin argues that the search for such connections between the social and the symbolic is both widely evident in a range of scholarship and a fruitful and important approach to the understanding of early Christianity.

Finally, Wayne Meeks responds to each of the essays, reflecting on the ways in which our understanding of the topics addressed in *The First Urban Christians* has developed, and indicating where his own views might now be refined, changed, or affirmed. Like the previous contributors, he not only looks back over the changes and developments in the social-scientific study of Pauline Christianity since the publication of that book, but he also indicates some of the future directions in which research may continue to develop. Meeks draws his response to a close by posing some broader questions about the value and purpose of socio-historical research, questions which should provoke all who engage in this kind of study to consider the *raison d'être* of their discipline, and their own view of its importance. Thus the volume concludes, appropriately, with a challenge to continue the kind of inquiries presented in *The First Urban Christians*, and to do so with an eye not only for the *minutiae* of historical detail but also for the wider significance of the task itself.

Chapter 1

WHITHER SOCIAL-SCIENTIFIC APPROACHES TO NEW TESTAMENT INTERPRETATION? REFLECTIONS ON CONTESTED METHODOLOGIES AND THE FUTURE

David G. Horrell

The modern phase of social-scientific criticism, though it has substantial earlier precursors and precedents,[1] began in the early 1970s, with the twin stimuli of Gerd Theissen's singularly innovative and influential essays[2] and the formation of a Society of Biblical Literature group devoted to the study of the social world of early Christianity.[3] Among the group's founding members was Wayne Meeks, who had already begun to draw on perspectives from the sociology of knowledge to develop an interpretation of the Fourth Gospel as a reflection and legitimation of a sectarian community alienated from the world (Meeks 1972). Many innovative works were published in the following years, such that already by 1980 scholars were offering overviews and bibliographical surveys of the state of research in this vibrant area of New Testament studies (e.g., Scroggs 1980; Harrington 1980).

The First Urban Christians, published in 1983, is a landmark study, representing the mature flourishing of this initial period of innovative activity. A wide-ranging and synthetic treatment of various central aspects of the social life of the Pauline congregations, it draws on a variety of sociological and anthropological

---

1   See esp. Hochschild 1999 on the earlier history of socio-historical (*sozialgeschichtliche*) exegesis. Judge 1960b is often cited as an important stimulus for the development of the modern interest in the socio-historical aspects of the Pauline communities. Theissen 1993: 19 n. 23, for example, states that "this little book deserves a place of honor in the history of modern sociological exegesis."
2   The initial cluster of essays was published between 1972 and 1975 and collected in Theissen 1979 (3rd ed., 1988). For English translations of the key works, see Theissen 1982; Theissen 1993.
3   For a fuller outline of the modern emergence of social-scientific approaches to the New Testament, see Horrell 2002: 3–15.

perspectives, as well as works in Roman social history and New Testament studies, to construct a picture of what life was like for those "ordinary" people who joined the Christian movement. The work of Theissen is a notable influence at a number of points, particularly in the chapter on the social level of the Pauline Christians.[4]

In terms of the book's methodological stance, Meeks declares that his approach is that of a social historian (p. 2). The use of social-scientific theory is "suggestive, rather than generative in the manner of the experimental sciences" (p. 5). Rejecting the idea that such an inquiry into the lives of the early Christians might aim "to discover or validate laws about human behavior in general," Meeks describes his approach as "analogous to Clifford Geertz's description of the social anthropologist's task as an ethnographer, a describer of culture. The description is interpretative" (p. 6).

The use of social science in the volume is, as Meeks puts it, "eclectic. I take my theory piecemeal, as needed, where it fits" (p. 6). If there is an overall theoretical orientation, it is that of a "moderate functionalism," where "the sort of questions to be asked about the early Christian movement are those about how it worked" (p. 7). Thus, Meeks draws on a variety of approaches and theories—from Mary Douglas and Victor Turner on ritual, to Seymour Martin Lipset, Gerhard Lenski, and others on status indicators and status inconsistency—where they seem potentially to illuminate the facets of early Christianity under consideration.

Reactions to *The First Urban Christians*, insofar as they relate specifically to its methodological stance,[5] reflect in part an emerging difference between those, like Meeks and Theissen, whose approach was labelled that of a "social historian," and others, notably Bruce Malina, John Elliott, et al., who became known as the "social scientists." Thus Theissen declared himself "deeply impressed" with Meeks's book (Theissen 1985: 113), while Malina and Elliott criticized its lack of consistent theoretical foundation (Malina 1985; Elliott 1985).[6] Elliott, for example, argued that "Meeks's entire enterprise would have gained considerably in methodological clarity and perhaps also cogency if he had identified his theories and their sources, explicated his conceptual models, and clarified his sociological as well as historical and theological premises" (Elliott 1985: 332). This distinction between the so-called social historians and the so-called social scientists—though I shall argue that it is an unhelpful and intellectually unsustainable one—became

---

4 Meeks 1983: 51–73 (repr. in Horrell, ed., 1999b). For discussion of this topic, see Bruce Longenecker's chapter below.

5 I leave aside reactions to the more substantive topics and proposals, which are discussed in the following chapters.

6 See also Stowers 1985 for an extensive engagement, which stresses the need for critical examination of methods and theories used, and criticizes, among other things, the functionalism of Meeks's study, the use of the concept of status inconsistency, and its tendency to find ritual everywhere in the imagery of the texts. For criticisms of functionalism, see also Horrell 1996: 33–38.

embedded in the different Society of Biblical Literature groups that emerged during the 1980s.[7]

Before addressing some of the methodological issues at stake in this distinction, I shall first set the scene by sketching what seem to me key developments in socio-historical and social-scientific approaches to New Testament interpretation since the mid-1980s.[8]

1. Key Developments since the 1980s

First, there has been a continued diversification in the range of approaches used and the spread of topics addressed. Some studies orientated to social issues and topics in the study of earliest Christianity—such as the social status of the leaders of the Pauline communities—while interacting with the work of Theissen, Meeks, and others, have resolutely avoided using theories or models from the social sciences (Clarke 1993; cf. also Winter 2001). Other studies have drawn on social theory, such as the constructionist sociology of knowledge represented by Peter Berger and Thomas Luckmann, to study such phenomena as institutionalization (MacDonald 1988).[9] Some recent studies have begun to focus particularly on the economic dimensions of earliest Christianity (Meggitt 1998b; Friesen 2004), and on the political aspects of early Christianity's existence in the Roman Empire (e.g., Horsley, ed., 1997a, 2000a, 2004b). Some have looked to psychology, and specifically social-psychological approaches to understanding group identity, to analyze the role of early Christian texts in constructing a new sense of identity (Theissen 1987; Esler 1998a, 2003). Perhaps most notable of all is the development of interest in anthropology, a trend captured in a comment by Dale Martin, writing in 1993: "most scholars engaged in social approaches to the New Testament claim to find sociology less and less helpful and anthropology and ethnography more and more interesting" (Martin 1993: 115). This turn to anthropology is especially exemplified in the work of Bruce Malina and the Context Group, to which I will return below. My point here is simply to illustrate, albeit very briefly, the wide range of topics and approaches which use or represent some kind of socio-historical or social-scientific engagement with the New Testament. It would be impossible to establish any kind of common approach, method, or focus to define the field.

My second observation is an extension of the first: many of the themes, approaches, and topics that were innovative in the period prior to *The First Urban Christians* have since become well-established in the mainstream of New

---

7   See further Osiek 1989: 268–74, and Martin 1993: 107–10.

8   I make no pretense to offer a bibliographical survey here. For broader studies and bibliographies, see Elliott 1993; Horrell, ed., 1999a; Blasi, Duhaime, and Turcotte, eds., 2002.

9   MacDonald's study also draws heavily on *The First Urban Christians*.

Testament studies. In 1972 it was novel to talk about John's gospel as representing a sectarian community; now that kind of label would be routinely adopted and discussed.[10] (Ironically, though, as is often the case, just as such designations become widely accepted as "standard," so some start to question whether the terminology is useful or apposite at all: there has been a significant challenge in recent years to the deeply rooted assumption that the Gospels were written for specific local, "sectarian," communities;[11] and, more directly related to Meeks's work, one may also question how cogent it is to speak of "Pauline communities," as if there were Pauline congregations ideologically and physically distinct from other early Christian congregations: see Horrell 2008.) Similar things could be said about the development of an essentially sociological understanding of Paul's arguments about the Jewish Law: James Dunn's influential proposals have made discussions of the social function of boundary markers in defining identity central to the ongoing debate on this long-established topic (Dunn 1983). Ben Witherington's series of socio-rhetorical commentaries exemplifies this integration of social-scientific perspectives into the mainstream, popular voice of the discipline. Both Witherington and Vernon Robbins, independently, it seems, have fused social-scientific and rhetorical approaches and, in Witherington's case, used this fusion as a basis to interpret the whole range of New Testament texts.[12]

In short, to use the famous, now almost clichéd, phrase of Robin Scroggs (Scroggs 1980: 166), to a considerable extent there has indeed been a rejoining of "body and soul," such that in New Testament studies generally there is very frequently the engagement with the kind of social aspects of early Christian life that Meeks found so lacking in the discipline as he entered it (cf. Meeks 1983: ix, 1–2; Meeks 2002: xi–xxviii). This diffusion of concerns and approaches originally associated with the innovative attempts to develop a sociologically informed reading of the New Testament indicates the success of the movement: the kinds of questions Meeks and others had in view, in works such as *The First Urban Christians,* are now established facets of the range of issues central to the discipline. It also illustrates, though, the impossibility of identifying clearly or meaningfully what does and does not "count" as an example of a social-scientific approach to the New Testament.

My third observation, however, runs somewhat counter to the previous two, which have stressed the diversity and integration into the mainstream of broadly social-scientific concerns. I mentioned above the increasing focus on anthropology rather than sociology among those interested in the social dimensions of

10　Also influential on the use of the sect model was an early study by Robin Scroggs (Scroggs 1975; repr. in Horrell, ed., 1999a).

11　Bauckham 1998. For challenges to the "sectarian" reading of John, see Barton 1993; Barton 1998, esp. 189–93.

12　See Robbins 1999a, 1999b; Witherington 1995, the first in a series of socio-rhetorical commentaries that now covers almost the entire New Testament.

earliest Christianity. There is one book which exemplifies this turn to anthropology, and has indeed provided the basis for a specific, model-based method of
social-scientific interpretation: Bruce Malina's *The New Testament World: Insights
from Cultural Anthropology*. First published in 1981, this book "was written in
particular for the student beginning to study the New Testament" (Malina 1981:
iii), lacking the detailed notes and bibliography typical of the scholarly mono-
graph but including, at the end of each chapter, a section with questions and texts
intended to allow the reader to test the proposed model or hypothesis. Despite this
student-focused style, Malina's book was ground-breaking, setting out a series of
models of the pivotal values of ancient Mediterranean culture, which contrasted
sharply with the cultural values of modern Americans.[13] These models depict the
key values of honor and shame, dyadic rather than individual personality, the perception of limited good, distinctive rules of kinship and marriage, and a set of
purity rules to distinguish clean and unclean.[14] The aim of the book was to enable
its readers to appreciate the strangeness and difference of that Mediterranean
cultural context, thus correcting the tendency (on the part of Americans in particular, as the primary audience for the book) to make ethnocentric and anachronistic
assumptions in interpretation.

Malina's book has provided the foundations for an approach to understanding
the New Testament in its cultural context pursued by the Context Group.[15]
Formally begun as such in 1989, but building on long-standing collaboration
between Malina, Elliott, and others, including Jerome Neyrey, John Pilch, and
Richard Rohrbaugh, the Group has met annually since 1990 and its members
have published, individually and collaboratively, a wide range of diverse works.[16]
It is important to stress, however, that, despite the influence of Malina's ground-
breaking work, there is a diversity of method and approach among those who
participate in the Context Group.

---

13   Hochschild takes the book's character as a *Lehrbuch* to indicate that the social-scientific approach
was already institutionalized and accepted in the mainstream of the discipline: "Textbooks always
presume a certain degree of institutionalization of a research movement. In this respect this book is not
only exemplary of a cultural-anthropological interpretation of the New Testament, it is at the same
time an indication of the growing acceptance, in a period of less than ten years, of the use of social-
scientific models in New Testament exegesis" (Hochschild 1999: 225, my trans.). I think this underes-
timates the innovative character of Malina's book, the style of which probably reflects Malina's
institutional context rather than the factors Hochschild suggests.
14   The third edition of the book (Malina 2001) adds two new chapters, on envy and the evil-eye, and
on the evolution of the Jesus groups.
15   See Esler 2004: 52–54 for a member's comments on the fundamental influence of Malina's
models on the Context Group's approach.
16   For an initial orientation to this output, see Elliott 1993: 29–30. Further bibliography at: http://www.
contextgroup.org/bibliog/bibliogall.doc (accessed December 15, 2008). See Esler 2004 for an (occasionally defensive) account of the Group's origins and work. Some publication dates, however, need
to be corrected: Malina's *New Testament World* and Elliott's *Home for the Homeless* were published in
1981, not 1978, and Theissen's book on the *Soziologie der Jesusbewegung* in 1977, not 1974 (p. 49).

What interests and concerns me here, in the context of a discussion taking its initial point of departure from Meeks's book, is the claim made, particularly by Malina, that the kind of approach practiced by members of the Context Group is properly "social-scientific," in a way that others are not. Indeed, it may in part be the strong claim to the label "social-scientific" on the part of Malina and some others in the Group, and their sometimes strident criticism of others' work, that in part accounts for the reluctance of others to claim the label.

2. WHAT COUNTS AS SOCIAL-SCIENTIFIC WORK? BRUCE MALINA'S CRITERIA

There are various facets to this claim, as presented by Malina. First, there is the insistence on the use of models as the only proper and recognizably social-scientific method. In a recent essay, Malina defines a social-scientific approach as follows:

Social-scientific interpretation of New Testament documents involves reading some New Testament writing by first selecting a suitable model accepted in the social-scientific community, and using the model to form adequate scenarios for reading the document in question (Malina 2002: 3).[17]

An associated principle for such biblical interpretation is that "if a social-scientific model is called into question or rejected by reputable social scientists, we would do well not to apply it in social-scientific interpretation" (Malina 2002: 15 n. 1).[18]

Second, there is an insistence on a distinction between social history and social science: "As a rule, social-scientific interpretation of the Bible is confused with social history . . . 'Social description' and 'social history' are no more 'sociology' than 'policy' and 'politics' are identical" (Malina 2002: 15 n. 2).[19] What counts as social-scientific interpretation should be defined by the standards of the social sciences themselves: "Use of the social sciences in biblical interpretation should

---

17 Cf. also Malina 1982: 231–37; Elliott 1986: 3–9; Esler 1987: 6–9; Esler 1994: 12–13; Esler 1995a: 4–8.

18 Cf. also Malina 1982: 240, though more cautiously expressed there: "Models borrowed from the social sciences have to be good social science models. For purposes of biblical scholarship, the assessment of social science models would have to follow the criticisms of social scientists as well as the degree of fit with the area under consideration."

19 A number of authors are listed as evidencing the "unfortunate" tendency to import these "imprecisions . . . into the lexicon of biblical scholarship," including "the works of Barton, Holmberg, Kee, Malherbe, Meeks, and . . . Peterson [sic] . . . and, most recently, see Horrell 1999" (Malina 2002: 15 n. 2). The quotation given in the main text above is also found in Malina 1982: 241, where he comments that "[i]t would be unfortunate if these imprecisions in terminology would be imported into the lexicon of biblical scholarship." Twenty years later, Malina clearly senses that his fears have been realized.

at least be acceptable to and recognizable by social scientists and by undergraduate students who take courses in the social sciences" (Malina 2002: 15 n. 2).[20]

Third, there is a confident rejection of works that fall outside this definition of social-scientific research. For example, in an edited textbook outlining resources for social-scientific interpretation (Rohrbaugh 1996)—from the Context Group perspective—Malina provides a bibliography in his guide to "Understanding New Testament Persons." Here, certain works are asterisked as "inadequate for a valid understanding"; they are cited "as examples of outdated or dead-end approaches to the subject" (Malina 1996b: 56–57). The list includes Meeks's *The First Urban Christians* and Theissen's *Psychological Aspects of Pauline Theology*. Malina elsewhere criticizes Abraham Malherbe scathingly for his attempt to claim the label "sociological" for his work.[21] This tendency to criticize harshly—as failing to adopt a proper social-scientific method —work which stands outside the methodological scope of the Context Group's approach is matched by a similar tendency simply to ignore works which do not cohere with the method. In the recent co-authored *Social-Science Commentary on the Letters of Paul* (Malina and Pilch 2006), for example, the bibliography does not list anything by Meeks, Theissen, Bengt Holmberg, Dale Martin, et al., though it does include twelve items by Philip Esler, fourteen by Malina, and sixteen by Pilch. This is presumably because the works of the "social historians" are deemed to have failed—absolutely, it seems—to grasp the crucial cultural values central to ancient Mediterranean culture, and so cannot even begin to provide appropriate "reading scenarios."

In what follows, I want to mount a critique of this stance, not by criticizing *per se* the constructive work or methodological approach of the Context Group, but by questioning the grounds on which the attempt to distinguish such work from other social-scientific or socio-historical work is based.

3. A Critical Response

I have elsewhere outlined my reasons for finding a model-based approach open to question, in dialogue with Philip Esler, and will not repeat myself here.[22] My main observations are simply that: (a) a good deal of contemporary social science, whether in anthropology or sociology, does not appear to proceed according to the

20   Cf., again, Malina 1982: 241. The remainder of the note (in Malina 2002: 15–16 n. 2) reasserts some of the standard supposed distinctions between history and sociology, that the former is characterized by "implicit, arbitrary, and unsystematic" conceptualizations and an untheoretical, narrative approach, while the latter uses explicit and systematic concepts and is interested in underlying structures and cultural values. Cf. also Malina 1985: 346. I have elsewhere addressed many of these issues, which seem to me, at best, a dated caricature of the distinctions between the two disciplines. See Horrell 1996: 18–32.

21   Malina 1996a: 217–41, esp. 226–28.

22   See Horrell 1996: 9–18; Esler 1998b; Horrell 2000; Esler 2000.

method Malina presents as the standard for social-scientific interpretation, i.e., by *first* outlining a model and then proceeding to consider if and how the data fit; (b) insofar as social scientists do talk of models, they are generally regarded as simplified or idealized representations of real-world phenomena which are constructed in order to summarize key features of a series of empirical cases.

I happen to agree with Malina, Elliott, and others, that there is considerable value in outlining a coherent and explicit theoretical framework at the outset of one's work; this, one might recall, formed the main basis for their criticism of Meeks's book. I do not agree, however, that such theoretical groundwork is equivalent to, or best described as, selecting and presenting a model. But even this stance, as we shall see, does not by any means represent a "standard" for social-scientific inquiry.

Malina is right to be cautious about biblical scholars using models or theories that are rejected by contemporary social scientists. In interdisciplinary work there is always the danger that one will be using out-of-date or flawed material from the discipline in which one is less at home. However, just as the outline of social-scientific methodology presumes far too great a unanimity of approach in the social sciences, similarly, to propose that no model be used if it "is called into question or rejected by reputable social scientists" implies a level of agreement among social scientists that seems far from the case: profound empirical, methodological, and theoretical debates characterize many contemporary disciplines, not least the social sciences, which are in many ways deeply contested, particularly since the advent of postmodernism. (It is perhaps worth imagining the implausibility of a corresponding statement on the part of a social scientist seeking to use methods from New Testament scholarship. To insist that no New Testament method be used if it "is called into question or rejected by reputable" New Testament scholars would rule out almost every approach adopted in contemporary scholarship, given the realities of today's diverse and highly contested discipline.)

As with the previous points, so Malina's insistence on a sharp distinction between social history and social science is based on a conviction about the nature and methods of the social sciences. Any social-scientific method of New Testament interpretation must be "acceptable to and recognizable by social scientists . . ." in terms of its methodological stance.

One reasonable way to probe what might count as an acceptable method would seem to be to examine some recent works produced by social scientists and see what method they adopt. The following examples are by no means claimed as representative or somehow "standard" in terms of method. Indeed, part of my point is to reject the very idea that there is anything like a single "social science" method.

My first example is from the field of sociology, and specifically the sociology of religion. Grace Davie, Professor of Sociology at (as it happens) my own university, the University of Exeter, is one of the most prominent contemporary sociologists of religion. The work which first established her profile is *Religion in Britian since 1945: Believing without Belonging* (Davie 1994). In this book, Davie presents a wide range of empirical material relating to the changing patterns of religious belief and participation in religious (and other) institutions in post-war Britain. The subtitle summarizes her main thesis: that levels of religious belief (belief in God, etc.) remain high, but that levels of participation in institutional religion have declined—at the same time as participation in *all* kinds of institutions has declined, suggesting that some wider cultural change is in view, rather than a simple rejection of (established) religion. *After* the presentation of the pertinent material, Davie offers a "theoretical postscript" in the final chapter, in which she attempts to make sense of the material in terms of a theory of religion and its changing role in modern society.

In a subsequent work, *Religion in Modern Europe: A Memory Mutates* (2000), Davie broadens the scope of her interest to religion in Europe. The opening chapter of the book presents a series of facts and figures about the profile of religion in modern Europe. In the second chapter she asks, "How, then, can we begin to interpret the mass of data presented so far?" (Davie 2000: 24). Three possible approaches are outlined: Steve Bruce's secularization thesis, José Casanova's work on the nature of religion in the modern world, and Danièle Hervieu-Léger's approach to religion as collective memory. It is this latter approach that Davie finds most fruitful and develops in her work.

In terms of method, Davie nowhere appears to talk of models, and certainly does not open her work by setting out the models she is going to adopt. She does, as we have seen, draw on theories of religion and its role in modern society in order to make some sense of her data, but neither describes these theoretical frameworks as "models" nor uses them to preface her presentation of data.[23]

My point is not to claim that Davie's method is standard, nor that it is not open to critique (e.g., Bruce 2002: 104–105). But however vigorous the debate or the methodological critique, it would be nonsense to claim that Davie's work did not "count" as recognizable social science.

My second example comes from the field of anthropology: David Sutton's *Remembrance of Repasts: An Anthropology of Food and Memory*. Sutton's book is primarily an ethnographic study of "the relationship between food and memory on the island of Kalymnos, Greece" (Sutton 2001: ix). Through extensive observation and recording of everyday activities and conversations around food—from

---

23   It would be possible, following an argument often made by Malina, Esler, and others, to suggest that writers such as Davie do in fact have an implicit framework for the interpretation of data, which might better be made explicit at the outset, and which we might call a "model" (cf. Malina 1982: 231–32; Esler 1994: 12; Esler 1995a: 4; Elliott 1985: 334; Elliott 1993: 40–48). The relevant point here, though, is that social scientists such as Davie—whose methods Malina et al. claim we should be following—do not explicitly proceed in this way nor describe their theoretical frameworks as models.

buying and growing to cooking and eating—Sutton develops a rich analysis of the ways in which food practices constitute an important form of cultural memory and a crucial site for the sometimes conflictual encounter between the local and the global, the traditional and the modern. The first main chapter of the book considers ritual, as "a key site where food and memory come together" (p. 19). Sutton touches briefly on some relevant theoretical resources, such as Paul Connerton's treatment of social memory, and mentions recent anthropological debate about the definition of ritual (pp. 19–21). But there is no "model" of ritual set out, no set framework for the inquiry. The chapter swiftly moves, then, to a description of some of the ways food functions in everyday life on the island. Subsequent chapters deal both with classic topics in anthropology, such as gifts and exchange, and with themes such as the role of sensory memory in the construction of worlds. Throughout, Sutton's discussion is theoretically informed—in that he weaves into his ethnographic description broader theoretical and conceptual discussions that can offer some ways to make sense of the data—but it is primarily focused on a rich description of the multifarious ways in which food plays a significant role in everyday life on the island. There is nowhere, so far as I can see, where he refers to models, nor does he make any attempt to set out from the outset the chosen models that will shape and guide his investigation. As he puts it, his plan is "to be fairly eclectic in suggesting possible paths and theoretical approaches, illustrated primarily through my Kalymnian material," with which to address the topic of food and memory (Sutton 2001: 15). His approach, in short, is that of "theoretically informed ethnographic exploration" (Sutton 2001: 163). Here, we might suggest, we find a sort of intuitive eclecticism not dissimilar to that espoused by Meeks.

These examples, chosen simply *ad hoc*, could, I suggest, be multiplied almost indefinitely. But, as I have stressed, my intention is not to claim that these particular works represent a "standard" social-scientific methodology, nor to deny that one might also find social-scientific work which proceeds through an explicit and developed use of models. My point, rather, is simply to illustrate that established and recognized social science proceeds in a variety of ways, does not necessarily adopt a model-based approach, and is, in fact, highly diverse in its methods and theoretical commitments. There is an enormous range of work and of theoretical and practical approaches, from empirical studies of religious beliefs and attitudes in sociology of religion to postmodern literary ethnography in anthropology, from experimental observation of group behavior in social psychology to Marxist economic history, and so on.

Indeed, the point can be sharpened and, at the same time, broadened. In and beyond the so-called social sciences themselves there are hardly clear disciplinary boundaries: When does sociology become philosophy or politics? What distinguishes human geography from sociology or anthropology? Do postcolonial and cultural studies belong in the field of the Arts, in departments of literature, or are they facets of contemporary political science? How can history be defined over against economic history, historical geography, or historical sociology? While some set of core convictions and approaches can generally be argued to lie at the heart of each of these distinct disciplines, these are often more the product of the history of scholarly communities rather than intellectually sustainable distinctions, and in individual cases it is often hard to see why one researcher's work belongs in one particular discipline rather than potentially in various others. Moreover, as I have already hinted, the appropriate methods and character of these disciplines are themselves profoundly contested: the postmodern critique of traditional ethnography, for example, has led to fundamental questions about how anthropology should conceive itself as a discipline (see, e.g., D. C. Moore 1994; Rubel and Rosman 1994). Generalizations about the distinctions between "social science" and "history"—in terms of the former's systematic, model-based or theoretically conscious approach and the latter's untheoretical, narrative focus on individuals and unique events—clearly fail to do justice to either set of contemporary disciplines, with the diversity of theoretical and philosophical commitments in each.

To return to the domain of New Testament studies and the implications of the discussion above, it is not my intention here to imply or develop any critique of the substantive work presented by Malina and other members of the Context Group (and again I stress the diversity of work undertaken by participants in the Group).[24] Rather, the key point is to argue against the dismissal of other types of social-scientific work on the grounds that they fail to conform to a recognizable and model-based mode of social science research. That latter claim is simply unsustainable, and unhelpful too, since it avoids rather than engages in methodological debate.

This does not mean, of course, that methodological debate is unhelpful or inappropriate, quite the contrary. But the arguments about whether, say, something more like a Geertzian ethnographic "thick description" is preferable to an approach based on a broader, more generalized model of the central values of a certain culture are arguments about the strengths and weaknesses of different kinds of social-scientific research, not about what counts as proper social science.[25] Indeed,

---

24   Though it does seem to me that there are critical issues to be raised, at the broad theoretical level. For example, in a penetrating review, Justin Meggitt (Meggitt 1998a) suggests that Malina's work (Malina 1996a) presents a rather homogenized view of the ancient and modern Mediterranean, and disturbingly depicts negative stereotypes as characteristic not only of ancient but also modern Mediterraneans/Arabs, an approach subjected to powerful and classic critique in Said's *Orientalism*. For a developed and polemical critique along these lines, see now Crossley 2008, chs. 3–4. For a critical engagement with the topics central to Malina's models of Mediterranean culture from the perspective of a literary ethnography of the Gospel of Matthew, see Lawrence 2003.

25   For an argument in favor of the former approach, see Garrett 1992. For the opposing view, see Esler 1995a: 5–8; Esler 2004: 57–58.

the debate on this topic in biblical studies mirrors similar debates in the social sciences, as well as in other disciplines, such as ancient history.[26]

The implication of my argument, then, is that the enormous diversity of work in contemporary New Testament studies that employs, or is influenced by, some aspect of work from the social sciences all represents, to a greater or lesser extent, a kind of social-scientific or socio-historical approach. Since the kinds of questions and approaches introduced by the pioneers of social-scientific criticism have spread into the mainstream of the discipline, it is impossible to draw any boundary around what does and does not count as social-scientific work—just as it is impossible to say, for example, where history gives way to historical sociology or historical geography. Moreover, there is no sustainable distinction to be drawn between what is "social science" and what is "social history."

All that is to be welcomed, in my view, even if it makes it harder—perhaps now impossible—to offer any kind of comprehensive survey of contemporary social-scientific interpretation. It also makes it harder to talk about the kind of methods and approaches that might appropriately inform future work on the New Testament from a social-scientific perspective, since the field is potentially so diverse and unbounded; the range of possible disciplinary connections is huge. Nevertheless, as a way of drawing positive consequence from my argument for a broad, loosely defined, but vigorously debated notion of social-scientific interpretation—and despite the risk of simply promoting one's favorite perspectives—I shall conclude by suggesting a few possible areas for fruitful ongoing development.[27]

4. Suggested Areas for Fruitful Development

First I mention *literary ethnography*. While ethnography has traditionally involved fieldwork, the literal and geographical immersion of the anthropologist into a foreign culture—a kind of participant observation impossible for the student of ancient texts—a turn toward literature in some anthropological studies has opened up possibilities for ethnographic readings of New Testament texts to be informed by, and to interact with, readings of *texts* by anthropologists. These New Testament readings would be concerned to immerse themselves into the world constructed

---

26 See, e.g., Cartledge 1994: 5, on the distinction between ancient historians "who believe it is possible and fruitful to generalize across all modern Greece (and sometimes, more broadly still, to 'the Mediterranean world', for example)" and those who believe "that such comparison should be used chiefly to highlight fundamental cultural difference rather than homogenize heterogeneous cultures." See further Horrell 1999b: 19–21.

27 In this closing section I draw heavily on an unpublished paper presented by invitation to a session on "The New Testament and the Social Sciences After Thirty Years: Retrospect and Prospect," in the Social-Scientific Criticism of the New Testament Section, Society of Biblical Literature Annual Meeting, Philadelphia, November 20, 2005. I would like to take this opportunity publicly to thank the Chair, Dennis Duling, and other members of the Committee, for that kind invitation.

and presented by a particular text, not read in glorious isolation but seen in the light of other materials, both contemporary and distant, and to analyze the ways in which the text deals with areas classically the focus for anthropological study: power, religious practice, exchange, kinship, gender, and social stratification (cf. Lawrence 2003, 2005). Such approaches—and here I reveal my own bias and methodological preferences—are likely to be somewhat closer in approach to the Geertzian mode of thick description than the model-based generalized picture of culture, but this does not mean that a broader picture of the key traits of a wider cultural context cannot valuably inform the investigation, only that the researcher will be equally and especially attentive to the distinctive facets of the constructions of culture found in any given text.

Second I would point to what we might very loosely call *Marxian economic and social history*. I deliberately use the label Marxian rather than Marxist for these approaches, since, especially insofar as they are useful for the study of early Christianity, they will reflect (I would suggest) not a doctrinaire Marxism but rather the *influence* of Marx and Marxist studies in a focus on the economic dimensions of life, on doing history "from below," and on class conflict, popular culture, and popular protest. Marxist approaches as such have never gained very much attention in the field of social-scientific criticism of the New Testament, though this is less true in continental Europe than in English-speaking scholarship, and also less true in the case of political approaches to the Bible influenced by liberation theology. As James Crossley has pointed out, the major movement of Marxist historians, who were so influential in history-writing around the 1960s, was largely ignored in New Testament studies, primarily, Crossley argues, because New Testament scholars, mostly Christians, were ideologically opposed to Marxism and the kinds of historical analysis it fostered (Crossley 2006: 5–34). It is interesting, for example, that Meeks briefly mentions Marxist approaches to early Christianity from a former generation, only to swiftly dismiss their potential on the grounds of their "reductionist" view of religion (Meeks 1983: 3).[28]

Some scholars have, for some time, pursued a radical approach to the New Testament influenced by the approach of historical materialism, as well as by liberation theology and feminism. One thinks in particular of Luise Schottroff and Wolfgang Stegemann in Germany and, in the USA, Richard Horsley and the influential SBL groups fostered and facilitated by him, with their focus on emancipatory readings of the New Testament, and on issues of power, empire, and politics.[29] More recent studies, without in any way being explicitly or strictly Marxist as such, have also begun to show the value of attending to the specifically

---

28   Though note the attention given in Scroggs 1980: 177–79. See also Dale Martin's comments in his essay below.
29   See, e.g., Schottroff 1985 (ET in Horrell, ed., 1999a); Schottroff and Stegemann, eds., 1984; Gottwald and Horsley, eds., 1993; Horsley 1993; Horsley, ed., 1997a. On materialist exegesis as a dimension of social-scientific interpretation, see also Hochschild 1999: 228–32.

economic dimensions of early Christianity, in ways informed by the radical histo-rians such as E. P. Thompson (notably Meggitt 1998b) and in ways concerned to highlight the unacknowledged influence of contemporary (consumer) capitalism on the approaches to (or neglect of) economic poverty in studies of the Pauline churches (Friesen 2004).

Third I would point to *iconological studies*, or to *studies of New Testament iconography*, that is to say, studies of the meaning and impact of New Testament (textual) images in the light of their visual representation in their wider cultural world. Archaeology, of course, throws up lots of examples of visual depictions which "formed" the cultural and social world which the auditors of the New Testament texts inhabited. Moreover, there are various theoretical perspectives—from semiotics and structuralism to social constructivism, and so on—which can help us to conceptualize and analyze the reception and impact of images, visual and textual. A recent volume edited by Annette Weissenrieder, Frederike Wendt, and Petra von Gemünden (Weissenrieder, Wendt, and Gemünden 2005) sets out some of these theoretical resources and contains a number of suggestive and insightful studies of specific texts and images (cf. also Lopez 2008). For example, Philip Esler interprets Paul's athletic imagery against the background of visual depictions of Greek athletes; Hanna Roose provides an indication of how John's readers might have understood the image of Babylon the whore, given material representations of (aging) prostitutes in antiquity; Harry Maier interprets the integrative imagery of Colossians (3:11) in the light of visual representations of Rome's conquering and incorporating achievements. These few examples indi-cate too how this innovative approach has the potential to draw together a number of strands in existing work: archaeology, studies of the New Testament in its Roman imperial context, classic theoretical resources such as Peter Berger and Thomas Luckmann's work on the social construction of reality, and so on.

Finally, I want to highlight the potential of *postcolonial studies* for understand-ing the New Testament in its socio-historical context. Here in particular it is impossible to pin the approach (postcolonialism) down to a specific disciplinary location. Indeed, insofar as it has one, it is often in departments of literature. Yet it—or rather, the diversity of theories, approaches, and topics that fall under this broad umbrella—has considerable relevance to the study of the ways in which the early Christians negotiated their existence in the Roman Empire. Much of the energy in postcolonial biblical studies has been focused on examining the ways in which (readings of) the Bible served—and serve—to legitimate the interests of modern colonial powers and on considering how readers in colonial and post-colonial contexts can and do generate their own (counter-)readings of the text (see, e.g., Sugirtharajah 2002). Yet postcolonial theory also has considerable potential for helping us to analyze the ways in which the New Testament texts, in various ways, represent strategies of both accommodation and resistance to empire. This is especially so given that postcolonial theory, on certain construals at least, is concerned not only with the situation after the (ostensible) end of colonial rule but equally with the period following the time of initial colonization (i.e., the "post" may be construed in two somewhat different senses; see Gandhi 1998: 3). James Scott's studies of the forms of resistance found among peasants, and other subordinate groups, most often hidden and covert rather than open or violent, have already provided fruitful resources to inform studies of New Testament texts (e.g., Horsley 2004a; Carter 2004). Postcolonial writers such as Homi Bhabha offer valuable ways to explore the profoundly complex and ambivalent relationship between colonizer and colonized.[30] Scott infamously quotes an old Ethiopian proverb: "when the great lord passes, the wise servant bows deeply and silently farts" (Scott 1990: v). Bhabha speaks of a "sly civility" (Bhabha 1994: 93–101). Put more prosaically, there is a whole range of possible strategies of resistance, from overt and forceful rebellion to silent, "internal" opposition, practiced alongside what may, to all intents and purposes, be fully conformist behavior. These kinds of theoretical resources may help us to develop more nuanced analyses of the relationship between church and empire, as it is variously depicted and promoted in the New Testament texts, rather than the somewhat blunt alternatives of opposition or conformity that have sometimes characterized analyses to date.

If, then, we allow a broad, methodologically diverse notion of social-scientific interpretation to define the field and the future—something I have argued best fits the character of the contemporary social sciences on which we draw—these are (only) a few of the many possible directions in which New Testament study might fruitfully continue to develop. It will, I think, remain the case that a more socially grounded approach characterizes New Testament studies broadly, in a way that was not so twenty-five years ago: that, in part, represents an achievement of those who have energetically promoted this aspect of New Testament study. But given this fact, and the diverse directions in which future work will go, it will, I think, be harder and harder to draw any legitimate or meaningful boundary around "social-scientific" interpretation, defining what does and does not "count" as such. Nor should this fuzzy, indefinable world be a cause for our concern or regret: unlike sociologists, anthropologists, geographers, and historians, we have a defined body of texts and a circumscribed historical period that determine the central focus of our discipline. Determining what does and does not count as social-scientific criticism is unimportant and almost certainly unachievable. What matters much more is that we continue to forge the kind of interdisciplinary connections that will inform and invigorate New Testament studies, and continue to engage in vigorous debate about the strengths and weaknesses of our various methods and about the extent to which they make cogent historical sense of the varied phenomena of earliest Christianity.

---

30 See Bhabha 1994; Moore 2006: 109–10; Horrell 2007: 121–22.

Chapter 2

CONTOURS OF THE URBAN ENVIRONMENT

Peter Oakes

The five chapters of Wayne Meeks's *The First Urban Christians* that relate social issues to Pauline Christianity (namely, chs. 2–6) are underpinned by an initial chapter that sets out key aspects of the urban environment of Paul's churches. Even though the chapter is the longest in the volume (forty-one pages plus fifteen pages of endnotes), the vastness of the field required Meeks to be selective about which topics to bring up, especially as he wanted to give his picture a good amount of detailed support from both primary and secondary sources. After some brief, but wide-ranging, introductory sections he focuses on four main areas: mobility (physical and social); possible entry routes that a city might provide for Christianity; diaspora Jewish life; and specific cities in which Pauline Christian groups were established. He also includes a (sadly) short section on women in urban life.

The chapter stands up very well after twenty-five years. A key factor in this is that the 1970s saw the emergence of views about first-century society that broadly remain part of the scholarly consensus. In particular, Meeks was able to draw on the work of Ramsay MacMullen, whose *Roman Social Relations* (MacMullen 1974) remains a standard study. Meeks also undertook work in collaboration with Robert L. Wilken (Meeks and Wilken 1978), another scholar with continuing influence. However, there has been a deluge of work on Greco-Roman society in the past quarter-century, especially as social issues have moved more and more to the center stage of academic activity. Moreover, there are parts of the chapter, especially on the study of particular sites, where Meeks is (often unavoidably) dependent on work that was already quite old by the time of his book. On Philippi, for example, his main source is now more than seventy years old (Collart 1937).

The selectivity of Meeks's approach also raises a broad issue that we will attempt to tackle in this essay. His initial approach to characterizing the urban environment is nicely dynamic and comprehensive. He introduces the Greco-Roman city by tracing the entry and increasing influence of Romans in the cities of the Hellenized eastern Mediterranean (Meeks 1983: 11–16). This approach not only describes but also explains key factors such as the dominance of local aristocracies (used by the Romans as a means of control), the degree of uniformity in urban life across the region, and the variety of responses of people to Rome. However, this broad-ranging kind of explanatory introduction is soon succeeded by more fragmentary topics, as noted above. Each of these topics is of particular value for Pauline studies, so Meeks is very reasonable in foregrounding them. However, as a result of this choice, Meeks does not offer, despite the title of the chapter, a sustained general description of a Greco-Roman urban environment, either in physical terms—what a city looked like—or in social terms—which groups lived there and how they related to each other. Some of these points are discussed, piecemeal, at various points in the book, but no overall model, or range of possible models, is presented. Throughout the book, Meeks presents an excellent range of aspects of cities and their inhabitants, but the absence of an overall picture makes it hard to gauge how well Meeks's pieces fit together. Do they add up to a coherent and credible pattern of first-century urban society? Conversely, are there any crucial gaps in Meeks's urban pattern? Of course, presentation of an overall model does not prevent a scholar's view from being incorrect. However, it does make it much easier to assess. Maybe more importantly, an overall picture of the urban environment provides a contextual framework that enables particular social elements, such as those provided throughout *The First Urban Christians*, to be better understood by being properly located in an overall pattern.

How could we go about offering a useful general description of the Pauline urban environment, while also offering a way to understand specific Pauline cities? One approach would be to offer a general theoretical model, with variation for a number of ideal types of city. Particular actual cities could be described in terms of how they related to the general model and specific ideal types. In a forthcoming essay, I suggest a patronage model of urban structure, consider how it relates to ideal types such as "temple city" and "Roman colony," then briefly apply the model to Corinth in order to interpret some passages in 1 Corinthians (Oakes, forthcoming b). Here, we will take an alternative approach. We will begin with a particular town and take its urban environment as an initial model for Greco-Roman towns in general. We will then consider how specific towns fit with, or vary from, this initial model. Slightly counterintuitively, our initial model town will be a non-Pauline one, Pompeii. This is the best documented first-century town and shows many features that are common in Pauline towns. Having understood something of the urban environment in Pompeii, we will then think about ways in which Pauline towns were like Pompeii and ways in which they differed from it. We will use three examples: Philippi, Thessalonica, and Corinth. In considering the evidence from the four towns, we will also see a range of the scholarship that has been done in this area over the past twenty-five years.

1. THE URBAN ENVIRONMENT OF POMPEII

For the physical environment, we will use a framework that runs from a macro- to a micro-level: geography, topography, overall urban layout, streetscape, housing design. This is further complicated by incorporating changes over time. For the social environment, the framework will cover social structure, political structure, and economic structure. Each of these topics will necessarily be touched on only briefly, with a focus on a few of the potentially relevant points.

Physical Environment

Every town is a series of historical layers. To understand the town requires some thinking about the layers and how their interaction has produced the unique form of any given place. The following chronology represents the recent conclusions of Roger Ling, who dates the whole grid plan of the city very early.[1] In any case, the important characteristics of the following description of the environment are not dependent on the exact sequencing of the layers.

The southwest corner of Pompeii gives a clue to its topography and origins (see Figure 1 on the next page). The earliest discernable town is clearly marked by the irregular pattern of streets around the forum, sharply contrasting with grid plans of the rest of the town. The old town sat on a 30m high bluff overlooking the River Sarno close to the sea—a defensible position suitable as a port. The somewhat irregular street pattern of the old town suggests that it was not a Greek colony, as were other towns in the region, such as Naples. This point is supported by the absence of early Greek inscriptions (Ling 2005: 33).

The date of the earliest phase is unclear. In contrast, and contrary to the earlier scholarly consensus, it now seems likely that, by the sixth century BCE, the overall layout of Pompeii had taken its current shape. That shape looked much more like a Greek colony. Three phases of grid development had taken place (although much of the grid was not yet built upon). The first grid, of rhomboidal blocks of land, followed the "Via Stabiana" (a modern name), whose course was deter-mined by a fairly steep-sided valley just to the east of the old town. The second phase was north of the old town. Its grid was aligned with one of the two main roads (the "Via di Mercurio") that cross at the town center. The blocks were long rectangles, 120 feet wide, a standard Greek (and Roman) width. Some of the countryside to the north of Pompeii was probably divided into a grid on the same

---

1   For a more conventional view of the historical sequence see, for example, Herman Geertman's explanation (Geertman 1998: 18–20), although one notes that already, in another essay in the same book, Andrew Wallace-Hadrill is floating the idea of an early layout of the eastern streets, although not of the houses extant in 79 CE, on the basis of sixth century BCE finds (Wallace-Hadrill 1998: 49).

alignment. Evidence of this is provided by the discovery of five villas, oriented in this way. The third grid also had 120 feet wide blocks but occupied the east of the city and was lined up at right angles to the continuation of the east-west road through the forum, the "Via dell'Abbondanza." Again there are traces of field patterns (this time indicated by field boundaries) on this alignment to the south of the town. An irregular-shaped wall surrounded the town (Ling 2005: 29–33).

Despite these rather Greek patterns, the archaeological finds suggest that political control of the town at this period was more likely to be by Etruscans, the dominant group north of Rome. After the Etruscans were forced out of the area in the fifth century, local tribal (Samnite) control reasserted itself. This was maintained until the beginning of the first century BCE, although, as time went on, that control was more and more subordinate to the regional overlordship of Rome. Having said all this, the physical urban environment continued to develop in a largely Hellenistic way. There is an early temple to Apollo and another in the Greek Doric style. The Stabian baths follow a Greek pattern, featuring a colonnaded exercise area. A theater was built in the second century. Adjacent is another portico area

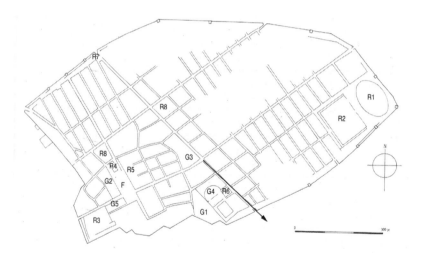

Figure 1. Features of the Greco-Roman urban environment of Pompeii. The outline of the very early town can be seen in the irregular streets around the forum (F). The arrow marks the valley that determined the orientation of the grid to the east of the early town. Hellenistic elements: G1—Doric temple; G2—temple of Apollo; G3—Stabian baths; G4—theater; G5—basilica. Roman colonial elements: R1—amphitheater; R2—exercise area; R3—temple of Venus; R4—temple of the Capitoline Triad; R5—imperial cult temple; R6—small theater, possibly used for meetings of colonists; R7—water supply control building; R8—baths. With thanks to Roger Ling for permission to use his drawing of the street layout.

for meeting or exercise. Near the central square a basilica was built. Major houses of this period also reveal evidence of Hellenistic taste (Ling 2005: 34–46).

After joining the Italian rebels in the Social War, Pompeii was besieged and defeated by Sulla in 89 BCE. In 80 BCE it became a Roman veteran colony. Colonists displaced the local elite in the governing of the town. The effect on the physical environment was most marked at the east end of the town. A large number of blocks of housing were demolished to make way for an amphitheater "for the perpetual use of the colonists," as its dedicatory inscription says (Ling 2005: 55). Later, more blocks adjacent to this were demolished to provide a large, colonnaded exercise area, in line with the Augustan program of military training for young elite men (Ling 2005: 70). Interesting changes also took place in the religious landscape. The most prominent site, overlooking the harbor, was given over to a temple to Venus, Sulla's patron goddess and now the patron goddess of *Colonia Cornelia Veneria Pompeianorum*. Under Augustus, the local elite greatly enhanced the temple of his patron god, Apollo. In the forum, the north end was taken over by a prominent temple to the classic Roman gods, the Capitoline Triad of Jupiter, Juno, and Minerva (Zanker 1998: 64). Over time, temples to the imperial cult appeared around the forum. More generally, the forum became more and more monumentalized. Another physical change in the Augustan period was the arrival of a water supply, brought by Agrippa's aqueduct and a local piping system, to elite houses, public fountains, and baths. Several new bathing establishments were built between then and 79 CE.

Moving our focus to street level, the urban environment was one of great mixture. Although some areas had more large houses than others did, elite houses were spread right across the town. They were mixed in with small houses, apartments, workshops, shops, and bars. One of the most common patterns, particularly on major roads, was for the grand (but fairly narrow) entrance of a mansion to be flanked by two shops, built into what would otherwise have been the two front rooms of the big house.

Design of large houses covered the gamut of possible combinations of the traditional Roman atrium area, the more Hellenistic peristyle gardens, and various service areas. The House of the Menander (I.10.4), for example, included all these, together with a bathing suite, a stable-yard that acted as a base for agricultural work, and a shop. Smaller houses quite often combined fairly traditional elements, such as an atrium, with commercial activities. The atrium of house I.6.7 is dominated by a fulling vat. Smaller workshops usually had limited living quarters either at the back or in a mezzanine space. Some houses were divided into apartments, although there were none of the large apartment blocks that one sees at a site such as Ostia.

The roads were paved. Pavements and stepping-stones were often provided, allowing at least some chance of keeping out of the mire that must often have covered the streets. The roads leading out of the town were lined with tombs.

These were sometimes of very large scale, volubly proclaiming the status and merits of the town's wealthy families.

Social Environment

The most prominent tombs proclaimed the honor of the town's elite. The grand entrances and semi-public spaces of their houses gave the same message. The message was even more direct in the inscriptions on temples and other public buildings, attesting the generosity of the benefactor who paid for it. All this culminated in the forum. At some point in the first century CE the town council decided that there were so many honorific statues in the forum that they needed sorting out. They did so by lining up all the equestrian statues on one side and the standing ones on the other side (Ling 2005: 72–73)! The town was centered on an area designed to honor the town's benefactors.[2] The people who acted as patrons in the town received honor in the forum, as well as the more daily honor that they received from their own personal groups of clients.[3]

As well as the civic elite, the forum honored more distant patrons. This could include Roman senators who had brought favor to the town, but increasingly it meant the imperial family. Statues and temples honored them for their patronage. More subtly, Rome's patronage was honored by the shaping of the forum in line with that at Rome, most obviously by the presence of a raised *capitolium* at the top end of the forum. Imperial cult temples were not the only ones that expressed patronage. The temples to patron deities of Roman leaders—Venus for Sulla and Apollo for Augustus—implicitly honored the patronage of those leaders. The temples also, like all temples, acknowledged the patronage of the deities themselves. This was particularly true of Venus, the patron goddess of the town. In a different sense, the human benefactors, who paid for the construction and running of temples, were also patrons and were honored by inscriptions on the site. More specifically, by paying for the cult, these human patrons were acting as brokers for higher patrons, the gods. In a similar way, inscriptions in the forum that honored external patrons at Rome also effectively honored the local elite as brokers who had given the town access to these higher patrons.

This patronage pattern was replicated on a smaller scale across the town. Each member of the elite was a patron with a network of clients. Many of those clients

---

2   For a recent exploration of this issue in relation to the setting of Paul's letter to the Romans, see Jewett 2007: 50.

3   There are complex theoretical issues in deciding what counts as patronage. I am using a broader social-scientific definition of the term (Eisenstadt and Roniger 1984: 48–49) rather than a narrower Roman one. My fundamental argument would be that to center the town on an area for elite display of honor in return for benefaction represents a patronage *system*. For a definition of this see Johnson and Dandeker 1990: 220–21. For a broader discussion of these issues see Oakes, forthcoming b.

would, in turn, have acted as patrons to clients of their own, providing, among other things, brokerage for access to elite patrons. In this way, the social fabric was largely an interlocking mesh of patronage networks.

Many at the lower social levels would rarely have experienced these networks as being beneficial to them. "Vertical" social ties will have predominated over "horizontal" ones—a key characteristic of a patronage network—but the dominant interactions would have been those of control, not benefaction: master to slave; landlord to tenant; creditor to debtor. However, even in these relationships there was an element of patronage. For example, a prominent aspect of control of urban slaves was the provision of a *peculium*. This was money that slaves were given as tips and which was regarded as their own, even though legally it belonged to their owner. As Alföldy's classic diagram of Roman society suggests, in its divisions between rural and urban as well as between free, freed, and slave (Alföldy 1985: 146), Roman society weakened the ties between groups at the same social level. A patronage-based society privileges vertical ties of dependence over horizontal ties of solidarity (Morris 1991: 46–47; Gellner 2006: 9–10). Even though formal patronage, in the Roman sense, was weaker outside specifically Roman society, patronage in the social-scientific sense was a dominant social structure across all Greco-Roman towns.

Political power in Pompeii was in the hands of a Roman elite group that was stable in ideological terms; however, in practical terms, its composition continually changed. This was due to the high mortality rate in the first-century world. Elite wealth quite often passed into the hands of freed slaves, who could hold prominent positions outside the decuriate, the town council, and whose freeborn children could themselves hold decurial positions. Willem Jongman documents this and also points out how the turnover among the elite is masked for us by the practice of freed slaves taking the family name of their former owners (Jongman 2007: 509–13). Of course, the relatively high turnover among the elite should not be taken as meaning high social mobility among the population. In a town council of one hundred, thirty children of freed slaves joining it in a generation would be a high turnover. However, it would involve a miniscule fraction of the slaves in the town. The best that most urban slaves could hope for would be a free but poor existence in later life, generally after giving much of their *peculium* back to their owner to buy their freedom. For the average freeborn poor Pompeian, the prospect of social mobility was even less apparent.

Elite income in Pompeii, and generally in the Greco-Roman world, was mainly from agricultural rents and produce. However, as Wallace-Hadrill (1991) has demonstrated, the elite were far more involved in local trade and urban rental than scholars have generally thought, having been misled by the impression given by Roman elite writers. The shops built into the front of elite houses were undoubtedly owned by the elite. Many must even have been run by slaves or freed slaves of the elite, with the income going into elite pockets. As Finley argued, much of the economic activity in the town will have been to provide goods and services for the elite (Finley 1985). The number of builders and decorators working in large houses at the time of the eruption is a good example of this. However, there was clearly also substantial economic activity among the nonelite. The clearest evidence of this is the large number of bars. These would have supplied food and drink primarily to the nonelite. Moreover, the customers of shops and bars included people from the countryside around Pompeii. This is demonstrated by Ray Laurence's analysis of locations of shops and bars, showing a particular favoring of roads leading into the town from outside (Laurence 2006).

The above points are intended to present a lightly sketched model. Much more could be said about the Pompeian urban environment that would be useful for understanding Pauline cities. Social structure within the household is a further vital field, particularly in relation to gender, age, and slavery. Pompeian domestic evidence has made a major contribution to the study of these areas in the last twenty-five years. This is seen particularly clearly in the 1997 collection, *Roman Domestic Space: Pompeii and Beyond* (Laurence and Wallace-Hadrill 1997). Some of this type of work is also presented in the September 2004 issue of *Journal for the Study of the New Testament*, devoted to domestic space. Also, the social significance of artwork within Pompeian houses has been explored by John R. Clarke (Clarke 1991, 2003), and in relation to study of early house-churches by David Balch (Balch 2008). More could valuably be said about demography, particularly on the social makeup of the population. I explore this issue and discuss a range of Pompeian evidence in a forthcoming book (Oakes, forthcoming a).

2. Variation One: Philippi

Meeks's description of Philippi still stands up well. In contrast to many commentators of the period (and later), he presents a good balance between the exceptionally Roman character of the colony, compared with others in the Greek East, and the persistence of a substantial non-Roman part of the population (Meeks 1983: 45–46). Since the classic 1930s and 1940s studies on which Meeks draws, progress in publishing the excavations at Philippi has been slow. There is a useful 1973 study by Demetrios Lazarides and an excellent study of the regional context by Fanoula Papazoglou (Papazoglou 1988). The long-promised publication of the official archaeological reports began in 1975 (Collart and Ducrey 1975) with a study of the amazing rock reliefs on the lower slopes of the acropolis (especially just above the theater). The largest group of these are of the goddess Diana and have inspired studies of early Philippian Christianity in that context by Valerie Abrahamsen (Abrahamsen 1995) and Lilian Portefaix (Portefaix 1988). Publishing of the official series has continued to be very slow since 1975. This has been mitigated by a number of articles in publications such as *Bulletin de Correspondance Hellénique, Archaiologikon Deltion* (in Greek), and the series *Ancient*

Macedonia, published by the Institute for Balkan Studies at Thessaloniki. Michel Sève has produced a major study on the development of the forum (Sève 1989, 1990), and Chaido Koukouli-Chrysanthaki has also published a useful article on the colony (Koukouli-Chrysanthaki 1998). However, the most valuable recent publication has been by Peter Pilhofer, who has produced an interim catalog of the Philippian inscriptions (Pilhofer 2000, with a new edition imminent). The scale and fascinating detail of the collection promise much for future contextual study of Paul's letter to Philippi. Pilhofer has produced his own contextual study of Philippians, which highlights factors such as the particular structures of office-holding among cultic groups in the town (Pilhofer 1995). Lukas Bormann uses the history of Philippi to raise issues relating to patronage in the interaction between Paul and the Philippians (Bormann 1995). Joseph Hellerman uses material on honor and shame to consider Phil. 2:5-11 (Hellerman 2005). My own work considers the social development of Philippi and contextual issues in relation to the suffering of the Philippian Christians and Paul's response to it (Oakes 2001).[4]

Physical Environment

The geographical reason for Philippi's initial settlement seems to have been the proximity of gold and silver mines with, more immediately, the presence of reliable springs. Topographically, the immediate location is a raised sloping shelf between a defensible hill and a wide marsh. A consequence of this formation was that the main local trade route could be controlled at this point. Of particular long-term significance was the vast fertile plain surrounding Philippi. The various areas of the plain needed differing amounts of drainage to bring them into use. This began under Philip II (382–336 BCE) and was finally completed only in the twentieth century.

Like Pompeii, Philippi was a Roman colony. However, it was also twice colonized previously: in 360 BCE by Greeks from the nearby island of Thasos and in 356 BCE by Macedonians led by Philip II, after whom the town was named from then on. Like Pompeii, the town had a somewhat irregular-shaped wall (although more rectangular than at Pompeii). Our main evidence is of the Roman street grid but the topographical constraints suggest that the Macedonian colony will have had a rather similar plan, with a dog-legged grid following the line of the main road, which became part of the Via Egnatia. Unlike Pompeii, Philippi had an acropolis, a fortified high-point, within the walls. This certified the town's

---

4   See chapter one (pp. 1–54) for references for the points below. On the physical environment, the landscape photographs are correct in the 2007 paperback ed. but were originally printed flipped the wrong way round!

existence as an independent Greek city. Of course, this was ironic, because the town was a dependency of the Macedonian kings. However, it demonstrates Philip's strongly Hellenistic ideology: his cities needed to be properly Greek. To this end, it was not surprising that he also provided the classic Greek cultural icon, a magnificent theater, built into the side of the hill on which the acropolis stands.

The arrival of the Roman colony in 42 BCE (reinforced in 30 BCE) did little to change the outlines of the urban space. However, over the following two centuries the colonial authorities transformed the center of the town into the most Roman of forums. The first major forum development took place under Claudius. The currently visible forum was established under the Antonines. As well as there being a prominent temple to the imperial family, the forum was dominated by the temple of the Capitoline Triad. The slope of the hill immediately above the forum provided the opportunity for a strong replication of the effect of the Capitoline Hill at Rome, looking down on all the business that took place in the town center. One more point of particular interest in Philippi's physical environment is the opportunity that the lower slopes of the hill provided for the practice of cults other than those celebrated in the city center (which was very close by). Cults of Isis, Diana-Artemis-Hecate, and Sylvanus are among those honored in shrines and in inscriptions cut into the rock (see references above).

Social Environment

The Roman veteran colony at Philippi was, politically and economically, more far-reaching in its effects than that at Pompeii. Although the political structures at Pompeii became Roman ones, and colonists initially occupied the leading positions, all the free Pompeians gained Roman citizenship within a few years, as part of the general resolution of the political situation in Italy. Moreover, many of the Samnite families kept hold of at least a substantial part of their property. At Philippi the native population were Greek or (culturally) Thracian. The veteran settlement, part of the proverbially vicious round of colonizations of 42 BCE, involved expropriation of huge amounts of farmland and no general grant of citizenship to the previous residents. This left a political structure in which all power resided among the Roman elite for the next two centuries.

By the time of the Roman colonization, the gold mines were exhausted. As Meeks rightly notes, the economy of the town was mainly based on agriculture (Meeks 1983: 46). However, he goes too far in claiming that this is "different from the other Pauline towns." Most small- to medium-sized towns, such as those in Galatia, were primarily dependent on agriculture. The colony's initial social structure was of a landowning Roman elite, several thousand small landowning Roman veterans and their families, and several thousand largely Greek workers in crafts, trades, etc. Over the century between colonization and the writing of Philippians and Acts, inscriptions relating to estates testify to a substantial concentration of landholding, which must have meant many (probably most) of the descendants of the colonist small-holders losing ownership of their land. Their families, together with freed slaves and their descendants, will have introduced a significant minority of Roman citizens into the groups of people engaged in craftwork, etc., in the town.

3. VARIATION TWO: THESSALONICA

The work of Peter Pilhofer extends beyond Philippi to Thessalonica. The published thesis of his former doctoral student, Christoph vom Brocke, is an invaluable study of that city (vom Brocke 2001). Correcting some aspects of the historical work by Rainer Riesner (Riesner 1995, also an important study), he distinguishes carefully between different phases of the development of the town to produce a convincing picture of its situation at the time of Paul's ministry. Vom Brocke then uses local epigraphic and coin evidence to make links between 1 Thessalonians and features such as the Cabirus cult. His work can to some extent be compared with earlier contextual work by Karl Donfried (Donfried 1985). Holland Hendrix also draws on local material in his work on Thessalonian honoring of Rome (Hendrix 1984). More recently, a number of studies have considered the social situation of the Thessalonian Christians and their relations with other people in the city (de Vos 1999; Still 1999).

Physical Environment

Thessalonica was a port city, the main base for trade in the northern Aegean. Like Philippi it ironically boasted the features of an independent Greek city: walls (again, roughly rectangular) and an acropolis. Like Philippi, the irony was that it was a Macedonian foundation, named after one of their queens. The topography was gentler than at Philippi: a reasonably steady slope up from the sea. This allowed a fairly regular grid pattern to be laid out from the beginning.

The disasters that befell Pompeii and Philippi (malaria from the marsh in the medieval period) were not replicated at Thessalonica so there is no large undeveloped area to dig up (Meeks 1983: 46). The most extensive set of remains is the *agora*. The extant buildings in the central square date mainly from the second century CE. Among the buildings is an *odeon* that may have been the meeting chamber for the town council. An Augustan inscription (*IG* X.2.1 no. 31) gives evidence of a Caesar cult temple. There was also a particularly prominent Serapeion. A final feature that says something about the nature of the city is a triumphal arch, built to celebrate the victory of Antony and Octavian at Philippi in 42 BCE (vom Brocke 2001: 41, 55, 59–60, 68).

Social Environment

In the first century CE, Thessalonica was a "free" Greek city. In another irony, its status as a free Greek city resulted from involvement in Roman action. It acted as the base in northern Greece for Antony and Octavian prior to the battle of Philippi. The stakes were very high for the city because Brutus and Cassius promised their soldiers the sacking of Thessalonica if they were victorious (Plutarch, *Life of Brutus* 46.1). Events went the other way and Antony and Octavian gave Philippi, Brutus and Cassius' forward base, to some of Antony's veterans. Thessalonica was honored with freedom, which essentially meant relief from some Roman taxes.

This, together with its status as capital of the Roman province of Macedonia, gave Thessalonica a double identity. Its constitution and citizenry were Greek. It had a largely Greek elite. Vom Brocke notes only forty-seven out of more than one thousand inscriptions as being in Latin (vom Brocke 2001: 99, including rather more Latin ones than Meeks notes, 1983: 212 n. 251): the contrast with nearby Philippi is very stark. Thessalonica had the governing apparatus of a council and popular assembly. However, it also had resident a Roman governor and his retinue. Even though he was technically not responsible for running Thessalonica, his influence must have been considerable. As Holland Hendrix notes in his work, Roman patronage of this Greek city was a key element in its identity (Hendrix 1984).

4. Variation Three: Corinth

Since *The First Urban Christians*, publication of archaeological work on Corinth has continued steadily, both in the *Corinth* series and in articles, especially in *Hesperia*. The twentieth *Corinth* volume marked the centenary of work there up to 1996 (Williams and Bookidis 2003). An influential, although controversial, study of Corinth was published by Donald Engels at the beginning of the 1990s, using Corinth as a case study to question some of the parameters of the *consumer city/producer city* debate that has dominated theoretical discussion of ancient cities since Finley (Engels 1990). A major recent collection edited by Daniel Schowalter and Steven Friesen gives a good picture both of some of the range of current archaeological work and of interests of New Testament scholars and other historians in this perennially fascinating site (Schowalter and Friesen 2005). The chapter by David Gilman Romano on urban and rural planning is particularly useful as an orientation to the city and its development (Romano 2005). How perennial the interest in Corinth is among New Testament scholars can be seen in the recent collection edited by Edward Adams and David Horrell, which gathers classic studies, with a few new ones, on the church at Corinth (Adams and Horrell 2004). Study of 1 Corinthians in particular has constantly gone back to issues about the place of Christians in Corinthian society (e.g., Chow 1992; Clarke

1993), or to more specific related issues such as the eating of food offered in the
Greco-Roman cults (e.g., Fotopoulos 2003). Murphy-O'Connor's classic study of
Corinth in Paul's time (Murphy-O'Connor 2002 [1983]) has had a particular
impact in its rooting of the church's issues about communal eating (1 Cor.
11:17-34) within the context of a real Corinthian villa. This approach has recently
been taken further by Horrell in a challenge to relocate the imagined dining space
to a socially more likely setting in rooms east of the theater (Horrell 2004). Bruce
Winter has produced a string of books and articles making substantial use of
Corinthian evidence in interpretation of Paul's letters (e.g., Winter 2001). Jorunn
Økland has made particularly creative recent use of archaeological details about
Corinthian cult practice to make fresh suggestions about the dynamics of the
passages in 1 Corinthians about women (Økland 2004). One particular Corinthian
contextual issue that Meeks discusses is that of the aedile Erastus and his possible
relationship to the person named in Rom. 16:23 (Meeks 1983: 48). Discussion on
this has continued steadily in the past twenty-five years, not least because the
question of whether an early Christian can be securely identified as a member
of the civic elite is one that raises sharp questions for various scholars' overall
constructions of the nature of early Christian communities within their urban
environments (Clarke 1993: 46–56; Meggitt 1998: 135–41).

Physical Environment

There are few places where the successive stages of a city's development have
interacted more oddly than at Corinth. Its reinstatement as a city, in the creation of
the Roman colony in 44 BCE, just over a century after its sacking, involved the
layout of an entirely new grid plan, carefully worked out on conventional Roman
lines. As usual, substantial space was allowed for the forum at the crossroads of
the *decumanus maximus* and *cardo maximus*. Or, rather, it worked the other way
round. Preexisting buildings from the classical and Hellenistic Greek *agora* were
still there. The colonial surveyors laid out the forum around them and placed the
crossing of the two key roads accordingly. However, they oriented the *cardo maximus* toward the port of Lechaion rather than trying to line it up with any of the
(slightly conflicting) orientations of the Greek buildings. This left the forum
sitting neatly in the colonial grid plan but with its buildings at strange angles to
the grid. Furthermore, when the Romans themselves built in the forum, they
followed one of the Greek orientations rather than lining the buildings up with
their own grid (Romano 2005: 30–41).

Given all that, it is no surprise that the colonial grid layout bore no relation
to the remaining irregular Greek city walls. As well as walls, Corinth had an
acropolis, the Acrocorinth. Temples were located in and around the forum and
at various other places, particularly on the slopes and summit of the Acrocorinth
(Bookidis 2005). What the colonial grid did relate to was a large area of centuriated

farmland, particularly to the north. Several schemes of centuriation were implemented before and during the first century CE (Romano 2005: 43–53). The effort put into these schemes may call into question Meeks's inference from Strabo of the economic insignificance of agriculture around Corinth (Meeks 1983: 48, citing Strabo, *Geog* 8.6.23, C382). So much space seems to have been centuriated that even if, as Strabo asserts, farming was difficult, it must have been a major component of the city's economic activity.

Social Environment

The ambiguity of the layout of the colony is reflected in the city's social structure. Just as the firmly colonial grid was adapted at its center to accommodate previous Greek alignments, Anthony Spawforth has shown that the firmly colonial senior political posts as *duoviri* were several times occupied by Greeks in the first century CE (Spawforth 1996: 174; discussed in Walters 2005: 408). Unlike Pompeii, where the populace in general became indistinguishably Roman soon after colonization, or Philippi, where colonial government was kept firmly in Roman hands, Corinth witnessed a more complex interaction of Roman and Greek culture and identity. Ultimately, particularly under the patronage of Hadrian, this eventuated in something of a re-Hellenization of Corinth in the second century CE.

Another of Spawforth's conclusions is that nine of the identifiable *duoviri* were descendants of freed slaves (Spawforth 1996: 169). It is hard to know how radically the initial composition of the colony, predominantly of freed slaves and poor freeborn citizens, will have affected the social environment over succeeding decades. The experience of Pompeii suggests that the effect was not likely to be very great. As we have noted, Pompeian families of wealthy freed slaves rapidly fitted into the social patterns of the existing elite. There is undoubtedly far more to be brought to light by archaeological study of Corinth. However, I would be quite surprised if it was shown that the social hierarchy of the city at the time of Paul's letters differed radically from that of Greco-Roman cities in general.

5. Conclusions

Looking at these three Pauline cities, it is evident that most types of feature of the Pompeian urban environment, both physical and social, occur in each place: the main exception being the Greek political structure in Thessalonica. Each city also has distinctive aspects. The Pompeian model provides a convenient and well-evidenced backdrop against which to see both the commonalities and the differences between the Pauline cities.

In the twenty-five years since Meeks's book appeared, scholarship has done little to undermine the fundamental points in his "urban environment" chapter.

The main change over the period has been a deepening and broadening of social study of the first century, as scholars have brought more and more tools and sources of evidence to bear. If we wanted to pick one issue to epitomize the changes that this has brought about, we might choose study of the social significance of space. From regional geography, to urban layout, to domestic interiors, work has explored the social shaping of space, and the ways in which that socially shaped space then affects lives. Space and power; space and honor: the brief comments above, on Pompeii, show one way into these topics. Because, in Pompeii, we have extensive supporting evidence to help us uncover aspects of how various spaces functioned, the town can provide a model to help in understanding aspects of the functioning of space in less well-preserved towns. Other scholars have pursued a range of other ways into spatial topics. Looking back across this quarter-century of scholarship, Meeks's description of the urban environment does look as though it somewhat underrepresents spatial issues. However, this is retrospect. Meeks's chapter remains an excellent study that has had, and continues to have, a positive and far-reaching impact in setting a context for Pauline studies.

Chapter 3

SOCIO-ECONOMIC PROFILING OF THE FIRST URBAN CHRISTIANS

Bruce W. Longenecker

1. MEEKS'S CONTRIBUTION IN CONTEXT

Interest in the socio-economic profile of the first urban followers of Jesus has a long history, having a strong foothold even in patristic literature of the early centuries CE.[1] But only recently has scholarly discussion about the issue taken on a controversial edge in an unprecedented way. The debate derives its importance not from some speculative interest in the size of the "wallets" of the first urban Jesus followers. Nor is it that their socio-economic level derives its primary utility in relation to the interpretative nuances of a few early Christian texts. Instead, the issue is central for understanding things like how early urban groups of Jesus followers may have attracted or deterred first-century urban dwellers and how those groups were internally constituted. In order to address issues of this kind, socio-economic factors need to be taken into full account, even if they may fall short of providing all-encompassing explanations.

Wayne Meeks's impressive *The First Urban Christians* stands tall in explorations of matters such as these. One of the most important contributions of that book is its consideration of the extent to which the rise of Christianity in first-century urban contexts was assisted by socio-economic factors. Since innumerable (other) clubs and associations existed within Greco-Roman urbanism, Meeks was interested in understanding what particular attractions early Christian groups might have offered urban dwellers, without resorting to sociological reductionism (see esp. Meeks 1983: 1–7). In this, Meeks sought to take full account of the fact that, in the ancient world (and today as well), a full register of a person's status

---

1 See, for instance, Origen, *Contra Celsum* 3; Augustine, *De divinatione daemonum* 10.14; Chrysostom, *de laudabis sancti Pauli* 4.11. On similar interest in 1 Cor. 1:26 by Theodore of Mopsuestia and Theodoret, see *Catenae Graecorum Patrum in Novum Testamentum* Vol. V: *Catenae in Sancti Pauli Epistolas ad Corinthios* (ed. John Anthony Cramer; repr.; Hildesheim: Georg Olms, 1967 [1841]), 30–31; *Pauluskommentare aus der griechischen Kirche* (ed. Karl Staab; 2nd ed.; Münster: Aschendorff, 1984), 174.

involved a blend of diverse factors, the economic being only one. Meeks alerted his readers to a variety of features that would have contributed to a person's social profile: ethnic origins, *ordo*, citizenship, personal liberty, wealth, occupation, age, sex, public offices or honors, and family heritage (pp. 54–55).

To what extent might status issues shed light on the rise of the early Christian movement? At the forefront of Meeks's proposals are people who were "status-inconsistent" in the Greco-Roman world. For Meeks, such people occupied "an ambiguous position in society," and groups of Jesus followers offered them a means to resolve their socially perceived status inconsistency. For any in this bracket, some indicators would have registered higher up the status scale while others would have registered lower down (cf. Hopkins 1965: 26). In Meeks's view, two intertwined factors would have served to attract status-dissonant middling urbanites to groups of Jesus followers, as opposed to other Greco-Roman associations. Meeks outlines this double-attraction in the final paragraphs of *The First Urban Christians*: (1) the Christian "good news" of divinely empowered "change" would have been attractive to "status-inconsistents," since the structures of society were generally stacked against beneficial change, and (2) the intimacy that transpired within groups of Jesus followers would have been attractive to status-inconsistents, since corporate intimacy would have offset the inevitable "anxiety" and "loneliness" of status-dissonant urbanites through the "emotion-charged language of family and affections and the image of a caring, personal God" (p. 191).

Meeks's thesis is derived primarily from evidence within Paul's corpus of texts, since that corpus, more than any other within the early stratum of Christian literature, testifies to the urban context of the first generation of the Christian movement (so Meeks 1983: 7–8). Accordingly, the second chapter of Meeks's book is entitled "The Social Level of Pauline Christians." This is a pivotal chapter, making a strong arc into the closing paragraphs of his book. Meeks's concluding explanation for the rise of early Christianity takes full account of the issues of socio-economic status that he explores in his second chapter. In fact, the end of the "social level" chapter concludes much as the book does, with the claim that "the most active and prominent members of Paul's circle . . . are people of high status inconsistency" (p. 73). Meeks then asks the pressing questions:

> Is that more than accidental? Are there some specific characteristics of early Christianity that would be attractive to status-inconsistents? Or is it only that people with the sorts of drive, abilities, and opportunities that produced such mixed status would tend to stand out in any group they joined, and thus to be noticed for the record? (p. 73)

Chapters 3–6 in Meeks's *The First Urban Christians* are very much directed at giving a "non-accidental" explanation for the presence of people of high "status inconsistency" in Paul's communities, noting how those communities offered resources to offset the deficits that accompanied status inconsistency. Those who found their middling form of "status inconsistency" to be offset in Paul's communities provided the resources for Christian corporate life, and consequently held the key to the expansion of the early Christian movement within the Mediterranean basin in the first century CE. In this way, Meeks's second chapter in many ways serves as a primary foundation for the whole of his project.

Criticism has been levelled at Meeks's attempt to explain the socio-economic attractions of early urban Christianity in relation to the resolution of "status inconsistency" (see, e.g., Pleket 1985). Since status inconsistency was arguably a phenomenon that pertained to a wide spectrum of people, it consequently fails to have the explanatory power that Meeks affords it in relation to a narrower band within that spectrum.

For instance, psychological factors such as "anxiety," which carry significant weight in Meeks's analysis of motivational bases, are not themselves restricted to middling status-inconsistents. Clearly, anxiety would have marked out the existence of low status holders who lived near or at poverty levels; moreover, we should not fail to recognize the extent to which the elite themselves were subject to anxiety. Few, if any, were ever removed from the precarious prospect of loss: "The fear of loss, of the downward mobility that was so common, was nearly universal," involving "deep-seated and often undifferentiated fears about powerlessness and lack of control in life" (Rohrbaugh 1984: 543). Philo of Alexandria makes the point with polemical acuteness when speaking to the elite with this rhetorical question and subsequent instruction: "Does everything succeed with you according to your wish? Fear a change" (*metabolen eulabou, Ios.* 144). The fact that the elite seem not to have sought shelter against anxiety in the earliest Christian communities suggests that scenarios placing anxiety about status front and center are not fully nuanced.

Meeks's discussion of "the social level of Pauline Christians" contributes to a dispute that was long-standing in 1983 and still continues today. Much of the scholarship dedicated to the issue in the twentieth century showed a marked indebtedness to Adolf Deissmann's analysis. Deissmann's postulate of a "close inward connection between the gospel and the lower classes" was understood (rightly or wrongly) to mean that early Christianity was a movement of and for the poor and destitute (Deissmann 1910: 403). So in 1975 John Gager could speak of "something approaching a consensus" within scholarship, with early Christianity being depicted as "essentially a movement among disprivileged [*sic*] groups in the Empire."[2] The point has been championed most starkly in relation to an economic profiling of early urban Christians by Justin Meggitt, who writes:

> The Pauline Christians *en masse* shared fully the bleak material existence which was the lot of more than 99% of the inhabitants of the Empire . . .

---

2   Gager 1975: 96. Holmberg (1990: 28) characterizes this view as maintaining early Christianity to have been "a religion of the slaves and the oppressed, made up of poor peasants and workers."

To believe otherwise . . ., given the near universal prevalence of poverty in the first-century world, is to believe the improbable (Meggitt 1998: 99).

But alternative emphases have also been strongly registered along the way. In 1960, for instance, Edwin Judge claimed that "the Christians were dominated by a socially pretentious section of the population of the big cities," with those "socially pretentious" members of the community supporting "a broad constituency" that included predominantly "the household dependants of the leading members" (Judge 2008 [repr.]: 43; cf. 119). In the early 1970s Wilhelm Wuellner argued that the earliest urban Christians "came by and large from fairly well-to-do bourgeois circles, with a fair percentage also from upper class people as well as the very poor" (Wuellner 1973: 672; cf. O'Day 1990: 263), while Jürgen Becker found early urban Christianity to have been driven by "a self-confident, urban bourgeoisie with entrepreneurial spirit and sizeable wealth."[3] And by the late 1970s and early 1980s, other strong voices were being heard along similar lines, including those of Gerd Theissen (esp. 1982), Abraham Malherbe (1977 [1983]), Robin Scroggs (1980), and of course Meeks himself. Instead of Christianity's primary appeal being seen in terms of its attractions for the poor, it was common to characterize the early Christian movement as having been comprised of socially diverse members who were supported in communities by its most prominent members. Those members were predominantly "the urban middle-status holders,"[4] who enjoyed an elevated socio-economic status (at least by comparison with the numerous poor).

Both sides of the debate have advocates among scholars twenty-five years after the appearance of Meeks's *The First Urban Christians*.[5] It is common to depict the two positions in terms of those who advocate the "new consensus" (i.e., Theissen, Meeks, etc.) over against the "old consensus" (i.e., Deissmann, etc.). But in fact, the differences between these two positions have at times been unnecessarily overdrawn.

I suggest this for two reasons. First, most scholars recognize a spread of some sort within the socio-economic profile of the early urban groups of Jesus followers, so that the debate often has most to do with particular nuances and refinements to the overall picture. For instance, when Theissen writes that the "majority of the members . . . come from the lower classes" but that "a few influential members . . . come from the upper classes,"[6] it is only the second clause about "a few influential members" that is in any way contentious for some.

---

3 Becker 1993: 168.
4 My translation of Schleich's "der städtischen Mittelschichten" (1982: 288; cf. 279).
5 Compare, for instance, Meggitt 1998 and Friesen 2004 on the one hand and Horrell 1996: 91–101 on the other. See now Horrell 2009 for a slight qualification to his earlier position.
6 Theissen 1982: 69. The word "class" is an unfortunate English translation of Theissen's original "Schicht," which, as Horrell rightly notes (1996: 95 n. 189), should be translated "stratum."

Second, the debate may have been overdrawn due to terminological variation within academic parlance. Arguably, for instance, some who speak of the attractions of early Christianity for the "lower classes" mean to include by that designation the vast swathes of people, all of which fell below the elite but at varying points. If the terms "elite" and "upper classes" can refer to those endowed with enormous amounts of status resources, the terms "the poor" or "the lower class" have at times been used to demarcate all the rest. This is where a lack of clarity can potentially arise, because a term like "lower class" can be used to demarcate either *status* deficiencies (more broadly) or *economic* deficiencies (more narrowly). Not unlike the ancient rhetorical practice of distinguishing between the few *honestiores* and the many *humiliores*, some scholars have adopted the discourse of "the lower class" to refer not simply to those at or near the poverty line but to a broad category of people, including those that others would describe as among the economically middling groups (see Friesen 2004: 324–26). Terminological ambiguity within scholarly discourse cannot account for all points of scholarly disagreement, of course. But it may go some way toward blunting what might at times look to be a debate unnecessarily entrenched in polar opposites.[7]

This point might be made, for instance, by comparing Meeks's position with Gager's. Although they are usually seen to fall on either side of the scholarly divide with regard to the economic level of earliest urban Christians, Meeks and Gager reconstruct the social function of the early Christian movement in much the same way:

> Those who were attracted to the Christian movement as a religion with unmistakably revolutionary implications were not those who stood at the very bottom of the social ladder, that is, the deprived in an absolute sense, but rather those with social aspirations who found their path blocked by the rigidity of the Roman social structure.

The words are Gager's in 1982,[8] but the position resonates well with Meeks's description of "status-inconsistents" in 1983.[9]

Meeks's position with regard to the social profile of Paul's communities has itself, it seems, been subject to occasional misinterpretation. Steven Friesen, for instance, understands Meeks to say that, despite having a broad membership from several social levels, Paul's communities "did not include the . . . lowest strata

---

7 The issue may involve more than simply terminological imprecision. It may also involve issues pertaining to the "sociology of knowledge." On this, see Rohrbaugh 1984: 530–31; Friesen 2004: 323–37.

8 Gager 1982: 262; cf. Gager 1975: 95.

9 Meeks (1983: 215 n. 20) identifies Gager's "relative deprivation" thesis as being "closely related" to his own "status inconsistency" thesis.

of society" (Friesen 2004 326 n. 10). But it is not clear that this description adequately represents Meeks's position. The relevant paragraph from Meeks is as follows:

> We have found a number of converging clues . . . that permit an impressionistic sketch of these groups. It is a picture in which people of several social levels are brought together. The extreme top and bottom of the Greco-Roman social scale are missing from the picture. It is hardly surprising that we meet no landed aristocrats, no senators, *equites*, nor . . . decurions. But there is also no specific evidence of people who are destitute—such as the hired menials and dependent handworkers . . . There may well have been members of the Pauline communities who lived at the subsistence level, but we hear nothing of them (pp. 72–73).

Meeks does not say that Paul's communities "did not include" the lowest strata of society (contra Friesen), only that there is "no specific evidence" of such people, allowing for the fact that "[t]here may well have been members of the Pauline communities who lived at the subsistence level." Hearing nothing about the destitute does not mean that the destitute were not present in Paul's communities; it means only that their imprint has not been left on the surviving material record.

Meeks is right to be skeptical about members of the elite being part of Paul's communities, but there is reason to be more optimistic about the data pertaining to the destitute within those communities. Regardless of whether we have "specific evidence," the grain of New Testament data runs in the direction of signaling that Paul's communities must have included a significant number of destitute members. This view is based not merely on the occasional reference to such people within Paul's letters (e.g., "those who have nothing," 1 Cor. 11:22), it is based primarily on those texts that demonstrate that Paul expected treasuries for the poor (or their equivalent) to be established within communities that he founded. Scholars have not always recognized the extent to which Paul's communities were engaged in extending relief to the poor, and consequently, I have tried to spell this out elsewhere.[10] Various New Testament texts testify to a strong presence of the urban-destitute-beyond-the-confines-of-a-household within Paul's communities, many of whom must have been attracted to such communities for whatever economic support those communities might have provided. This feature helps to explain, for instance, how Paul can laud communities like those in Thessalonica for their "work of faith and labor of love" that had been reported throughout the region of Macedonia and Achaia (as says Paul hyperbolically in 1 Thess. 1:3-10).

---

10   Longenecker 2007: 45–59. The case will be elaborated elsewhere; see Longenecker forthcoming b.

It is also important to note that Meeks's analysis works well if we imagine early Jesus followers to have been embedded within household structures. A typical household would have been comprised of a householder, the householder's family, and a group of servile functionaries. Many of those slaves would have been poor in and of themselves, although being embedded within a household would often have provided some relative security. Similarly, as a householder joined a group of Jesus followers, so too would those within the household (or those whom the householder designated).[11]

More recently, however, scholars have been toying with other organizational models as the context for the meetings of the earliest followers of Jesus.[12] In these cases, the influence of a householder is greatly reduced or altogether absent. For instance, David Horrell has noted "the considerable variety of possible types of domestic space—from country villas to peasant homes, smart town apartments to rooms behind or over a shop, not to mention the more ramshackle and temporary dwellings of the destitute." So he warns against imagining any of them as necessarily "typical" settings in the rise of the Christian movement: "NT studies should pay more attention to the varieties of domestic space in the urban setting of Corinth and other cities of the Roman empire, and consider these as possible settings for early Christian meetings" (Horrell 2004: 366, 369). While Meeks's reconstruction works especially well in relation to the household model, where (middling group) householders hold predominant forms of power, it will have less explanatory force when other models are adopted as heuristic models for considering the social context from which earliest groups of Jesus followers emerged.

As noted already, Meeks alerts his readers to the commonplace that status was multidimensional in the ancient world. Quite simply, economic profiling is only one dimension of status profiling, with a variety of other factors contributing to a full canvassing of status in the ancient world. With that said, however, Meeks's chapter on the "social level of Pauline Christians" includes a strong economic focus.[13] This is not necessarily surprising, nor is it illegitimate. It is arguable that, generally speaking, status was intricately connected to economic resources. Access to economic resources enhanced one's chances of status improvement,

---

11   Cf. Judge 2008: 44, 119, for whom the rise of earliest Christianity was primarily an urban phenomenon of household conversions.

12   Exceptions to the household conversion model are evident in 1 Cor. 7:12-16; 1 Tim. 6:1-2; and 1 Pet. 3:1-2.

13   All examples of status inconsistency in the final paragraphs of Meeks's book include an economic component (1983: 191): "independent women with moderate wealth, Jews with wealth in a pagan society, freedmen with skill and money but stigmatized by origin." Clearly, other dimensions of status might have been foregrounded in Meeks's study, not least issues of gender. While studies on gender have been copious since the publication of Meeks's volume, they will not be the focus of this article, since they were not the primary focus of Meeks's second chapter.

and improved status usually enhanced one's access to economic resources (cf. Veyne 1990: 44). So classicist Greg Woolf rightly notes that in the ancient world one's access to wealth was "one of the most explicit and formal measures of an individual's social standing and a key component of his public identity" (Woolf 2006: 92).

If economic profiling looms large in Meeks's analysis, it has also been the focus of some of the most stimulating discussions of status in the wake of Meeks's work. This is true most significantly of contributions by Justin Meggitt and Steven Friesen. Their analyses, however, lead to scenarios in which Paul's Christian communities are entrenched in poverty far more than the scenarios that Meeks, Theissen, Judge, and others seem to envision, or at least articulate.

Most challenging in this respect is Meggitt's *Paul, Poverty and Survival,* which appeared in 1998. Meggitt proposed that a scholarly paradigm has been constructed on the basis of an interlocking package of erroneous interpretations that are founded on a flawed methodology. Front and center in Meggitt's criticisms are those who adhere to the "new consensus," that is, those who imagine that people of some notable economic means were primary players in the constituency and development of earliest Christianity. In this, of course, Meeks is fully in Meggitt's rhetorical sights.

Whether in agreement with him or not, scholars immediately recognized Meggitt's work to be a major contribution to the field. Meggitt had thrown down the gauntlet so effectively that what had often looked like robust historical work might look a bit more like the results of an interpretative consensus that shared less-than-secure interpretative assumptions as it engaged with historical data. This is not to suggest that Meggitt's own historical reportage was free of interpretative elements. Most significantly, his reconstruction of the Greco-Roman world is shot through with a binary predilection that contrasts an extremely small group of ancient elite with a huge and relatively undifferentiated majority struggling at subsistence levels of existence. This binary model has itself come under heavy fire in classical studies and is not itself free of interpretative weaknesses (see further Longenecker 2009). Nonetheless, not without cause Meggitt's work has attracted significant attention in the decade since its initial appearance.[14]

Another important contribution was made by Friesen in 2004. His work is comprised of characteristics from both sides of the debate. On the one hand, Friesen proposed a seven-tiered scale of Greco-Roman economic levels: the three top levels demarcate the economic level of the various elite; the three bottom levels demarcate those whose identity is configured in relation to poverty; the middle level demarcates those with "moderate surplus." Accordingly, Friesen's model outlines economic levels in a much more nuanced way than Meggitt's binary presentation and gives a foothold for middling groups—much like Meeks's view

---

14   See especially the articles in *JSNT* 24 (2001).

of the ancient world. The chart of Friesen's economic levels, descriptors, and percentages is as follows:[15]

Chart Showing Friesen's Seven-Point Poverty Scale, with His Estimated Percentages

Scale	Description	Includes	%
ES1	Imperial elites	Imperial dynasty, Roman senatorial families, a few retainers, local royalty, a few freedpersons	0.04
ES2	Regional or provincial elites	Equestrian families, provincial officials, some retainers, some decurial families, some freedpersons, some retired military officers	1
ES3	Municipal elites	Most decurial families, wealthy men and women who did not hold office, some freedpersons, some retainers, some veterans, some merchants	1.76
ES4	Moderate surplus	Some merchants, some traders, some freedpersons, some artisans (especially those who employ others), and military veterans	7
ES5	Stable near subsistence level (with reasonable hope of remaining above the minimum level to sustain life)	Many merchants and traders, regular wage earners, artisans, large shop owners, freedpersons, some farm families	22
ES6	At subsistence level (and often below minimum level to sustain life)	Small farm families, laborers (skilled and unskilled), artisans (esp. those employed by others), wage earners, most merchants and traders, small shop/tavern owners	40
ES7	Below subsistence level	Some farm families, unattached widows, orphans, beggars, disabled, unskilled day laborers, prisoners	28

On the other hand, while Friesen's model has the potential to get beyond a binary model in its brute form, his own analysis betrays an indebtedness to binary presuppositions about the ancient world—much like Meggitt's. This is evident in the 7% he awards to ES4, which, as I argue elsewhere, should be increased to 17% or so, with other adjustments in tow (Longenecker 2009).

Chart Comparing Friesen's Percentages and My Proposed Percentages

	Friesen's Percentages for Economic Levels of the Greco-Roman World	Reworked Percentages for Economic Levels of the Greco-Roman World
ES1–ES3	3	3
ES4	7	17
ES5	22	25
ES6–ES7	68 (40, 28)	55 (30, 25)

---

15 Note that whereas Friesen 2004 identified these levels as "PS" levels (i.e., poverty scale levels), my own preference is to call them "ES" levels (i.e., economic scale levels), as in this chart.

Moreover, Friesen is critical of the views of Meeks and others, offering a clarion call to the discipline much like Meggitt's:

> the discipline of Pauline studies in the early twenty-first century appears to have no interest in why people were poor or how the Pauline assemblies dealt with economic injustice. Instead of remembering the poor, we prefer to discuss upwardly mobile individuals and how they coped with the personal challenges of negotiating their ambivalent social status (Friesen 2004: 336).

This is a constructive and important challenge for the study of early urban Christianity.

While inevitable weaknesses attend to models of the kind advocated by Friesen, the advantages of Friesen's model outweigh its potential disadvantages; ignoring Friesen's efforts is not a live option. In particular, with its variegated categorization, Friesen's taxonomy offers scholars a discursive framework from which to analyze data, in three helpful ways. First, its sevenfold construction assists in the avoidance of a simplistic binary modeling of the ancient world. Second, and relatedly, the scale is workable for practitioners in its relatively restricted number of differentiated levels; we simply do not have the relevant data to be much more refined in assigning economic levels (although ES4 should probably be differentiated into ES4a at its upper end and ES4b at its lower end).[16] Third, Friesen's adjusted scale offers a discursive frame of reference that goes a long way in avoiding the terminological imprecision that has often plagued scholarly debate (as noted above with regard to terms like "the lower class"). In view of these three advantages, the next generation of scholarship on the first urban followers of Jesus will do well to put a scale of this kind front and center in its deliberations.

With that in mind, the revised economy scale will serve as the basis for the following sections of this essay. So, section 2 gives brief consideration to prosopographic evidence with regard to named individuals from Paul's communities. Paul's rhetorical construction of his communities' general economic level is then considered in relation to the economic scale in section 3. Section 4 considers the issue that inherently drove so much of Meeks's own study—the extent to which the first urban groups of Jesus followers would have offered socio-economic attractions within their urban environment. A final section notes the effects of these matters on Meeks's overall thesis.

2. PROSOPOGRAPHIC EVIDENCE: LOCATING PEOPLE MENTIONED IN PAUL'S LETTERS

Socio-economic profiles of early Christianity usually include a prosopographic analysis of the status indicators that have made their way into early Christian

---

16 Contrast Friesen's revised economic scale, unveiled at Annual Meeting of the Society of Biblical Literature in 2007, which is comprised of 120 economic levels.

texts. These analyses normally focus on Paul's letters, where Paul at times speaks of individual Jesus followers in relation to one or two status indicators.

Prosopographic surveys are plagued by difficulties in knowing how to assess certain indicators. For instance, what factors would indicate that someone has "comfortable" economic resources? Perhaps travel? Or being an artisan engaged in a trade? Or being a householder? Or providing hospitality? Or having a slave? Or allowing a Christian group to meet in one's home? Or opening one's home to a collective of Christians groups? Such indicators are interspersed within Paul's texts, and none of them is a wholly reliable or transparent social indicator for composing a prosopographic profile.

A full prosopographic taxonomy will not be attempted here, however. This is for two reasons. First, a prosopographic analysis requires detailed consideration that word-restrictions preclude here. Second, although the data is handled differently by different interpreters, prosopographic analyses rarely differ all that much in their conclusions about particular individuals. Where they do differ, the differences are not all that significant.[17]

The second of these claims might seem surprising, but a simple trawl through three prosopographic analyses from the last three decades (i.e., those of Meeks 1983, Horrell 1996, and Friesen 2004) illustrates how relatively stable prosopographic analyses have been during that time, even across the "consensus" divide.[18] Similarities between Meeks and Horrell may not be particularly notable, since Horrell does not do much to differentiate himself from the "new consensus" that Meeks represents. Friesen, on the other hand, mounts a significant challenge to that consensus. Despite this, however, Friesen's prosopographic itemization does not differ in any significant measure from the sort of conclusions that Meeks himself drew. Of course, there are differences here and there. In general, Friesen errs on the side of depressing the prosopographic features, whereas Meeks errs on the side of inflating them. But despite these differences, Friesen's prosopographic conclusions with regard to specific individuals are not a world away from similar analyses by some that are firmly within the "new consensus."

In Friesen's estimation, for instance, up to seven individuals mentioned by Paul "can be classified as having moderate surplus resources," including: Chloe (if a member of a Pauline community) and Gaius at ES4; and Erastus, Philemon, Phoebe, Aquila, and Prisca at either ES4 or perhaps ES5 (Friesen 2004: 348). Once again, there are, of course, differences between Meeks and Friesen, as is generally the case when two scholars assess the same data.[19] But the differences

---

17   Where scholarly differences become significant is in relation to descriptors pertaining to the "wealthiest" among the Christian groups and in imagining how representative the wealthiest are within the constituency of the urban Christian groups; on this, see section 3 below.

18   Meeks 1983: 55–63; Horrell 1996: 91–101; Friesen 2004: 348–58.

19   For example, Meeks (1983: 57–58) includes Stephanas within this upper-band of the "wealthiest" Christians (relatively speaking, although lower than Erastus, Gaius, and Crispus), whereas Friesen (2004: 352) puts Stephanas in ES5 or ES6.

are not all that significant. With the exception of Erastus (Rom. 16:23) and perhaps one or two others,[20] neither scholar includes the elite of ES1–ES3 in the prosopographic mix of early Christian communities, and each has a spread of adherents from the middling groups downward. Perhaps there is more in common than is sometimes thought between those who challenge the "new consensus" and the more cautious advocates of the "new consensus." Here again is some evidence of how the scholarly debate can too easily be stereotyped and overdrawn.

In my view, a prosopographic analysis of individuals mentioned in 1 Corinthians, Romans 16, and Philemon (excluding other letters of Paul and the Lukan Acts of the Apostles)[21] suggests the following:

1. those who seem to fall within ES4 include Erastus (Rom. 16:23), Gaius (1 Cor. 1:14; Rom. 16:23), and Phoebe (Rom. 16:1-2);[22]
2. those who seem to fall within either ES4 or ES5 include Chloe (1 Cor. 1:11), Stephanas (1 Cor. 16:15-16), Philemon (Phlm.), and Crispus (1 Cor. 1:14-16; cf. Acts 18:8); and
3. Prisca and Aquila (1 Cor. 16:19; Rom. 16:3; cf. 2 Tim. 4:19; Acts 18:1-27) probably fall within ES5.[23]

If scholarly differences with regard to individuals mentioned by Paul are generally not all that significant, the differences become more interesting with regard to how scholars map out the proportion of those individuals in relation to the larger makeup of early urban groups of Jesus followers. To what extent are ES4 members indicative of the economic profile of urban Christian communities in general? If a rough guide is to be found in this regard, it involves a double approach: (1) taking into account Paul's rhetorical construct of his communities' economic

---

20   Meeks (1983: 59) puts Erastus in the position of a civic elite.

21   On the socio-economic levels of Paul's associates in Acts, see Friesen 2006, 2008.

22   These are presumably the kind of people whom Paul has in mind as exceptions when he writes that "not many of you hold influence or are well-born" (*ou polloi dynatoi, ou polloi eugeneis*, 1 Cor. 1:26). Limitations of space preclude discussion of the issue of whether the Erastus of Rom. 16:23 is the same person mentioned on a first-century CE Corinthian inscription. I think this to be unlikely. For a strong case against identifying the two as the same man, see Meggitt 1996. With regard to the socio-economic status of the Erastus of Rom. 16:23, the term *ho oikonomos tēs poleōs* places him in a position of some status, even though the term can also span socio-economic levels. Cf. Pleket 1985: 194: "[T]he true parallel for the status of such an *oikonomos* [i.e., the Erastus of the Corinthian inscription] is an inscription from Stobi (SEG XXIV 496), where a certain Diadoumenos *as slave* fulfills that function, rather than Hellenistic civic decrees which mention free-born and respectable *oikonomoi*." In my view, Erastus is likely to be comparable to the Augustales, whom I locate primarily in ES4a; see Longenecker 2009. The Augustales consisted predominantly of freedmen who, due to their servile past, were generally excluded from securing decurial posts but who, upon gaining their freedom and in view of the viability of their financial resources, were willingly conscripted and appointed by decurial patrons to enhance local civic life.

23   This is a lower category than many might imagine to be appropriate. But see Lampe 2003: 190–91.

location, and (2) making educated guesses about the potential attractions of those communities for different economic levels. Each of these issues is explored in the following sections of this essay.

3. PAUL'S RHETORICAL CONSTRUCTION OF HIS COMMUNITIES' ECONOMIC LEVEL

Most of the individuals whom Paul mentions by name, and whose economic profile can be tentatively reconstructed, seem to fall within ES4 or ES5. It is notable, then, that when he envisages the economic profile of his communities in general, Paul's descriptions seem to drop a level, gravitating toward the ES5 level primarily, with some resonance with ES6.[24] His descriptions usually exclude the categories on either side of these economic levels (i.e., ES4 and ES7).

Paul gives advice in 1 Cor. 16:1-2 about how Corinthian followers of Jesus should put a little aside every week in preparation for the collection. This advice makes the most sense if it is directed to those of ES5, and possibly ES6. Those among ES7 would have had nothing to put aside, while those in ES4 would probably have had resources that are out of alignment with the kind of advice that Paul offers.[25] So Paul's description of the Corinthian situation (along with that of his Galatian communities, also mentioned in 1 Cor. 16:1-2) rhetorically excludes ES7 and gravitates primarily toward ES6 and, especially, ES5. This does not mean that the Corinthian and Galatian communities had no representatives from ES4 and ES7, but simply that Paul is not addressing them primarily in this passage.

This instance resonates with the preponderance of other data. On those occasions when Paul's discourse includes an indicator of his audience's economic level, that level gravitates to ES5 especially. Of particular interest is the use of the phrase "work with your own hands." Of relevance are the following passages where this phrase appears: 1 Cor. 4:11-13; 1 Thess. 4:11-12; Eph. 4:28; and Acts 20:34-35 (the latter two with slight changes to the form). While the phrase might conceivably be appropriate to a variety of levels, it would exclude most in the ES4 descriptor (except upper-level artisans). In 1 Cor. 4:12 Paul makes use of the phrase in a list of entries meant to illustrate the extremely low end of status levels. In 1 Cor. 4:11-13, Paul offers a catalog of hardships to show that he embodies all that is held in disrepute according to cultural standards and expectations. He is nothing other than "the world's scum" (*perikatharmata tou kosmou*) and

---

24   This view refines that of Friesen: "The group references that have economic significance assume that most of the saints lived at subsistence level" (2004: 350). Instead of ES6, as Friesen implies, a higher economic register is often noted in Paul's group references.

25   Paul must have expected those at ES4 to be involved in his collection, but his advice in this passage does not apply to them primarily.

"the scrapings from everyone's shoes" (*pantōn peripsēma eōs arti*).[26] He counters these lowly status indicators with another that he expects to trump them all—that of Paul being the Corinthians' progenitor in faith (*patēr*, 4:15). The Corinthians are in the odd situation of being status-inconsistent with their own "spiritual father." For they imagine themselves to be enjoying overabundance (*kekoresmenoi este*), to have been made rich (*eploutēsate*), and to have been established as kings (*ebasileusate*), as ones who are strong (*ischyroi*) and honored (*endoxoi*). But Paul glories in his weakness and disrepute, marshalling evidence to prove his cultural dishonor. He has experienced hunger, thirst, homelessness; he has had a lack of proper clothing and has suffered abuse, persecution, and slander. Among these dishonorable entries Paul includes "working with our own hands" in 4:12 (*ergazomenoi tais idiais chersin*).

While most of the entries in Paul's catalog of vices in 1 Cor. 4:11-13 could well apply to ES7 situations, it would be wrong to assign, by association, the phrase "working with hands" to that same economic level. That phrase resonates with sub-elite levels ES6 through ES4 (ES4b more so than ES4a). The "working with hands" phrase may be at home in Paul's "low-status hardship list," but it does not drop to the bottom of that list like some other entries do. Paul incorporates his manual labor into the frame because it is a live issue among his audience (cf. 1 Cor. 9) and, relatedly, because manual labor was generally despised by the elite and used as a mark of inferiority by the rich who enjoyed overabundance and high-levels of social honor (see Finley 1974: 40–43). Accordingly, even if the phrase "working with hands" is rhetorically aligned here with ES7 descriptors, it is best taken as a descriptor of economic levels higher than ES7. Conversely, if the phrase resonates well at ES6 and ES5 levels, it nonetheless starts to become a bit thinly stretched as a descriptor of ES4, precisely in view of its rhetorical utility in Paul's hardship list.

A similar picture emerges in 1 Thess. 4:11-12, where Paul advises members of his communities "to work with your own hands, as we directed you, so that you may command the respect of outsiders and be dependent on no one (*mēdenos chreian echēte*)." Here Paul's advice seems targeted at those in ES5 primarily, with some resonance with ES6, but excluding ES7, who were in real need and were wholly dependent on others.

The passage is important beyond initial appearances, since Paul makes it clear that this advice replicates advice that he and his associates had given earlier ("as we directed you"). Meeks writes:

[T]his is a *paraenetic* reminder of instruction given the Thessalonian converts when the church was first organized there. It is not a unique admonition fitted to special needs of the Thessalonians . . . but represents the kind of instruction that Paul and his associates generally gave to new converts (Meeks 1983: 64).

---

26 The translation is that of Thiselton 2000: 344.

It is not surprising, then, that a similar economic characterization of Paul's communities is maintained in two other Pauline texts. The author of 2 Thessalonians advises that Jesus followers should "do their work quietly and to earn their own living" (2 Thess. 3:12). The author of Ephesians proposes that, as a consequence of joining Christian communities, "thieves must give up stealing" and must instead "labor and work honestly with their own hands, so as to have something to share with the needy" (Eph. 4:28). The double-tasked prospect of working with one's hands and sharing with others puts the rhetorical target above the level of ES7, being rhetorically centered primarily in ES5, and possibly ES6. Of course, both of these admonitions occur in disputed Pauline letters, but implications with regard to the economic characterization of Paul's communities are not undermined by that. Instead, if either one or both texts is/are thought to have been authored by someone other than Paul, we would simply have a consistent depiction of the economic characterization of Paul's communities across one or more authors alongside of Paul himself.

It is also notable that when the Lukan author imagined Paul to gather together with members of his communities, he too placed those members generally at the level of ES5. In Acts 20:34-35, when meeting with members of his Ephesian communities among whom he had lived for several years, Paul says: "You know for yourselves that I worked with my own hands to support myself and my companions. In all this I have given you an example that by such work we must support the weak (*dei antilambanesthai tōn asthenountōn*)."[27] The "weak" of Acts 20:35 must overlap considerably with the economically "poor," to the extent that the two are likely to be virtually identical. The Paul of Acts 20 is not speaking to people of ES7, and perhaps not to those of ES6. His scenario of working with one's hands to support oneself and in order to support the needy corresponds most closely to the ES5 economic level.[28]

In two instances Paul's economic register focuses on those who fell within ES7—a category included in the reference to "the weak" of Acts 20:35. In 1 Cor. 11:22, Paul discusses the situation of "those who have nothing" (*tous mē echontas*) in relation to the Corinthian observance of the Lord's Supper.[29] Here Paul's discourse focuses on, and seeks to negotiate, the disparity between those who fall

---

27   Gaventa (2003: 283) rightly notes: "As the book's most extended speech for those who are already Christian (cf. 11:5-17; 15:7-11, 13-21) and the last speech prior to Paul's captivity, this address occupies an important place in the book as a whole."

28   Paul's self-description in Acts 20 accords well with the same in 1 Cor. 9:12-18; 2 Thess. 3:6-10.

29   I interpret *tous mē echontas* in 1 Cor. 11:22 in absolute terms as "those who have nothing." Winter qualifies *tous mē echontas* in relation to the *oikia* of the same verse (1994: 203), so that the phrase differentiates between those with household connections and those without connections to householders. This is possible, and in either reconstruction the economic level of those referred to is likely to be much the same; the difference will simply be in whether *tous mē echontas* pertains only to those beyond households or might also include some within households. Meggitt's claim (1998: 119–20) that *tous mē echontas* refers to "those who do not have bread and wine" seems less likely.

within ES7 (and perhaps ES6) and those higher up the economic registry. This instance does not provide us with a rhetorical construct of the Corinthian's general economic profile, but shows Paul addressing a situation that involved particular individuals who fell predominantly within ES7.

Second Corinthians 8:1-6 provides us with another instance of Paul constructing an economic location of ES7 for some of his communities. There he describes the economic situation of Macedonian Christian communities (i.e., Thessalonica and Philippi). According to Paul, those communities had already given generously to the collection despite their "severe ordeal of affliction" and "extremely onerous poverty" (*hē kata bathous ptōcheia autōn*). Since Paul's advice of 1 Thess. 4:11-12 envisions a higher economic register for Thessalonian followers of Jesus than in 2 Cor. 8:1-6, it may be that in 2 Corinthians Paul is intentionally depressing the economic situation of the Macedonian congregations. This would have had the rhetorical effect, first, of accentuating Macedonian generosity in order, second, to motivate Corinthian generosity through emulation of the Macedonian communities. It is noteworthy, then, that Paul can shift his construct of Macedonian economic identity between ES7 in 2 Cor. 8:1-6 and ES5 (or so) in 1 Thess. 4:11-12, according to the requirements of rhetorical utility.[30]

A similar shift out of ES5 for purposes of rhetorical effect is also likely to be evident in 2 Cor. 8:14, although in this case moving up the scale rather than down it (as in 2 Cor. 8:1-6). Paul's depiction of the Corinthian "abundance" (*perisseuma*) in 2 Cor. 8:14 might be said to describe a community that falls predominantly within ES4 rather than ES5 and below. But this rhetorical construct must be interpreted with some caution. Paul is likely speaking of Corinthian "abundance" in terms relative to the Jerusalem communities. Or the reference to "abundance" might be a subtle way of arm-twisting those few in ES4 from within the Corinthian communities, seeking a generous donation from them for Paul's collection efforts (having already instructed those in ES5, and perhaps ES6, in 1 Cor. 16:1-2). Either way, the term is probably being used with an extra dose of rhetorical spin in this case and should not be used to raise the general profile of the Corinthian communities beyond a general average of ES5, with some falling into higher and some into lower categories.[31]

In general, then, Paul seems to address his communities as if they were comprised primarily of people belonging to ES5. At times the rhetorical target is broad enough to incorporate both ES5 and ES6, but when advice about working with one's hands is combined with exhortations to support others in need, ES5 seems

---

30   It is possible, of course, that when Paul says "Macedonia" he is thinking primarily of Philippian instead of Thessalonian Christians. But this is not the impression his Corinthian audience would have received, unless the one who delivered and (presumably) read the letter pointed it out to them.

31   Other indicators are also neutral economic indicators, such as the fact that some Corinthian Christians were engaged in lawsuits against others. Lawsuits in themselves are not indicative of economic location. See the evidence assembled by Meggitt 1998: 122–25, 152.

to be most in Paul's sights—or at least, his hortatory pressure comes to bear most notably on them. At times Paul moved the level of economic characterization up or down from that point, for rhetorical effect, or when addressing particular people or people groups. But in general, ES5 seems to be where his own mental averaging of his communities seems to gravitate most naturally.

4. Economic Levels and Affiliation Attractions

As Meeks notes, "motivational bases for becoming part of the *ekklēsia* would likely vary from one member to another" (1983:77). And identifying possible "motivational bases" requires an attentiveness to socio-economic location. While socio-economic factors alone will not provide a sufficient explanation for the spread of the early Christian movement and the promulgation of its good news, we need nonetheless to consider the extent to which such factors may have played some part in that spread.

We should guard against the assumption that the only "motivational bases" worthy of note are those of the middling-status artisans and householders. In this regard it is important to query the widespread assumption that Pauline communities really had very little concern for offsetting the condition of the poor in general (see Longenecker 2007: 46–49). If this assumption proves incorrect, then alongside a middle-class artisan and household constituency should be included those beyond the security of households and in economically vulnerable positions. Paul's communities were comprised of members ranging throughout ES4 through ES7, with some at the lower end of the socio-economic scale being members on their own initiative rather than by reason of an attachment to a householder who had joined the group. For this reason, consideration of "motivational bases" needs to be extended beyond the middle-status holders to include also those beyond household structures—not least, the poor.

Arguably, the early Christian movement offered a great deal to impoverished urbanites right from the very start, especially those beyond the relative security of a household. If Paul's communities took initiatives to care for the poor, and if they gathered to share food and drink in corporate dinners and other occasions, it is relatively easy to see what economic attraction such communities would have held for people in ES6 and ES7 who fell beyond the structures of a household. Moreover, this dimension might have distinguished groups of Jesus followers from other urban associations, since Greco-Roman associations did not accumulate their membership from among ES6 and ES7 levels (see below). While economic benefit is probably not a *sufficient* explanation for Christianity's attractions among those in ES6 and ES7, it would nonetheless have been a powerful means of attraction, alongside any other "non-economic" factors that might be tabled.

At the other end of the economic scale, the early Christian movement seems to have had little attraction among the elite of ES1 through ES3. As Edwin Judge noted half a century ago, early Christian groups "did not draw upon the upper order of the Roman ranking system . . . Their social needs were very amply gratified by the exclusive circles to which they were admitted" (Judge 2008 [repr.]: 37). By the late first century CE at the latest, this situation began to change (Lampe 2003: 139). Before that time, it is unlikely that they had much of a presence within urban groups of Jesus followers.[32]

If there is relative clarity with regard to the attractiveness (or otherwise) of early Christianity for those at either end of the economic spectrum, more convoluted is any attempt to theorize the possible attractions of early urban Christianity for those in the middle of the economic scale. In relation to both ES4 and ES5, it is best to proceed by analogy with Greco-Roman *collegia* or associations, for which we have enough data to extrapolate somewhat in relation to groups of early Jesus followers. Such associations were numerous in the first century, and early urban Christianity shared some significant similarities with them.

In a world where identity was calculated in relation to social honor, establishing oneself as a benefactor of an association would have had some obvious attractions. This was true especially for those at the upper end of the middling groups (i.e., ES4a). They would have had both the resources and the motivation to act as an association's benefactor. Being a benefactor of a *collegium* had its own rewards in a number of ways. First, it allowed one to be the equivalent of "a big fish in a (relatively) small pond" (cf. Kloppenborg 1996: 18). Second, it would have enabled the benefactor to increase in social visibility, since *collegia* benefactors were frequently honored by the members of associations in ways that increased their public honor. Consequently, and third, sponsoring an association would have increased the benefactor's chances of entering into an advantageous patronage relationship with a more prominent patron, on the grounds that the benefactor would have had influence within sectors of the populace.

By analogy, we might well imagine similar attractions having motivated some to establish themselves as benefactors of urban groups of Jesus followers. Early Christian communities might well have served as vehicles for social honor for some ES4 figures engaged in the never-ending hunt for "honor capture" that marked out Greco-Roman urbanism.

It needs to be noted, however, that other factors might have made the prospect of becoming a benefactor of an urban Christian group less than wholly appealing. Three will be mentioned here. First, there is a difference between the economic profile of *collegia* in general and urban Christian groups. While there were *collegia* whose membership included rather poor sectors of society (e.g., funerary associations),[33] *collegia* members generally were "drawn from the upper echelons

---

32 It would be hasty, however, to exclude their presence altogether from early groups of Jesus followers, at least from the middle of the first century onward.

33 Note, however, Kloppenborg's case (1996) that funerary associations were not prominent in the first century CE.

of the urban *plebs* and can best be characterized as 'employers' rather than 'employees'" (Patterson 2006: 255). This characterization would place the primary membership of *collegia* within ES5 and ES4 (perhaps ES4b especially), with the *collegia*'s benefactor standing higher up on the economic spectrum (ES4a and higher). As John Patterson has demonstrated, the fact that *collegia* members were not normally drawn from among the needy is both "implied by the costs involved in belonging to a *collegium*" and "reflected in the level of generosity shown to *collegia* members as part of formal distributions or banquets" (Patterson 2006: 255). Patterson's case cannot be fully presented here, except to note that he identifies *collegia* members as "the wealthier elements within the *plebs*." He makes the point in relation to mounting levels of urban growth:

> [U]rban growth led to increasing profits for artisans and traders of the city, leading to an increasing influence on their part and a growing differentiation between them and the destitute . . . Part of this additional wealth financed the development of *collegia* (Patterson 2006: 261).

Describing *collegia* members as primarily artisans and traders who were differentiated from the destitute and who enjoyed the increasing profits of urban growth, Patterson places them squarely within the ES5 and ES4 economic levels.

If honor were ascribed to benefactors of *collegia* whose membership usually fell predominantly within ES5 and ES4 economic levels, it is not clear that similar forms of honor could be expected for benefactors of Christian *ekklēsiai* whose profile included significant levels of ES5 members as well as high percentages of members from ES6 and ES7. Accordingly, the prospect of a member of the elite establishing a patronage relationship with a benefactor of a Christian association comprised primarily of people in ES5 through ES7 may not have been as attractive as patronage connections with sponsors of other kinds of associations.

Chart Comparing the Economic Levels of *Collegia* in General and Christian Groups

Level	*Collegia* in General	Christian Groups
ES4	Predominant Membership Levels	
ES5	Predominant Membership Levels	Predominant Membership Levels
ES6		Predominant Membership Levels
ES7		Predominant Membership Levels

Second, those who sought to establish a relationship of benefaction with a Christian "association" might soon have been repulsed by a general lack of the ascribed honor they expected from those within that association. In this regard it is, of course, impossible to attribute to early Christian communities anything more than a general proclivity toward "culturally transgressive" norms. Certain texts from the early Christian movement reflect how, on some occasions, honor was ascribed within groups of Jesus followers in ways that adhered relatively well with normal social codes. But in each case, the texts' authors are quick to point out that the Christian good news frequently runs contrary to the cultural canons of honor. In the early days of the Christian movement's spread into Mediterranean urban contexts, there is little to suggest that members of Christian *ekklēsiai* were expected to follow their sponsor through the streets among an entourage that publicly proclaimed their sponsor's merits. No lists of honor pertaining to early Christian benefactors are evident in the literary or archaeological data of the earliest Christian movement. Instead, communities of Jesus followers remembered their Lord as having defamed those engaged in honor-bound benefaction and patronage practices, all the way up the socio-economic scale, including "the kings of the Gentiles" (Luke 22:25-26). Instead of engaging in patronal relationships that escalate the honor of those higher up the socio-economic scale, the Jesus tradition promotes relationships that escalate the honor of those at the bottom of the scale (cf. Luke 14:12-14). As Halvor Moxnes says about early Christian passages such as these, "Compared to Hellenistic and later Christian texts, it is remarkable that there is no expectation of reciprocity, not even in the form of gratitude from the poor . . . This is the end of a patron-client relationship in a traditional sense."[34] It is little wonder, then, that Paul called the Christian good news "foolishness to the Gentiles" (1 Cor. 1:23), precisely because that news was frequently interpreted to run contrary to normal codes of social honor.

Third, prospective benefactors of early Christian groups might have been hesitant to establish themselves as sponsors because of the potentially dubious reputation of the Christian movement with regard to the Roman imperial order. A little more than a decade after the publication of Meeks's *The First Urban Christians*, historians of the early Christian movement began revisiting this issue with vigor, asking about the extent to which the Christian good news included a politically subversive or anti-imperial dimension. Romanism was primarily an urban phenomenon, and the Roman imperial cult was at the heart of Roman urbanism in the provinces that the Christian movement was spreading across. Within urban contexts, social advancement was generally inconsistent with anything anti-Roman.

In this light, the relationship between social advancement and adherence to the Christian good news might well have been seen as inversely proportional in certain contexts. The more subversive the early Christian movement appeared, the less attraction it would have held for those enthralled by honor and advancement within Roman urbanism. And at the heart of the good news that Paul proclaimed lay the drama of one crucified on a Roman cross. Throughout the Mediterranean

---

34 Moxnes 1988: 133. See also Meggitt 1998: 175 n. 103.

basin, crucifixion was the recognized punishment for those convicted of antisocial and, ultimately, anti-Roman sentiment. Crucifixion not only removed anti-Roman criminals but promoted fear among the populace and reenacted Roman victory over the nations. In urban contexts of highly charged pro-Romanism, it is not difficult to imagine that "some aspects of early Christian communal life . . . could be seen as politically or socially destabilizing" (Wilson 1996: 3). At times in its early history, the Christian movement was seen as part of the civic problem, holding back urban progress and the Roman program.

The degree to which the gospel of early Jesus followers was politically subversive is an issue currently entangled in debate and cannot be entertained in any detail here. For our purposes, however, the point is simple: The extent to which potential benefactors would have considered the early Christian gospel to have a subversive religio-political dimension (rightly or wrongly) might well have approximated the extent to which the same prospective benefactors would have been hesitant to act as sponsors of Christian groups in urban contexts engulfed in pro-Romanism.

In light of these three factors, sponsoring a group of Jesus followers might have been a less attractive prospect for prospective benefactors than sponsoring some other association or group (of which there were numerous varieties). When faced with the prospect of sponsoring an urban Christian group, one would have had to weigh up both the potential advantages and the potential disadvantages in relation to the register of his/her social honor. Various factors were thrown into the socioeconomic mix and would have been synthesized in different ways by different people in different situations. While sponsoring a group of Jesus followers might have had some aspects of potential attraction, it might also have introduced considerable vulnerability to any in the ES4 economic level who were also immersed in the quest for civic honor and status advancement (esp. those in ES4a). For this reason, there is not necessarily a direct route from isolating socio-economic motivations for sponsors of Greco-Roman *collegia* in general to the isolation of socio-economic motivations for sponsoring early Christian urban groups. Often, in fact, many in ES4 must have imagined that involving themselves in the Christian movement would have added to their status inconsistency within the civic arena rather than reducing it.

To someone in ES5, an urban Christian group might have had some of the same benefits as other associations—i.e., enjoyment of resources (food, drink, conviviality) provided by more economically secure benefactors.[35] Moreover, there

---

35 Cf. Meeks 1983: 104: "For many members, especially those of the humbler social strata, the Christian assemblies and meals provided a more than adequate substitute for benefits, both physical and social, that they might otherwise have obtained from membership in collegia of various sorts or from the various municipal festivals." This "motivational base" for "those of the humbler social strata" pertains especially to those at ES5, for whom membership of *collegia* was something of an option; it is less evident as a motivational descriptor of those below ES5, who had no such option.

is little to suggest that urban Christian groups, unlike other associations, had a membership fee that was paid to the association's treasurer to enhance the goals of the association.[36] Perhaps we are to imagine a scenario in which those in ES5 could enjoy the benefits of a benefactor's generosity without being expected either to make membership payments or to be involved in public acclaim of the benefactor. Such a group could well have been attractive to people at this economic level, more so perhaps than *collegia* of other sorts (although Paul's communities shared similarities with other groups as well).[37]

On the other hand, from around 53–57 CE Paul targets ES5 members (along with ES4 members, no doubt, although they are not specifically targeted in his letters) with the financial responsibility of raising funds for the collection for the Jerusalem poor (1 Cor. 16:1-4).[38] This might have been a variation on an established expectation that, instead of paying membership fees, ES5 members would contribute to the offsetting of the material needs of the poor within Paul's communities. In general, then, while there might have been additional attraction to join a Christian group (i.e., lack of a membership fee), someone in ES5 might have found joining an urban Christian group to have similar economic dynamics to any (other) association in the urban marketplace.

These considerations of socio-economic factors pertaining to the attractions (or otherwise) of the early Christian movement are not exhaustive, nor can they be so within the constraints of this volume.[39] But they are indicative of some of the kinds of socio-economic factors that urbanites of the first century CE might have taken into account when entertaining the notion of whether or not to join a local group of the early Christian movement.

5. REFERENCE GROUPS AND STATUS REALIGNMENT

If it is the case that joining a group of early Jesus followers might have *increased* the problem of "status inconsistency" for some middling-level urbanites (as outlined in section 4 above), does this make untenable Meeks's general thesis about status-inconsistents finding status resolution within groups of Jesus followers? Not necessarily. Instead, it might simply heighten the significance of what early Christian groups offered to those middling-group urbanites. What was on offer included the kind of things that Meeks outlines in the chapters that follow his chapter on the social level of Pauline Christians. In short, the early Christian

---

36   Are association fees what Paul has in mind in 2 Cor. 9:7 when contrasting generosity in Christian communities with payments made "reluctantly or under compulsion" (*ek lypēs ē ex anagkēs*)? Cf. Justin, *Apol.* 1.67.6; Tertullian, *Apol.* 39.5.

37   See Edward Adams's essay below.

38   On the dating of Paul's collection efforts, see Longenecker forthcoming a.

39   A fuller consideration of socio-economic factors will appear in Longenecker forthcoming b.

movement must simply have offered something quite attractive to such status-inconsistents if they were willing to brave the prospect of further status inconsistency within the civic order in order to enjoy the benefits of the Christian groups. The more it was the case that status inconsistency would have been compounded by participation in a group of Jesus followers, the more things like fictive kinship within those groups becomes significant in our understanding of the rise of the earliest urban Christian movement.

This highlights the importance of reference groups for understanding the growth of the early Christian movement. Reference groups are those groups or arenas that people prioritize as most valued in terms of defining their identity and status.[40] The rise of Christian household groups might best be attributed to the fact that some people in the Greco-Roman middling groups must, to some extent, have shifted their primary reference group away from the burgeoning, highly stratified, and agonistic civic arena and toward the fledgling, intimate, and expectant fellowships of Jesus followers.[41] This shift in primary reference groups helps to explain how joining a group of Jesus followers might at one and the same time have had two different consequences for middling-group members of the Greco-Roman world: (1) the potential for status reduction within the civic arena, and (2) the potential for status realignment within the corporate context of early Christian groups. Meeks rightly emphasized the second of these; that emphasis is heightened further when the first is kept firmly in view.

Precisely because the benefits of belonging to an early Christian group must have had significant attraction, Meeks's project does not stop where *The First Urban Christians* ends. Instead, it extends into those books that Meeks went on to write: *The Moral World of the First Christians* in 1986 and *The Origins of Christian Morality* in 1993. In one sense, these three books belong together as a triumvirate, in that they showcase the "moral world" of the early Christian movement as holding the key to the historical success of that movement. As Meeks writes toward the end of *The Origins of Christian Morality*:

Perhaps . . . it was in certain of their social practices that the Christian groups most effectively distinguished themselves from other cult associations, clubs, or philosophical schools—[1] their special rituals of initiation and communion,

---

40 Meeks explains a reference group anecdotally (1983: 215 n. 20): "I am not likely to feel oppressed nor are the people who matter to me likely to snub me because I shall not ever receive a peerage in the British realm." In this example, Meeks's reference group is shown not to place a particular value on the peerage status within Britain, even if other reference groups might; Meeks's reference group values other markers of identity instead.

41 Elsewhere Meeks notes two types of shifts in reference-group loyalties (1986: 14): "I may . . . convert [from one group to another] because the world of the other community has come to seem truer to me than that of my former society. Or I may be forced into the new setting and only gradually come to understand and adopt its world view." For my own narrative attempt to explore reference-group shifts with regard to early groups of Jesus followers, see Longenecker 2003.

[2] their practice of communal admonition and discipline, [and 3] the organization of aid for widows, orphans, prisoners, and other weaker members of the movement (1993: 213).

For some middling-level urbanites, and for many others at lower socio-economic levels, such things as these may well have offset the relentless quest for honor capture in the civic arena and provided the basis for status realignment in spirited groups of the first urban Christians.

Chapter 4

FIRST-CENTURY MODELS FOR PAUL'S CHURCHES: SELECTED SCHOLARLY DEVELOPMENTS SINCE MEEKS[1]

Edward Adams

Wayne Meeks's overview of possible "models" for the Pauline churches from Paul's social environment, in the chapter "The Formation of the *Ekklēsia*," is one of the most cited and influential parts of *The First Urban Christians* (pp. 75–84); it has been called "a touchstone in the field" (Horsley 2005: 377). By "models" Meeks means *comparative* models or "analogies" (p. 84); he looks at four Greco-Roman social formations to which the Pauline *ekklēsiai* "bear at least a family resemblance" (p. 74): the household, the voluntary association, the synagogue, and the philosophical or rhetorical school. In the same chapter, Meeks also makes use of the modern social-scientific "model" of the sect in analyzing the social structure of Paul's churches. Here, however, I want to focus on what Meeks has to say about first-century models and to look at how scholarly discussion in this area has progressed in the years following the publication of *The First Urban Christians*. Thus, this essay summarizes Meeks's comments and then reviews subsequent scholarship relating to households, associations, synagogues, and schools (in this order) as potential analogues to Paul's churches. The treatment of scholarship since Meeks is necessarily selective, and I focus on developments and contributions that strike me as particularly significant and/or interesting (such as recent discussion of the domestic context of ecclesial gatherings). I also draw attention to Richard Horsley's view that Paul intended his churches to constitute an "alternative society" within the Roman Empire. Finally, I offer a few brief reflections of my own on the use of first-century social models to illuminate Paul's churches. I begin, then, with a précis of Meeks's discussion.

---

1   Like the other essays in this volume, an earlier draft was submitted for discussion at the symposium in Durham, and I am grateful for the feedback I received from my fellow participants in this project on that occasion. Thanks also go to Prof. John Barclay for helpful suggestions. I am especially indebted to the editors of this book for their comments and advice as I deliberated over the final shape of this piece.

1. MEEKS ON MODELS FROM PAUL'S SOCIAL ENVIRONMENT

Meeks looks in turn at each of the selected social models, beginning with the household. He observes that private houses functioned as the meeting places of the Pauline groups (p. 75). Paul uses the expression *hē kat' oikon ekklēsia* (Rom. 16:5; 1 Cor. 16:19; Phlm. 2) to designate a house church and to distinguish it from "the whole church" (*holē hē ekklēsia*) in a given location (Rom. 16:23; 1 Cor. 14:23) and from the *ekklēsia* as a translocal phenomenon (e.g., 1 Cor. 11:16; 16:1, 19). The house church, Meeks states, was the "basic cell" of the movement (p. 75), and its core was usually an existing household, which was a larger social entity (including slaves, freedmen, tenants, etc.) than the modern Western family.

The assimilation to the household had certain implications for the churches (pp. 76–77). As a place of meeting, the house provided a measure of privacy and stability. As a social structure, the household offered a ready-made "network of relationships," both within and beyond the household, which facilitated the expansion of the movement. However, the existence of more than one house church in a city could give rise to factionalism, as seems to have been the case at Corinth. The household influenced the organization of the *ekklēsiai*, with the head of the household naturally exercising some degree of authority over the group. In the later Pauline letters of Colossians and Ephesians, there is a greater attempt to pattern relationships in the churches according to the hierarchical order of roles in the household (Col. 3:18–4:1; Eph. 5:21–6:9—the so-called *Haustafeln*).

The household model, though, cannot account for every feature of Paul's churches (p. 77). The hierarchical structure of the household cannot explain the power exercised by the apostle and his coworkers within the larger movement or by charismatic individuals in the local group. Nor can it enlighten believers' sense of belonging to a worldwide people.

Meeks finds important correspondences between the Pauline churches and the voluntary associations or *collegia* (pp. 77–78). Both were small groups that fostered close interpersonal relationships. In both, membership was voluntary. In both, members often shared a common trade or craft. Both depended on the patronage of wealthier benefactors. Both valued rituals and held common meals. A prized service offered by many associations, especially the *collegia tenuiorum*, or funerary societies, was proper burial for deceased associates. Meeks thinks it likely that the Pauline groups in similar fashion made provision for the burial of departed members (cf. 1 Thess. 4:13–5:11; 1 Cor. 15:29).

Yet, for Meeks, there are key differences, which outweigh the similarities (pp. 78–80). First, "the Christian groups were exclusive and totalistic in a way that no club nor even any pagan cultic association was" (p. 78). The Christian "sect" demanded an allegiance from its members that displaced all other commitments. Correspondingly, there was "a deeper motivational basis for association" (pp. 78–79). Individuals tended to join voluntary associations for social fulfillment;

those who joined Christian groups were looking for "salvation" more comprehensively. Second, clubs tended to be socially homogeneous; the Pauline groups, on the other hand, exhibited a more varied social composition and allowed for "equality of role," which is hardly evident among associations (p. 79). Third, there is "the almost complete absence of common terminology" for the Pauline assemblies and the private associations (p. 79). A fourth difference is the "extralocal linkages" of the Pauline movement; associations functioned as relatively self-contained local units (p. 80). In his book *The Moral World of the First Christians*, Meeks makes the additional point that in contrast to the churches, associations were not so concerned with regulating the ethical conduct of their members (1986: 114).

In Meeks's view, the diaspora synagogue provides "the nearest and most natural" analogy to the *ekklēsia* (1983: 80). There are a number of similarities. Paul's congregations shared with the synagogues the sense of belonging to a larger body, the "People of God" (p. 80). Paul's use of the word *ekklēsia* seems akin to the usage of Greek-speaking Jews, though there is no evidence to indicate that the term was ever applied to a particular Jewish community.[2] Both groups met in private houses, though Meeks thinks that in the cities in which Paul operated, Jews already possessed buildings devoted exclusively to the community's functions. The kind of activities that characterized their meetings—prayer, the reading of Scripture, common meals—were probably similar. Moreover, the Pauline Christians adopted the sacred texts as well as many of the beliefs and traditions of diaspora Jews (pp. 80–81).

But again, there are telling differences (p. 81). Paul does not use the word *synagōgē* to describe the assembly of believers, and his terminology for community leaders is different. In the Pauline churches, women had a greater role than they did in the synagogues, more equal to that of men. Above all, ethnicity was not, as it was in the synagogues, a basis of membership.

Turning finally to the philosophical or rhetorical school, Meeks notes that Justin Martyr and other later apologists presented Christianity as a "philosophy." In more recent times, he observes, Edwin Judge has argued that the Pauline churches would have been viewed by contemporaries in certain respects as "scholastic communities" (p. 82).[3] Meeks sees some value in comparing philosophical schools with Pauline groups. The Pythagoreans (as described by Iamblichus in the late third century CE), and, especially, the Epicureans bear certain resemblances to the Pauline communities. But they do so, he thinks, only insofar as they are "modified households or voluntary associations" (p. 84). Although the Pauline groups seem to have had interest in philosophical and rhetorical issues, such interests were not "constitutive of the movement" (p. 84).

2   But see now Runesson, Binder, and Olsson 2008: 260–63 (nos. 201–203).
3   Judge 1960a.

Meeks thus comes to the conclusion that "none of the four models . . . captures the whole of the Pauline *ekklēsia*, although all offer significant analogies" (p. 84). He credits the household with providing "the basic context within which most if not all the local Pauline groups established themselves" (p. 84). However, in his view, the structures that characterized Paul's churches were "worked out by the Pauline movement itself" and may have been "unique" (p. 84).

In the bulk of the remainder of the chapter, Meeks investigates the Pauline letters for evidence relating to the fostering of internal cohesion and the creation of boundaries against outsiders, looking especially at the "language of belonging" and the "language of separation" (pp. 84–97). A final section focuses on the construction and promotion of a translocal sense of identity, an awareness of belonging to "a worldwide people" (pp. 107–10). As the chapter progresses, it becomes clear that Meeks regards the modern sociological category of "sect" as more helpful in illuminating and explaining the social formation of Paul's groups than any of the models available in the contemporary Greco-Roman world.

Meeks's comparative analysis is clearly not intended as an exhaustive discussion of the question. He simply lays out in a succinct way the similarities and differences as he sees them in order to show that while the chosen models have some things in common with Paul's churches, "none of these categories quite fits" (p. 74). Richard Ascough, in his book, *What are They Saying About the Formation of the Pauline Churches?*, provides a full survey of scholarship on the different institutions as potential analogies to Paul's communities. He deals with each of the four institutions considered by Meeks. He treats the household in the introduction and then devotes a chapter each to synagogues, philosophical schools, and associations. He also gives a chapter to the ancient mysteries, which do not figure in Meeks's treatment (Ascough 1998: 50–70). Although Meeks's brief sketch has largely been superseded by Ascough's book, Meeks's work continues to be a standard reference point for discussion in this area.

2. THE HOUSEHOLD CONTEXT

Meeks regards the household as a "model" of a different order to the others he considers: it is for him more a *formative* model than an analogical model, being the "basic context" in which Paul's churches were set. Ascough agrees and sees the household as the "base" and "foundation" of the Pauline churches (Ascough 1998: 9). The importance of the household for the social formation of the early churches is well recognized by scholars. Since the early 1980s, the early Christian "house church" has been attracting serious scholarly interest.[4] For Meeks, the

---

4 Banks 1980 (rev. ed. 1994); Klauck 1981; Branick 1989; White 1990, 1996; Blue 1994; Osiek and Balch 1997; Gehring 2004. It should be noted that the term "house church" can denote either a Christian *group* that meets in a house or the *house* in which the group meets (cf. Gehring 2004: 18–19, 27).

household context involves both the *house* as physical setting and the *household* as social structure. L. Michael White has underlined the significance of the house as a meeting place. In his monumental two-volume study, *The Social Origins of Christian Architecture*, White explores the evolution of Christian places of worship in the first three centuries, from unaltered private houses (house churches) to domestic buildings specially adapted for Christian worship (*domus ecclesiae*) and then to larger, hall-type structures. He argues that the "house church setting" was basic to Paul's mission (White 1990: 105–107). Private houses provided not only places for the churches to meet but also places for Paul and other missionaries to stay and use as bases for their missionary operations. White also argues that houses as meeting places had a major influence on patterns of worship in the early churches (pp. 107–109). According to White, at least in the cities of the Aegean coast, "assembly was regularly convened in the dining room of the house" (p. 107). The communal meal thus became "the central act that served to define the worshipping community, the church (*ekklēsia*) in household assembly" (p. 109).

Roger Gehring's *House Church and Mission* is the fullest treatment of the subject of the house church in the New Testament to date. He similarly gives attention to the "architectural significance" of the house as meeting venue (findings summarized in Gehring 2004: 288–91), but also explores the significance of the household as social structure, reinforcing and extending Meeks's observations. He sees household patterns as influencing the organizational and leadership structures of Paul's churches (pp. 295–300).[5] The owners of the homes in which the groups met would have become the leaders of the congregations. The well-organized household became, by the time of the Pastoral Letters, the model for the well-ordered church (p. 298). He sees the household as influencing norms and values in the churches (pp. 291–95). The household codes, as found in Colossians and Ephesians, represent a "socioethical correspondence to *oikos* structures" (p. 291), and he regards early Christianity's embracing of the household as a key factor in its long-term success. In adopting the household structure, the churches assimilated to the wider order of society. This had "a positive effect not only for the spread of the gospel; it also enabled continuity, duration, and tradition" (p. 292). Gehring recognizes that house churches had their "shadow sides," such as the social tension created by the existence of several house groups in one city (pp. 225–26), but overall he regards the influence of the household in the origins and development of early Christian communities as positive (p. 226), and he contends that the house church model has ecclesiastical relevance today (pp. 300–11).

Not all, of course, would view the impact of the social structure of the household on the early churches so favorably. Stephen Barton, for example, in an article

---

5   The importance of the household for leadership in the Pauline churches is underscored by R. Alistair Campbell in his study of "the elders" (Campbell 1994).

published in 1986, states that the contribution of the household model to ecclesial formation "was not always constructive" (1986: 225).[6] He thinks that Paul himself, while valuing the model, was also aware of its problems. Household patterns were proving to be divisive at Corinth, and in 1 Corinthians, Paul attempts to restrict their intrusion into church life. The apostle gives prominence to models and metaphors other than the household: temple, field, dough, body, etc. (p. 239). But more significantly, where the apostle sees conflict between church and household, he tries to draw a boundary line between them, separating *ekklēsia* space from *oikos* space (1 Cor. 11:17-34; 14:33b-36).[7] For Barton, though, Paul does not go far enough in distancing himself from household ideology (1986: 243).

A focal point for scholarly debate about the merits and demerits of the household model has been its significance for early Christian women. While some, such as Gehring (2004: 210–25), see it as providing leadership opportunities for women in the congregations, others see it as reinforcing male dominance. A recent study of women in the household setting of early Christianity finds evidence "both for women's leadership, solidarity, and participation in communal life at all levels and at times for women's powerlessness and suffering" (Osiek and MacDonald 2006: 249).

On the house as physical setting, an interesting discussion has arisen over the question: In what sort of domestic spaces did Pauline house churches meet? Attention to this issue has partly been motivated by concerns about the social level of the early Christians. When envisaging house churches, scholars have tended to imagine believers meeting in a traditional Roman *domus*, with *triclinium* (dining room) and *atrium*, provided by a wealthy member of the congregation. However, in more recent discussion, other domestic possibilities, less dependent on well-to-do patrons, have been considered.

Robert Jewett argues that many Christians would have lived in *insulae* or tenement buildings, the cheap form of housing used in densely populated cities, especially Rome. He posits that in such buildings, "tenement churches" as he calls them, would have developed. He thinks that believers would have met

within the *insula* itself, either using one of the workshop areas on the ground floor, or using temporarily cleared space used by Christian neighbors in upper floors. In either case the church would not be meeting in space provided by patronage, but rather in rented or shared space provided by the members themselves (Jewett 2007: 65).

---

6   In Barton 1994, he focuses attention on the relativization of the natural family in the Jesus movement.

7   On Paul's attempt to distinguish *ekklēsia* and *oikos* space and its gender implications, see further Økland 2004: 131–67.

Since such groups would not have depended on a patron/householder, they are likely, in Jewett's view, to have developed a more communistic social structure, which he calls "agapic communalism" (2007: 67; in contrast to the "love patriarchalism" characteristic of house churches, which takes for granted the hierarchical order of the household, and society at large, but offsets social differences by fostering mutual love and respect).[8] Jewett suggests that the groups mentioned in Rom. 16:14-15 and the Christian community at Thessalonica were tenement churches.

Justin Meggitt, in his epochal study, *Paul, Poverty and Survival*, stresses the abject poverty of the vast majority, over 99%, of the Empire's population (1998: 50). He states: "Nearly all urban dwellers lived in . . . lean-tos, 'shanties', *insulae*, *tabernae*, and shared houses, or slept rough in the street" (p. 66). There is little reason to believe that the domestic circumstances of the early Christians were any different: "[e]ven if a Pauline Christian owned his/her own home, it might well be little more than a shack or lean-to" (p. 121). He thinks that Christian groups were actually quite small, in which case we need not suppose that hosts required large houses: "virtually any habitation would have sufficed" (p. 121 n. 227).

David Horrell (2004) takes issue with Jerome Murphy-O'Connor's use of the excavated Roman villa at Anaploga (in the environs of Corinth) as a model for imagining the domestic setting of the Corinthian Christian community (Murphy O'Connor 2002: 178–85). Murphy O'Connor supposes that this is the kind of house in which Gaius would have lived, and thus in which the whole church (estimated at 40–50 persons) would have assembled (cf. Rom. 16:23), with the better-off members meeting and eating in the *triclinium* and the others gathering in the *atrium*. Persuaded to some extent by Justin Meggitt's thesis, Horrell doubts that any member of the Corinthian church would have owned a house like this. He thinks that the buildings on Corinth's East Theater Street offer a more plausible, if still imagined, alternative. Two of these buildings seem to have served as premises for the preparation and sale of cooked meats; they also seem to have had an upper level for residential purposes (Horrell 2004: 364–65). These structures, Horrell suggests, represent a more realistic setting for Christian gatherings at Corinth and fit with an understanding of the Corinthian Christians as not belonging to the social elite, but, *contra* Meggitt, not all living at subsistence level either. The buildings on East Theater Street constitute the kind of space occupied by "small traders and business folk," not too different in social level from Prisca and Aquila and also Paul himself (p. 367). Meetings could have been held in an upstairs room, in which "it would by no means be impossible to cram in 50 or so people" (p. 367).

David Balch (2004) argues that the *domus* remains a credible setting for Pauline house churches. Drawing on the work of Andrew Wallace-Hadrill (1994), Balch

---

8   Cf. Theissen 1982: 107.

argues that the archaeology of Pompeii does not support Meggitt's contention that the vast majority of people were living in absolute poverty. Meggitt's analysis "might lead one to expect a few wealthy villas owned and inhabited exclusively by the 1 percent to be surrounded by slums for the 99 percent," but what one finds is a huge range of house sizes bridging the gulf between luxury villas and humble *tabernae* (Balch 2004: 32).[9] Against Meggitt's claim that the Pauline churches were necessarily small, Balch points out that Pompeian *domūs* could have accommodated numbers in excess of forty persons (p. 41). At the same time, Balch acknowledges that the *insula*, or multistory apartment block, archaeologically exemplified by the huge *insula* in Herculaneum, should equally be considered typical space for house churches.[10] Applying the evidence of Pompeii and Herculaneum to Corinth, he imagines various scenarios (p. 40): Chloe's people (assuming they are her slaves), worshipping "in a service section of Chloe's *domus*" or "in a shop of her *insula*"; Crispus, Gaius, or Stephanus, arranging worship "in the representation area of their *domus* or *insula*"; Paul plying his trade in a shop within a *domus* owned by Prisca and Aquila, a shop that could have led directly into the house where the congregation worshipped.

One may wonder how far the wide distribution of house sizes at Pompeii can be assumed for the Empire as a whole, but there does seem to be a growing consensus among experts in the field that gradations in housing were Empire-wide. Simon Ellis writes: "there was a wide variety of housing, including types of houses which were occupied by those who were neither aristocrats nor peasants or artisans" (2000: 112). This variety blurs "the social distinctions which often form the basis for histories of the Roman world." Yet caution should still be exercised when applying Vesuvian data to other parts of the Empire. Balch's attempt to visualize some of the Corinthian Christians meeting in an *insula* runs aground on the fact that there is no archaeological evidence for this type of housing in Corinth (Horrell 2004: 361).

This caveat aside, the more recent concern to think beyond the *domus* when envisioning domestic spaces for early Christian meetings that we find in the work of Balch and others represents an important step forward. Clearly, there is more work to be done along this line, and the expanding body of literature on housing in the Roman era offers a rich set of resources for the task.

Researchers on Roman housing tend now to use the category "houseful" rather than household when considering the inhabitancy of domestic buildings,

---

9   Wallace-Hadrill places the Pompeian evidence he samples into four quartiles (1994: 80–82). Units in the lowest quartile are small shops or workshops, which would in many cases have served as living quarters. The top quartile contains the elite residences, the largest of which have between twenty and thirty-six ground floor rooms. The third quartile includes what Wallace-Hadrill identifies as the "average" size of Pompeian house; most houses in this band (60%) have an atrium.

10   This represents a change of mind from his previously held view that the *domus* was the primary setting of house churches (Osiek and Balch 1997: 16–17).

a "houseful" being understood as "a group unconnected in family terms except by coresidence" (Wallace-Hadrill 1994: 92). Research indicates that many houses, including *domūs*, were not occupied by households as such, but by persons unrelated by family ties. This has a significant bearing on the household model as it is generally understood and used by New Testament scholars because it calls into question the assumed link between house as meeting place and household as social structure. The ramifications of the distinction between household and "houseful" for the study of early Christian house churches have yet to be teased out, but at the very least it seems to make it more possible for us to imagine house churches that were *not* formed out of existing households.

White (1990: 105) and others (e.g., Snyder 2003: 128) recognize that the early Christians did not meet *exclusively* in houses. However, relatively little research attention has been given to the nondomestic options for ecclesial gatherings available to and utilized by the early Christians: shops, workshops[11] (both of which could double up as domiciles), warehouses,[12] open spaces, etc.[13] Study in this direction, which I hope myself to pursue, might necessitate some qualification of the view that the household (as both material space and social structure) was the "basic context" in which the early churches were set.

3. ASSOCIATIONS

Since the publication of *The First Urban Christians* there has been a revival of interest in the *collegia*. Prominent in calling for renewed attention to this ancient social formation (certainly in English-language scholarship) has been John Kloppenborg, who co-edited with Stephen Wilson the volume *Voluntary Associations in the Graeco-Roman World*, the result of a five-year project conducted by the Canadian Society of Biblical Studies (1988–93). In his essay in that volume (1996a), Kloppenborg offers a threefold classification of the associations: those linked with a household (domestic associations), those formed around a common trade (professional associations), and those devoted to a particular deity (cultic associations).[14] Richard Ascough has since argued for a basic twofold distinction between religious and professional *collegia* (2003: 41). Domestic associations, in his view, "were not formed simply as being part of the household but had as their

---

11   Murphy-O'Connor (2002: 192–98) imagines Paul working in one of the excavated workshops in Corinth's North Market, attracting converts as he did so. This workspace, he conjectures, could have been used as ecclesial space (195–96).

12   Cf. the gathering in a warehouse in *Acts of Paul* 11.1.

13   Siri Sande offers a brief but intriguing exploration of the nondomestic possibilities (giving particular attention to bathhouses): Sande 1999 (in Norwegian).

14   Kloppenborg (1996a: 21) points out that *collegia tenuiorum*, associations established purely for the sake of burial, did not legally exist until the time of Hadrian. However, many if not most associations took care of the burial of their members.

focus the worship of a particular deity" (2003: 24 n. 41); he would thus include them within the religious category.

Various scholars have undertaken comparison of associations and Pauline/early Christian churches.[15] Kloppenborg's and Ascough's work in this area is especially relevant to our interests because both interpreters engage critically with Meeks. In a seminal essay published in 1993, Kloppenborg argues that "there was a broad spectrum of forms of *collegia*, broad enough that most of the particularities seen in the Pauline churches could fit comfortably within that spectrum" (1993a: 231). Against Meeks's observation that there is hardly any common terminology between the associations and Paul's churches, Kloppenborg points out that while *ekklēsia* was not an especially common designation for associations, some associations *were* called *ekklēsiai*, and in an urban setting "the term would almost certainly be understood (by all involved) as one of the names for a voluntary association" (1993a: 231). Moreover, while Paul's letters lack some of the more common terms for officers in the associations, the terms that Paul does use, *episkopos*, *diakonos*, and *prostasis*, are all attested for *collegia* (1993a: 232). Against Meeks's claim that the Pauline churches were more socially inclusive and varied than the associations, Kloppenborg points out that some associations were quite inclusive, with slaves and free functioning more or less on the same level (1993a: 235). Furthermore, the assumption that Paul's churches were all equally inclusive and socially varied must be challenged: while the social composition of the church at Corinth seems to have been mixed, the Thessalonian church may have been quite homogeneous (1993a: 235–36). What Kloppenborg finds distinctive is the density of "brother" language in Paul's churches, which is quite rarely attested for the associations (1993a: 237–38).

In his study, *Paul's Macedonian Associations*, a revised version of his 1997 doctoral dissertation completed under Kloppenborg, Ascough reiterates his adviser's points against Meeks and addresses the other dissimilarities between the associations and Paul's churches alleged by Meeks. Responding to Meeks's claim that the Pauline groups were "exclusive and totalistic in a way that no club nor even any pagan cultic association was," Ascough points out that while for Paul being baptized into Christ excluded other kinds of religious allegiance, the Corinthians took a rather different view (2003: 88). Christians at Corinth seem to have participated with nonbelievers in communal meals in various settings, including pagan temples (pp. 90–91). Also, while it is true that the associations generally did not demand exclusivity, *de facto* they would have received it from their members (p. 88). Bearing in mind the cost of membership fees, many members would simply have been too poor to join more than one! Moreover, there are instances of more overtly exclusive associations. The regulations for an association in

---

15 Kloppenborg 1993a, 1993b, 1996b; McLean 1993; Schmeller 1995; McCready 1996; Ascough 1998, 2003; Clarke 2000: 59–77, 153–60; Harland 2003.

Philadelphia, Egypt (dating to the first century BCE) state that, "it shall not be permissible for any one of them . . . to leave the brotherhood . . . or to join another brotherhood" (p. 90). Also, an inscription dating to the late first or early second century CE in Sardis warns officials of the cult of Zeus not to participate in other mysteries (p. 89).

Ascough is especially critical of Meeks's contention that the associations did not have the extralocal links that were characteristic of the Christian groups. On the one hand, there is evidence of stronger translocal links among associations than Meeks and others think (pp. 93–100). Some inscriptions indicate that associations of foreigners maintained contact with their place of origin; others point to contact between associations in various locales (p. 100). On the other hand, the extralocal links of the Pauline churches have been much exaggerated. Although Paul saw his communities as connected, his churches did not appear to perceive the connections, and "Paul never assumes that his own communities were in contact with one another" (p. 106). Paul's churches and the associations "were both locally based groups with limited translocal connections" (p. 108). In response to Meeks's claim that associations were not so concerned with morality, Ascough observes that some associations did promote the display of virtues among their members (p. 65). There may have been a difference in rhetoric, with Pauline churches emphasizing sanctification and other associations stressing the need for moral purity in order to participate in cultic activity, but the distinction is not critical since "in both instances maintenance of moral codes was required" (p. 66). Again, associations and Pauline *ekklēsiai* were not as different as Meeks supposes.

After addressing these and other alleged problems in using the voluntary associations to understand the formation of Pauline communities, Ascough looks specifically at the evidence relating to Paul's churches at Philippi and Thessalonica. He argues that the Philippian church is analogous to a voluntary association of the religious type, while the Thessalonian church, which he thinks was mostly composed of males, resembles a professional association.

The research findings of Kloppenborg and Ascough show that Paul's churches and the *collegia* have more in common than Meeks had estimated. Yet, in their efforts to demonstrate the commensurability of the two, both Kloppenborg and Ascough overexploit what seems to be exceptional evidence. The term *ekklēsia* is found in only a few instances as a designation of an association (Ascough 2003: 74). This is a very slender basis on which to claim that in an urban context *ekklēsia* would have been understood by everyone concerned as specifying an association. Horsley (see below) is surely right that in an urban setting, the word *ekklēsia* would have suggested, in the first instance, the civic assembly. More overtly exclusive associations, on the data provided by Ascough, seem to be very exceptional, and what is excluded is participation in another association (and not necessarily *all* other associations; cf. Ascough 2003: 90). This falls short of the level of exclusiveness Paul demands of the Corinthians. There is nothing comparable in the evidence cited by Ascough to the sharp demarcation between the *ekklēsia* and the world that Paul insists upon in 1 Corinthians (1 Cor. 5:10; 6:1-2; 7:29-30, 33-34; 11:32).[16] Even so, as a result of Kloppenborg's and Ascough's investigations, the relevance of the associations to the study of Paul's churches can no longer be in doubt.

4. Diaspora Synagogues

Of the four institutions considered by Meeks as models for Paul's churches, the diaspora synagogue (as far as I can see) has been utilized the least in subsequent scholarship within this area. The main comparative study is James Burtchaell's *From Synagogue to Church*, in which he maintains that there was "continuity in community organization from the hellenistic Jewish synagogue to the early Christian church" (1992: 339). However, his thesis has generally failed to persuade. According to Ascough (1998: 21–23), Burtchaell assumes the continuity he seeks to prove, and his case is undermined by the differences he is forced to acknowledge between the Jewish and Christian communities (in membership, leadership, and nomenclature).[17]

The relative lack of research analysis focusing on the relationship between the synagogues and the Pauline/early Christian churches is probably related to the debates and uncertainties that have in recent years surrounded the ancient synagogue.[18] Yet, synagogue research is currently booming, and two recent developments in the field are noteworthy in the present context. The first relates to synagogue architecture. Donald Binder (1999) and Anders Runesson (2001) have challenged Michael White's view that the earliest diaspora synagogues (like house churches and *domus ecclesiae*) were private homes subsequently adapted for meetings (White 1990: 60–101). According to Binder (1999: 314), the synagogue at Delos was either built originally as the cultic hall of a pagan association in the second century BCE and subsequently transformed into a synagogue or constructed from the outset as a synagogue. Either way, it was not a modified domestic structure. Runesson (2001: 188) has argued that the synagogue at Ostia was purpose-built as a synagogue in the second half of the first century CE (cf. Runesson 1999). White contests Runesson's interpretation (White 1999), and

---

16   See further Adams 2000: 105–49. Ascough also seems to underplay the evidence and possibilities for communication *between* churches (cf. 2 Cor. 1:1; Col. 4:16; 1 Thess. 5:27), on which see Thompson 1998.

17   For further criticisms, see Clarke 2000: 166–67; Gehring 2004: 192–93.

18   For a detailed review and assessment, see Catto 2007.

the issue remains a subject of debate (Runesson 2002).[19] The discussion about the form of the first-century synagogue is an ongoing one, no doubt with many twists and turns to come, but one can perhaps detect a move in scholarly opinion toward acceptance of the existence of independent synagogue structures (in addition to meetings in private houses) in this period, which would effectively support Meeks's claim that while the practice of meeting in houses was an expedient for Jews in many places, in some cities, they "had probably already advanced to the stage of possessing buildings used exclusively for the community's functions" (1983: 80).

In his book *Conflict and Identity in Romans*, Philip Esler agrees with Meeks's assessment on the basis of ancient literary references (mainly in Philo) and appeals to the synagogue building at Ostia, as interpreted by Runesson, as material evidence for the presence of purpose-built synagogues at nearby Rome (Esler 2003: 88–97). He thinks it likely that Jews (or as he prefers "Judeans") in first-century Rome would have worshipped in buildings similar to and even grander than the Ostia structure (p. 97). This architectural context would have contrasted sharply with the simple domestic setting of early Christian gatherings, and such a pronounced spatial differentiation between the communities would have been "a powerful stimulus for the development of a distinctive identity for Christ-followers in toto" (p. 106). The architectural contrast would have contributed to the strained relations between Jews and Christians in the capital underlying Paul's letter to the Romans. Esler's reconstruction is intriguing, but without direct archaeological support from Rome itself it remains, to some extent, unproven.

The second development is the growth in interest in the relationship between synagogues and *collegia*. Peter Richardson maintains that diaspora synagogues were modelled on associations (1996), especially in terms of their architecture (2004: 207–21). Whatever the precise origins of the synagogue buildings at Delos or Ostia (domestic or otherwise), as functioning synagogues, they fit with local architectural styles for association buildings. He concludes: "While Jewish communities might form a discrete subgroup among other associations, they adopted architectural forms that were part of a common vocabulary of buildings from the same period and met a variety of communal needs, like other associations" (2004: 221). Binder (1999: 486–87) is more cautious in his assessment of the relationship between the two institutions, admitting significant overlap especially on the architectural side, but pointing out that the synagogues had greater privileges than the *collegia* and that the functions of the synagogue were more extensive than those of the associations. (Binder sees the Jerusalem temple as the model for the synagogue.) Runesson places synagogues within the general category of *collegia*, but observes that synagogues had a special status (2001: 469). The exact nature of the relationship between synagogues and associations

---

19   White is leading a new investigation of the site, which it is hoped will deliver new knowledge.

is thus debated, but that the former closely resemble the latter is increasingly being acknowledged.

5. PHILOSOPHICAL SCHOOLS

The analogy between Paul's churches and philosophical schools or schools in general has been explored by several scholars.[20] Loveday Alexander (1994, 2001) pursues the comparison from the standpoint of Galen, the Greek doctor who wrote toward the end of the second century CE. Galen "provides an invaluable . . . perspective on the schools from the viewpoint of an acerbic contemporary observer" (1994: 63); he is also the first pagan writer to draw an explicit comparison between Christian groups and schools. Galen includes medical sects among schools, which Alexander regards as important. Widening our definition of Hellenistic schools, she feels, may help to rid this social model of its limitations when we focus exclusively on philosophical groups (1994: 77). Although Galen belongs to a later time than Paul, Alexander thinks that his viewpoint is pertinent because he identifies "a pattern that can be observed throughout the history of the schools in the Hellenistic and Roman periods"; in modern terms, he is developing a "cross-cultural model" (2001: 105). From Galen's observations, it emerges that schools were much less scholastic and "rational" than we might have imagined (1994: 77); disinterested faith and uncritical loyalty to the founder were expected of learners. There was a strong sense of group identity and teachers would strenuously defend partisan viewpoints (rather than encourage free intellectual inquiry). In these respects, Hellenistic schools bear positive comparison to the Pauline movement. Galen also indicates that teaching was normally conducted in a public place, thus creating a two-tier audience: the inner ring of disciples and an outer ring of onlookers or interested enquirers (1994: 76). Alexander believes that a two-tier pattern of instruction, albeit in more "private" locations, was characteristic of Christian discourse in the first two centuries (1994: 81). (She finds little evidence for public evangelism.[21]) Paul seems to envisage some such scenario when he expects outsiders to be present at Christian meetings (1 Cor. 14:23-25), hoping that what they see, hear, and learn may cause them to cross the line from outsider to insider. Alexander makes clear that she does not think that the school type can explain every feature of Paul's churches. Nevertheless, she deems it a more fitting model than others that have been suggested, including household and association (1994: 82).

Clarence Glad in his book, *Paul and Philodemus: Adaptability in Epicurean and Early Christian Psychagogy,* takes up the comparison between Paul's

---

20   Alexander 1994, 2001; Glad 1995; Mason 1996; Stowers 2001.
21   So also Stowers 1984.

communities and Epicurean groups. The main focus of his study is Paul's style of community-nurture, which, he argues, conforms to a pattern of psychagogy, meaning "guidance of the soul," witnessed in Epicurean schools (cf. Meeks 1983: 82). When dealing with the "weak," both at Corinth and Rome, Paul is gentle and compassionate, but he is more forceful and overbearing when dealing with recalcitrant and obstinate members of his churches (Glad 1995: 328). This adaptability is characteristic of Epicurean psychagogy. Glad's broader thesis is that there is "a basic congruity between the Pauline communities and the Epicureans as it relates to the communal pattern of mutual participation by community members in exhortation, edification, and correction" (p. 8). Glad is not arguing for "cultural borrowing or direct influence or reaction"; his aim is to bring to light a "shared communal practice among Epicureans and early Christians" (p. 9) integral to both groups. He points out that both were often "lumped together" by outside observers from the second century onward (both were charged with atheism, secrecy, separatism, etc.) and suggests that this linkage may have rested to some extent on an awareness among outsiders of correspondences in the psychagogic practices of both communities (pp. 335–36). However, Glad offers no evidence that a similarity in this area was actually noted (or parodied) by contemporary witnesses.

Stanley Stowers identifies "seven closely connected areas in which the Hellenistic philosophies and Pauline Christianity possessed similar features" (2001: 89): both involved conversion, in the sense of "a dramatic reorientation of the self" (p. 91); both offered a "technology of the self" (p. 92); in both, the main practices were intellectual (p. 93); etc. Stowers wants it to be clear that he is not arguing that Pauline Christianity was a philosophy (p. 89). But though it did not derive from philosophy, it nevertheless shared "the structural features that made it philosophy-like" (p. 100). There are, of course, differences (pp. 100–101). Those belonging to a philosophy associate as friends, whereas in Pauline Christianity we find the rhetoric of fictive kinship. Also, rituals play a more important part in Pauline Christianity than in the philosophies. But one should not exaggerate these differences. Since the kinship is fictive and not genuine, it closely resembles friendship, and the ritual element in early Christianity was very minimal by ancient standards. However, as Horsley notes, it is not evident that all the points of comparison identified by Stowers are central features of Paul's concerns for his churches. Indeed, most "seem to emphasize the individual self and intellectual practices far more than Paul does" (Horsley 2005: 380).

6. AN ALTERNATIVE SOCIETY

In Horsley's view, the four institutions discussed by Meeks have even less value as comparative models than Meeks thought. In fact, Horsley believes that Meeks did not go far enough in stressing "the distinctive features of the *ekklēsia* that Paul advocated within his letters" (2005: 381). Paul viewed his assemblies as "local communities of a broader social order in-the-making that stands [*sic*] as an alternative to the Roman imperial order" (2005: 393).

For Horsley, it is highly significant that the chief term Paul uses for the movement as a whole as well as for specific local communities is *ekklēsia*. Although the term came to Paul by way of the LXX, where it had a specialized sense (the assembly of all Israel), its primary meaning in his imperial context was the citizen assembly of the *polis* (1997b: 208). The civic assembly involved activities, such as praise, acclamation, and discussion of issues affecting the citizenry, "which were also some of the principal activities that Paul's communities carried on at gatherings of the 'assemblies'" (p. 209). Horsley thus deduces that, "Paul evidently understood the *ekklēsia* of a Thessalonica or Corinth . . . as the political assembly of the people 'in Christ' in pointed juxtaposition and 'competition' with the official city assembly" (p. 209).

Horsley turns to 1 Corinthians as a "case study" of Paul's attempt to foster an alternative society (1997c: 242–52). He identifies a number of ways in which Paul tries to implement his social vision. The apostle insists that the Corinthian assembly conducts its internal affairs in complete independence of "the world" (esp. 1 Corinthians 5–6). By prohibiting the Corinthians' eating of food sacrificed to idols, Paul cuts them off from involvement in essential forms of social interaction in Roman society. Paul undermines the dominant patronage system (esp. 1 Corinthians 9) and indicates that the community "should embody economic relations diametrically different from those in Roman imperial society" (p. 249). Through his instructions about the collection for the church in Jerusalem (1 Corinthians 16), Paul encourages a style of "international economic reciprocity" perhaps "unique" in the Empire (p. 251). The letter as a whole, for Horsley, is an attempt to build up a "new society alternative to the dominant imperial society" (p. 244), grounded upon an apocalyptic perspective that regards the imperial order as a world that is passing away (1 Cor. 7:31; see further Horsley 2000b: 93–102).

Horsley's view of Paul's churches as the apostle himself conceived of them resonates with Meeks's more "sectarian" analysis of Pauline Christianity, though Horsley's emphasis on the anti-imperial dimension is different. Horsley concentrates on *Paul's* vision of community, which begs the question: How far did Paul's churches actually embody his radical vision? The Corinthian church, as reflected in 1 Corinthians, hardly assimilated it at all. Paul's heavy stress on the boundaries between the church and the world in this letter (unparalleled in his other letters) is to a large extent a reaction to the lack of distinction in this area he perceives at Corinth (Adams 2000: 85–103). We may also ask: Does Paul express a single, unified vision for his congregations, evident across his letters? First Corinthians is particularly amenable to the interpretation given to it by Horsley. I have argued myself that in this epistle, Paul endeavors to construct a community "*distinct* from the larger society, embracing alternative forms of sociality, patterns of living and community ideals" (p. 149). However, in looking at Romans, I concluded that here Paul advances a vision of ecclesial *"solidarity* with the larger society" (p. 220). The evidence of Romans, to my mind, challenges any view that throughout his letters, Paul *consistently* promotes the *ekklēsia* as an "alternative society," or at least, as a society that manifests its alternativeness in its direct opposition to the imperial order. In Romans 13, Paul legitimates the ruling order in the strongest possible way (pp. 204–207).[22]

Although Horsley is critical of the attempt to describe the social structure of Paul's churches by comparison with other contemporary groups and institutions, he does himself identify a Greco-Roman model for these congregations—the civic assembly, which for Horsley is a model that Paul exploits in order to counter. How Horsley reconciles his view that Paul intended his assemblies to imitate and to compete with the civic *ekklēsia* with his claim that Paul wanted his churches to constitute a "new society" with "distinctive" and "unique" features is not fully clear.

7. CONCLUSION: COMPARING PAUL'S CHURCHES WITH FIRST-CENTURY MODELS

As the foregoing critical review shows, in the twenty-five years since the publication of Meeks's *The First Urban Christians*, there has been considerable scholarly interest in possible analogues for Paul's churches from the Greco-Roman environment. This interest has been stimulated to a significant degree by Meeks's seminal discussion of the topic. No consensus has been reached on what is the "best" first-century model for the Pauline churches. Such lack of agreement is hardly peculiar in a discipline that thrives on debate and dissent; it does not invalidate the comparative exercise, though it may raise questions about fixating on any one, particular model.

The comparison of Paul's churches with relevant first-century social formations aids our understanding of the social character of the Pauline enterprise and has its place in the social analysis of Paul's mission, along with the application of methods drawn from the social sciences. Indeed, ancient comparative models might be seen to have an advantage over social-scientific "models" precisely because they are drawn from Paul's social-historical context. However, one should not be misled into thinking that when dealing with ancient models one is dealing with "pure" social-historical phenomena, while social-scientific paradigms are scholarly constructs. The data relating to Greco-Roman social formations are subject to scholarly collation, presentation, and interpretation (and the data

---

22   I am not persuaded by attempts (e.g., Elliott 1997; Jewett 2007: 780–803) to make Rom. 13:1-7 fit with an anti-imperial reading of the letter.

itself, both literary and material, is not value-free), and scholarly work on these institutions is subject to new discoveries in the field, shifting trends and even ideological bias, as a recent study of modern scholarship on the Roman *collegia* has shown (Perry 2006).

Scholarly discussion of analogies to Paul's churches has often been based on a generalized view of "Pauline Christianity,"[23] and it seems to me that more careful distinctions need to be made when handling the Pauline evidence. It is important to distinguish between the *ekklēsiai* as Paul would like them to be and the *ekklēsiai* as they really were (though our access to the latter is only through Paul's letters),[24] and also between the *ekklēsiai* as their members viewed and understood them and the *ekklēsiai* as they were perceived and categorized by outside observers. Furthermore, one should be prepared to recognize variation at each level. Thus, the Corinthian Christian community might have been viewed by outsiders as a harmless domestic cult, whereas the Thessalonian church might have been seen as a dangerous *haeresis*. The Corinthians may have thought of their group as a club,[25] participation in which did not preclude continued involvement in other associations and social networks;[26] the Galatians, on the other hand, having suffered a loss of social identity through their conversion to Christ,[27] may have sought to model their congregations on the synagogues, which might have seemed to them (to borrow Meeks's wording) "the nearest and most natural" social analogue. Paul *may* have wanted the Corinthian Christ-believing community to be an alternative *ekklēsia* (in the sense of civic assembly), but, if so, this was clearly not his aim for the churches at Rome.

Different analogies thus may be applicable at different levels. However, focusing on the differences between the various institutions when assessing their value as analogies to Paul's churches (whether as Paul construes them, as their members viewed them, or as outsiders perceived them) may be rather at odds with scholars' increasing recognition of the overlapping nature of households, associations, synagogues, and schools.[28] In the light of this emerging emphasis, perhaps more attention should be given in the comparative enquiry to the "generic" features of first-century groups (e.g., each involves the coming together of people on a regular basis; each is a distinct unit with a sense of social identity; in each members have or develop relatively close ties with each other; each has its own norms and ethos; in each meeting takes places in a regular physical setting,

---

23 For social variations within "Pauline Christianity," see Barclay 1992.

24 As Horrell (2008: 190) writes, "the historical churches, even as Paul allows us to glimpse them in his letters, never conformed neatly to . . . Pauline ideals, whatever the Apostle might have wished." Horrell questions the appropriateness of calling the churches to which Paul wrote "Pauline communities," since they evidently did not see themselves as "Pauline" (p. 196).

25 Barclay 1992: 71.

26 Harland 2003: 184.

27 Barclay 1988: 58–59.

28 See White 1990: 143–44; Clarke 2000; Harland 2003.

relevant to the group's activities; each imitates to some extent patterns in the wider civic arena).[29] If the most telling similarities between the Pauline churches and the different comparative models are at the generic level, the quest for the single, most appropriate first-century analogy may be somewhat misguided.

One wonders, in any case, how much more can be gained by comparing "Pauline Christianity" broadly conceived with one particular ancient model. A more fruitful approach may be to focus on a particular aspect of group organization or a specific area of group practice and to compare Paul's churches with other first-century groups on this point. Andrew Clarke's (2000) comparative study of leadership practices in Paul's churches and Greco-Roman civic institutions and Dennis Smith's (2003) treatment of early Christian community meals in relation to formalized dining in philosophies, clubs, etc., are suggestive in this respect.

Returning to Meeks, although a number of his points of similarity and difference are in need of revision, especially with regard to early churches and the associations, it seems to me that his overall conclusion—that though each of the suggested models can be meaningfully compared with the early churches, none offers an identical match—remains sound and would probably command general assent. As he puts it in *The Moral World of the First Christians*, the *ekklēsia* "was all the old things that observers in the first century might have seen in it: a Jewish sect, a club meeting in a household, an initiatory cult, a school. Yet it was more than the sum of those things, and different from the mere synthesis of their contradictory tendencies" (1986: 120).

---

29   For the synagogues' conformity to such patterns, see Clarke 2000: 103–41.

Chapter 5

ORGANIZATIONAL STRUCTURES AND RELATIONAL STRUGGLES AMONG THE SAINTS: THE ESTABLISHMENT AND EXERCISE OF AUTHORITY WITHIN THE PAULINE ASSEMBLIES

Todd D. Still

One may liken chapters 3 and 4 of *The First Urban Christians* to either side of the same coin. If the coin were to signify Pauline churches in general, chapter 3 could be said to constitute the coin's obverse and chapter 4 its reverse. While the former chapter focuses on the formation and character of Paul's congregations, the latter concentrates on the organization of and the relational dynamics within these fledgling Christian groups.

What is true of the volume in general is no less true of chapter 4 in particular: Wayne Meeks treats a complex topic (in this instance, Pauline church "governance") with literary clarity, intellectual curiosity, socio-historical sensitivity, and academic acumen. Meeks's examination of the "organizational dimension" or "structure of authority" (p. 111) within the churches of Paul is both instructive and stimulating.[1] Even as Meeks acknowledges his scholarly debt to the then recent monographs of John Howard Schütz (1975) and Bengt Holmberg (1978), we, too, may express appreciation for his volume as a whole as well as for this specific part of that sum.

At the outset of the fourth chapter, Meeks seeks to address the matter and manner of governance in the Pauline assemblies. To do so, he first considers Paul's account of the conflict between himself and other Christian leaders in Jerusalem and Antioch recorded in Galatians 2 (pp. 111–13). He then reads 1 Thessalonians, Galatians, 1–2 Corinthians, and Colossians as epistolary exercises in "social control" (pp. 113–31). Based upon inferences drawn from the

---

1   Although I speak of "Pauline churches" and the like throughout this essay (as does Meeks throughout his work), the recently published piece by Horrell 2008 calls into question the employment of such phrases without heavy qualification.

interpersonal and congregational conflicts Paul reports and addresses in these letters, Meeks concludes chapter 4 by exploring the wielding of authority in the Pauline assemblies. Discontent with merely describing those who possessed power, Meeks probes the ways and means employed by those empowered to lead (pp. 131–39).

I will begin this essay by offering a synopsis and analysis of Meeks's chapter on governance. Thereafter, I will consider subsequent academic work that is germane to the subject under review. Finally, I will seek to make a modest contribution to the ongoing conversation on this topic by treating other relevant Pauline passages and by highlighting the apparent correlation between the organizational, operational tensions that typified the churches of Paul on the one hand and the dialectical thought-patterns of the apostle on the other.[2]

1. REVIEW AND RESPONSE

As Meeks enters into what he describes as "the obscure territory of the structure of authority" in churches founded by Paul and his associates, he does so with two primary questions in view: (1) What sorts of persons had authority in Pauline assemblies? (2) Why did congregational members follow their leadership (p. 111)? Meeks's answer to these questions requires roughly thirty pages. He devotes the bulk of the chapter (twenty pages) to describing and explaining how Paul dealt with conflicts between persons and among congregations in his letters. He then examines precisely who led these assemblies and how they sought to do so.

At the outset of the chapter's first section entitled "Dealing with Conflict," Meeks explains that he will not so much focus upon the matters under dispute as he will upon Paul's responses to the conflicts arising. This intent is evident in Meeks's treatment of Paul's meeting with the Jerusalem "pillars" and his subsequent dispute with Peter in Antioch (see Gal. 2:14; cf. Acts 15:1-29). Noting that the flash points were circumcision and *kashrut*, Meeks moves on to ask what these differences between early Christian leaders might tell us about the emerging organization of the nascent movement (see further, e.g., Taylor 1992).

He culls the following observations relative to church governance from these two episodes (p. 113): (1) In but twenty years after Jesus' crucifixion, believers in Jesus (at least in Jerusalem and Antioch) had emerged as a "distinct sect among the Jews." They had their own (*ad hoc*) leaders who sought to settle group conflicts internally and had begun to reach out to Gentiles and to count them among their membership. (2) Christians in one locale were concerned about the beliefs and behaviors of "brothers and sisters" in other places. There was "a concern

---

2   I am aware that my essay is more exegetically oriented than others in this volume. The same may be said of chapter 4 in *The First Urban Christians* when compared to other chapters in the book.

for unity and conformity." (3) Conflict resolution was relational ("meeting and talking"), not formal, even if ongoing disputes would lead to the empowerment of people and the formalization of processes to deal with volatile issues and individuals.

Meeks admits that these conflicts involving Paul reveal precious little "about the specific organization of Pauline Christianity" (p. 113). They do, however, expose the relational cracks and crevices that were developing between Paul and other early Christian leaders. Paul's decided differences with other prominent figures in Jerusalem and Antioch on the Gentile question (described by Meeks as "Paul's defeat in Antioch") served as "the starting point for his formation of a more clearly distinct and self-conscious missionary organization of his own" (p. 113). Even as Paul's conflict with (Jewish-) Christian leaders over Gentile converts served as a stimulus for his more expansive mission among the nations, these disputes serve as a suitable segue for Meeks to consider Paul's contacts with his churches through letters.

Meeks selects five Pauline letters to read with intergroup discord and deviation in view. He begins with what he and a large majority of other New Testament scholars regard to be Paul's earliest extant letter, namely, 1 Thessalonians. Although Meeks finds no detectable traces of internal conflict in 1 Thessalonians, he commences his extended treatment of congregational discord evinced in Paul's letters with 1 Thessalonians (pp. 114–15). He does so in an effort to highlight the significance of Pauline emissaries (Timothy in this instance) and to point out how Paul could exercise "social control" via written communication. Meeks maintains that 1 Thessalonians "shows how Paul fashioned the letter into an instrument for extending through time and space his instruction of converts" (p. 115). In addition to extensive and expansive thanksgiving, various statements regarding *mimesis* and the reiteration of *paraenesis* lace this missive. Instructions concerning Jesus' *parousia* and its implications for Christians also feature in the letter.

If intergroup conflict is (all but) absent from 1 Thessalonians, it is at the fore of Galatians. Indeed, the clash between Paul and those whom he dubs "agitators" over matters of Jewish praxis, especially circumcision, relative to the Galatian congregations founded by Paul and comprised by Gentiles is what occasioned this finely crafted, fiery communiqué. Given the complexity of Paul's autobiographical, theological, and ethical argumentation in Galatians, Meeks contents himself with drawing attention to the various types of appeals contained within the letter (pp. 115–17).

First he notes Paul's appeal to his *revelatory commission* to preach the gospel as an apostle to the nations (so Gal. 1:12, 16). Related to his apocalyptic call in particular is *Paul's personal experience* in general. His activities both prior to and subsequent to his revelation indicate Paul's belief in the divine origin of his revelation and proclamation. No less important to Paul was the *experience of his Galatian converts*. His story was inextricably linked to theirs; hence, Paul is at pains throughout the letter to impress upon the fledgling, foundering fellowships in Galatia that they were in "danger of committing irreparable folly" and should thereby remember and return to the spiritual judgments that were formerly theirs (p. 116). Meeks identifies *Scripture* as Paul's fourth and final major source of appeal in Galatians. Far from ancillary or peripheral to the letter, Scripture is an integral, constitutive part of Paul's "extremely subtle argument" in Galatians 3–4, wherein "an ingenious interplay among several texts serves as the fundamental warrant" (p. 117; cf. Hays 1989, 2002).

The Corinthian correspondence features prominently in chapters 2–3 of *The First Urban Christians* and is no less prominent in Meeks's treatment of governance. In fact, Meeks devotes over one-third of his fourth chapter to sifting and sorting through issues pertaining to the intergroup conflict that marks these lengthy and lively Pauline letters (pp. 117–25, 127–31). At the outset of his extended treatment of the complex web of discord evident throughout 1–2 Corinthians, Meeks notes the recurrence of the terms *power* (*dynamis*), *authority* (*exousia*), and their derivatives in the Corinthian letters. Furthermore, he suggests that even as power was important to the addressees it was no less important for Paul to attempt to alter their perception of power. Given that the congregational conflict in Corinth revolved around assertions and interpretations of authority, the Corinthian letters serve as prime fodder for Meeks in this chapter.

Meeks commences his perceptive and expansive discussion of intergroup conflict in Corinth by noting the factions that had arisen among the Corinthians due to the fact that some members favored and followed Paul whereas others preferred the learned rhetorician Apollos (p. 117). If Paul managed in 1 Corinthians to diffuse such factions and curb such comparisons, 2 Corinthians 10–13 reveals that there were missioners, whom Paul sarcastically labels "superlative apostles," who were willing and able to assail his authority. In the aforementioned chapters, Paul employs his considerable epistolary skills in an effort to recast authority and to regain credibility among the assembly (p. 118).

Infighting regarding figureheads in Corinth was accompanied by internal struggles that Meeks traces to social and financial disparities between members on the one hand and charismatic endowments and manifestations (particularly *glossolalia*) among members on the other (pp. 118–22). If the former tensions were most evident at meals (see 1 Corinthians 8–10; 11:17-34), the latter were made manifest at worship gatherings (see esp. 1 Corinthians 14). Having surveyed the conflict-laden landscape of the Corinthian church, Meeks offers these sage summative remarks:

> We are left then with more suspicions than positive evidence for the interactions among the authority of apostles and their loyal adherents, the authority of wealth and position, and the authority of the spirit-possessed in Corinth. Probably there were conflicts not only between persons but also between different kinds of authority. Undoubtedly the real alignments were more complex than any picture we might construct (p. 122).

If the intergroup conflict among the Corinthian Christians was complex and multifaceted, Meeks contends that Paul's responses to this internal discord were no less complicated. Given that canonical 2 Corinthians is a literary puzzle that renders tenuous the sequencing of Paul's contacts and correspondence with the church in Corinth, Meeks once again resigns himself to cataloging the kinds of appeals that Paul makes in his surviving letters to the assembly (pp. 122–25). Writ large, the Corinthian letters constitute Paul's attempt to (re-)establish his standing and authority in the church by transforming the congregation's conception of power. Tools in his literary kit include: persuasion through irony, sarcasm, metaphor, and diatribe; correction through appeal to (traditional) language and experiences known to the readers; and reinterpretation of Corinthian linguistic slogans and spiritual claims (pp. 122–23).

While letter writing itself is an "implicit claim to authority," Meeks notes that explicit claims to authority also appear in 1–2 Corinthians. Paul typically makes such pronouncements relative to his establishment of and sacrificial care for the church. Closely related is Meeks's important observation that Paul sets forth dialectical interpretations as well as undialectical assertions of power in his letter to the Corinthians. Paul's dialectical structuring of weakness and power is most clearly seen in the *peristasis* catalogs that recur in the letters, which, in turn, are congruent with his proclamation of the crucified and risen Christ. When Paul does baldly assert his power, which he is sometimes wont to do, he can only wield his way and win the day when the assembly wittingly and willingly yields to his authority. In addition to Paul's multidimensional appeals to authority, he can also lay claim in 1 Corinthians to divine gifting, Christian tradition (including "commands of the Lord"), Pauline church customs, and general societal expectations (pp. 123–25).

For a final epistolary example where there is evident conflict over authority, Meeks turns to Colossians (pp. 125–27). Persuaded by Walter Bujard's (1973) stylistic study of the letter, Meeks understands Colossians to be pseudonymous. Be that as it may, he regards as real "the specific conflict that occasioned the letter" (p. 126). In order to combat the mystical claims and ascetic practices of the "philosophers," the author of Colossians appropriates Paul's "apostolic authority and personal example" (p. 126). Furthermore, Meeks draws attention to Colossians' use of traditional *paraenetic* materials focused upon baptism. Finally, the letter's emphasis upon group cohesion and harmony is noted. The Christian community is to cultivate "peace and loyalty," even as the Christian household, in contradistinction to the "philosophy," is to be characterized by "stability and harmony" (p. 127).

Before seeking to synthesize his considerable interpretive spadework regarding power and authority within Pauline assemblies, Meeks engages in one additional exegetical exercise (pp. 127–31). Returning to 1 Corinthians, he examines in its literary context the text where Paul instructs the church to remove from its midst a man who is living with his father's wife lest he further sully the purity of the community (5:1-6a, 13). Meeks's interest in this passage extends beyond the disciplinary action that Paul recommends the assembly take toward the man. He also wants to note how Paul employs the same disciplinary procedure in dealing with an offender in both 1 Cor. 5:1-6a and in 2 Cor. 2:5-11 (a passage where Paul implores the community to restore a punished, penitent "deviant"): the majority or main body of the gathered assembly acts in concert with Paul's recommendation (see further South 1992). As Meeks perceptively observes: "What is at issue is not just an egregious case of moral laxity, but also a tension between local, charismatic authority and supralocal, unitive governance through the apostle and his itinerant associates. Paul does not relax that tension" (p. 128).

Having treated in some detail a number of Pauline texts where interpersonal and intergroup conflict are front and center, Meeks devotes the final pages of chapter 4 to inferences that one may draw from these passages pertaining to authority in the Pauline assemblies (pp. 131–39). His section subheadings, "Leaders" (pp. 131–36) and "Warrants for Authority" (pp. 136–39), mirror the two questions that drive this part of Meeks's work: Who makes the rules, and why should one follow them?

Meeks begins his commentary upon leaders in the Pauline churches with the grouping "apostles," wherein he gives Paul pride of place as "the chief figure in the records that we have of these little groups" (p. 131). Lest this be perceived as special pleading, Meeks suggests, "It is because of the extraordinary personal authority exerted by this man that we have his letters as the earliest extant Christian writings" (p. 131). Within the letters themselves, Paul offers himself as a model to be emulated and issues commands to be followed. That being said, "[B]y his 'biography of reversal' and his application of the Cross as a metaphor to his own mishaps and sufferings, he transforms that commonplace [i.e., the propensity of Hellenistic moralists to set forth themselves as exemplars and guides] into something new" (p. 131).

If Paul linked his apostleship to a Christological revelation and a divine commission to preach the gospel to, and to start churches among, the Gentiles, he was far from the only "itinerant, charismatic" authority in earliest Christianity. In addition to the original Jerusalem apostles, who seemingly "had little or no direct authority so far as the Pauline churches were concerned" (p. 132), Paul speaks of a number of others as apostles in 1 Cor. 15:5-9 (cf. Rom 16:7). In his letters to the Corinthians and the Galatians we discover that Paul "locked horns" with other itinerants who were regarded as apostles, even if Paul thought them to be people who distorted the gospel and were unworthy of the salutary title. Meeks also mentions the "apostles of churches" (note 2 Cor. 8:23; Phil. 2:25; 1 Cor. 16:15-18) at this point in his discussion, suggesting that their authority was likely "derivative and limited" not unlike the "'apostles' of the rabbinic court" (p. 133).

Next, Meeks turns to consider Paul's "fellow workers" (pp. 133–34). In addition to cataloging those Pauline coworkers specified in the letters and the various capacities (coauthors, envoys, patrons, evangelists, instructors) in which they served, Meeks iterates that the Pauline mission was a "collective enterprise" and suggests that Paul may have learned this approach to mission and evangelization from Barnabas. The corporate, even collegial, nature of this enterprise, Meeks maintains, was particularly successful in urban centers. He also observes that people worked more (e.g., Timothy) and less closely (e.g., Apollos) with Paul and finds impressive the "complexity and fluidity of the network of leaders that tied the Pauline *ekklēsiai* together" (p. 134).

Meeks concludes his survey of leadership in the Pauline churches by considering local church leaders (pp. 134–36). At the outset he notes that in contrast to Greek and Roman private associations, early Pauline congregations had no formal offices or processes for selecting leaders. Although various Pauline passages indicate some variation and gradation in the roles and gifts of congregants (note 1 Thess. 5:12; 1 Cor. 12:8-10, 28-30; Rom. 12:6-8; Eph. 4:11), the focus is upon function not status and freedom not formality. Even if Phil. 1:1 and Eph. 4:11 may signal some formalization of offices in Pauline fellowships, Meeks insists that "Roles do not become fully institutionalized . . . until the turn of the [first] century and afterward, as we see in the letter of Clement from Rome, the letters of Ignatius, and the Pastorals" (p. 135). Taken together, Meeks suggests that local authority was predicated upon "visible manifestations of Spirit-possession, position, and association with apostles and other supralocal persons of authority." He goes on to add: "These were not mutually exclusive, but tensions and conflicts could arise among them" (p. 136).

The last order of business for Meeks in this chapter is to consider various warrants for authority contained in Paul's letters (pp. 136–39). To begin he suggests that Paul and his converts shared a "common ethos" (i.e., a "fluid but recognizable set of beliefs, attitudes, and dispositions") that enabled "informal modes of control [to] predominate" (p. 136). Interpersonal meetings, congregational gatherings, and pastoral letters were typically persuasive and effective because of the relationships, experiences, symbols, and beliefs that the apostle shared with his churches. Meanwhile, the writings of Paul also indicate that he and his assemblies embraced certain norms advocated and embraced by a number of first-century Jews and "pagans."

When Meeks turns to identify "specific warrants" for enjoining obedience in Paul's letters, he discovers no less than six: authoritative position; divine revelation; a Christological and eschatological interpretation and appropriation of Scripture; Christian tradition and Pauline custom; guidance from and signs of the Spirit; and the crucifixion and resurrection of Christ as the paradigm for authentic power. While acknowledging the influence of each, Meeks contends that the authority of the Spirit in the Pauline communities and Paul's paradoxical "biography of reversal" are the most significant warrants of all (pp. 136–38).

Meeks concludes his treatment of governance in general and warrants in particular by observing how infrequently Paul communicates norms to his churches by setting forth specific rules. To be sure, Meeks acknowledges, specific ethical instructions would have been a part of early Christian baptismal catechesis. Yet, Meeks notes the general, suggestive nature of Pauline *paraenesis*. Furthermore, he observes that even when Paul does specify certain ethical expectations, he exercises interpretive freedom and anticipates congregational discernment. In summation, Meeks suggests, "The impression is one of great fluidity, of a complex multipolar, open-ended process of mutual discipline." He then goes on to posit that this "fluid structure of authority" may be explained in no small measure by the apostle's Christological and eschatological convictions (p. 139).

The "thick description" of chapter 4 that I have offered here is meant to draw attention to the manifold ways *The First Urban Christians* has increased our understanding of power and structure among Pauline believers. Furthermore, to ascertain more fully where subsequent work has gone and might go it is prudent to consider carefully previous, meritorious inquiries. Before moving ahead, however, it is appropriate at this point in the chapter to raise a few investigative questions and to offer a number of evaluative comments on chapter 4.

Setting certain exegetical quibbles to one side,[3] I will limit myself to four concerns arising from my reading and review. To begin, when remarking on 1 Thess. 5:12 and the three functions of leaders specified there, Meeks notes that the term *proistamenoi* may mean to "preside over" or to "act as patron or protector." Meeks opts for the latter. He partly bases this interpretive choice upon clues culled from the Corinthian correspondence. In Corinth, he contends, "a position of authority grows out of the benefits that persons of relatively higher wealth and status could confer on the community" (p. 134). Granting that this *may* have been the case in Corinth,[4] is it necessarily appropriate to extrapolate from the socio-economic situation of one Pauline congregation to that of another (cf. de Vos 1999; Ascough 2000)?

Similarly, Meeks remarks that "[Leadership] roles do not become fully institutionalized . . . until the turn of the [first] century and afterward . . ." (p. 135). While I concur with the conclusion that function trumps position in the Pauline churches and that with the exception of the Pastorals literary evidence for the formalization of church offices is sparse in the Pauline letters, the mention of the *episkopoi* and *diakonoi* in Phil. 1:1 (a verse that Meeks also considers; cf. Eph. 4:11) gives me cause for pause. Is it possible that other Pauline congregations also had people who bore such titles despite epistolary silence? Or, could it be that church offices developed faster in some churches of Paul than they did in others (cf. Gal. 6:6, another verse cited by Meeks)? (See further Campbell 1994.)

Recognizing that it may not be entirely fair or appropriate to critique an author for what he did not write, I wonder, nonetheless, whether it might have been beneficial for Meeks to consider in his discussion of conflict in chapter 4 the

---

3   For example, it is not as clear to me as it appears to be to Meeks and Malherbe that Paul's ethical admonitions in 1 Thessalonians 4 are "typical" (so Meeks 1983: 114). Cf. Still 2007: 209–11.

4   See more fully Bruce W. Longenecker's essay above.

additional category of "apostasy." Defection or disaffiliation, it seems to me, goes hand in glove with intergroup discord, deviation, and discipline (see Still 1999; Wilson 2004). Admittedly, Paul does not acknowledge, by name or otherwise, the defection of any single individual from one of his churches (cf. 1 Tim. 1:20; Pol., *Phil* 11.1). This fact notwithstanding, Paul does excommunicate from the Corinthian fellowship the man who has his father's wife (1 Cor. 5:1-13; cf. 2 Thess. 3:6-15), even as he regards certain Galatian Christians in danger of turning back to the *asthenē kai ptōcha stoicheia* (Gal. 4:9), submitting again to a yoke of slavery (5:1), and falling away from grace (5:4). Additionally, Paul dispatches Timothy to Thessalonica for fear of the same (see esp. 1 Thess. 3:1-5; cf. Phil. 2:16). Furthermore, the Thessalonian correspondence indicates that external conflict has internal consequences, be they good or ill (cf. Still 1999).

It is also worth asking at this juncture whether or not the picture of authority in Pauline assemblies is skewed by the fact that Meeks focuses primarily upon passages in Paul that are characterized by intergroup conflict. Although Meeks clearly expresses his rationale for doing so (see pp. 136–37), one may rightly wonder how reading Romans, Philippians, Philemon, and the disputed 2 Thessalonians with matters of power and structure in view might shape the composite portrait set forth in this chapter. We will engage in such an interpretive exercise in the course of this essay.

2. INTERPRETIVE TRAJECTORIES

The eighty-six endnotes accompanying chapter 4 indicate that Meeks did not conduct his work regarding "governance" in the Pauline churches in an academic vacuum (see pp. 230–35). Subsequent to the release of *The First Urban Christians* in 1983, however, there has been an explosion of publications in the field of Pauline studies. So much so, that space constraints preclude a full review of relevant literature here. It is possible, however, to note three areas where there has been fruitful exploration regarding the subject under discussion.

One angle that scholars have taken to probe relations between and among Paul and his congregations is the consideration of metaphors that he employs in his letters to describe his churches and himself. Drawing from and building upon the earlier work of interpreters such as Paul S. Minear (1960) and Robert J. Banks (1994 [1st ed. 1980]), scholars including Richard N. Longenecker (2002), Trevor J. Burke (2003), Reider Aasgaard (2004), Beverly Roberts Gaventa (2007), and Andrew D. Clarke (2008) have all made contributions to this fertile Pauline field. In his letters, Paul uses terminology from various domains, including building (e.g., "temple"), agriculture (e.g., "field"), domestics (e.g., "dough"), human existence (e.g., "body"), and family (e.g., "brothers and sisters") to speak to and about his congregations. He also draws from these metaphorical wells to depict himself and, at times, his coworkers (e.g., "master builder," "planter," "servant," "father," "mother," "teacher," "slave"). Taken together, these metaphors assist Paul and his churches to conceptualize and actualize their faith, roles, and relationships.

Since the publication of *The First Urban Christians*, not a few Pauline scholars have also studied the institutionalization of Pauline churches. Here the volume of Margaret Y. MacDonald (1988) merits special mention. Seeking to move beyond the sharp and theologically loaded dichotomies propounded by the likes of Rudolf Bultmann, Hans von Campenhausen, Eduard Schweizer, and especially Ernst Käsemann between Pauline *charismata* and "early Catholicism,"[5] MacDonald draws upon the work of biblical scholars such as Schütz (1975), Holmberg (1978), Theissen (1982), Meeks (1983), and Norman R. Petersen (1985) as well as upon the sociological insights of Peter L. Berger and Thomas Luckmann (1966) and Max Weber (as adopted by Holmberg) with Bryan Wilson's extensive treatment of sects thrown in for good measure (e.g., 1970) to trace the process of institutional development in the Pauline movement. Her project proceeds in three stages (community-building institutionalization [Paul's Letters]; community-stabilizing institutionalization [Colossians and Ephesians]; and community-protecting institutionalization [The Pastoral Epistles]). At each stage MacDonald compares four aspects of community life: attitudes to the world/ethics; ministry; ritual; and belief. Throughout her work MacDonald attempts to see elements of continuity between the writings even as she attends to what she views as transformative development (pp. 236–37). Later, related research by Ernest Best (1988), Anthony J. Blasi (1991), R. Alastair Campbell (1994), David G. Horrell (1997), Perry L. Stepp (2005), and Clarke (2008) also considers various facets and dynamics of leadership and congregational development in the Pauline mission (cf. more broadly Collins 1990; Maier 1991; and Burtchaell 1992).

Perhaps the most significant shift and important development in academic discourse with respect to our topic since the publication of *The First Urban Christians* pertains to Paul and his exercise of apostolic authority and pastoral power. While earlier forays into this subject tended to be rather sympathetic toward, if not overtly supportive of the apostle, appreciation for Paul is no longer a given. To be certain, Paul has had critics from the onset of his "Christian career," and criticism of the apostle has at times reached particularly shrill tones with scathing critiques from intellectuals like Friedrich Nietzsche and George Bernard Shaw (see esp. Meeks and Fitzgerald 2007: 228–71, 408–19). Nevertheless, direct attack on Paul's authority from within Pauline studies is a relatively new development.

If scholars such as Elisabeth Schüssler Fiorenza (1983) have discovered in Paul a complex, mixed legacy relative to matters of power and authority (cf. also Kittredge 1998 and Polaski 1999), other recent interpreters have seen little if any ambiguity whatsoever on this issue. Not a few contemporary interpreters,

---

5 Bibliographic particulars may be found in MacDonald 1988.

including Graham Shaw (1983), Elizabeth A. Castelli (1991), Stephen D. Moore (1994), James A. Smith (2006), and Joseph A. Marchal (2006, 2008), recommend reading Paul with more than a pinch of suspicion. On this view, the apostle employs oppression and exercises manipulation more often than not. Studies that look askance at Paul's (ab)use of power, however, have not gone unchallenged.[6] Presently, one may well wonder whether the current scholarly conversation regarding Paul's (mis)appropriation of power and position has arrived at something of a stalemate. One may also ponder whether there is any conceivable way to navigate this interpretive impasse. The wide-ranging proclivities, commitments, and contexts of scholars who are working and writing on either side of this great divide render *rapprochement* unlikely, even though the recently published study of Kathy Ehrensperger (2007) demonstrates that significant advances can still be made and common ground can still be found. Ehrensperger's study shows "that there is ample evidence for a differentiated perception of the dynamics of power in [Paul's letters] which cannot be subsumed under the notion of domination, or even appreciated when perceived only through the lens of theories of power as power-over" (Ehrensperger 2007: 196).[7]

3. EXTENDING THE INVESTIGATION

Since it is not possible for us to interview Paul, his coworkers, or members of his churches in an effort to understand more fully the structure and exercise of authority among them, our first and foremost recourse is, of course, to Paul's surviving letters. In his chapter on governance in the Pauline churches, Meeks gravitates toward those Pauline texts that are typified by interpersonal and congregational conflict. In this section I will expand upon Meeks's inquiry by treating pertinent passages from Romans, Philippians, Philemon, and 2 Thessalonians respectively. In particular I will focus my inquiry upon various "inferences" that may be drawn from these letters regarding "leaders" and "warrants for authority."[8]

Romans

There are apparent tensions between Jewish and Gentile Christians (see esp. 11:11-24) as well as between "weak" and "strong" believers (14:1–15:6) living in

---

6   See esp. Best 1986, 1988; Banks 1994; Carson 2004–05; Park 2007; Clarke 2008. Cf. Still 2003b.

7   For a recent treatment of power from a theological perspective, see Sykes 2006.

8   In this section my interaction with the voluminous secondary literature on letters under discussion will be necessarily limited. For bibliographic resources on Romans, see Jewett 2006; on Philippians, see Still 2008; on Philemon, see Still 2005; on 2 Thessalonians, see Weima and Porter 1998.

Rome.[9] Moreover, Paul fears that he will encounter opposition from unbelievers when he arrives in Jerusalem (15:31). That being said, conflict does not feature in Romans as it does in Galatians, 1–2 Corinthians, or even Colossians. Therefore, Paul's self-presentation and instructions are not colored by conflict to the extent that they are in the aforementioned letters. For our purposes, the other major factor that we need to remember when reading Romans is that Paul was writing to fellowships in Rome that he did not found.[10]

Be that as it may, Paul commences his protracted letter to "God's beloved in Rome" (1:7) by noting his status as a *doulos* and an *apostolos* (1:1). Paul refers again to his apostleship in 1:5 (cf. 11:13) and does not shy away from stating his longing to share a *pneumatikon charisma* (1:11) and to preach the gospel in Rome (1:15). Furthermore, near the conclusion of Romans, Paul links the bold reminders he has issued to his audience throughout the letter to the grace God has given him as an apostle and a minister of the gospel (15:15-16).

Romans 16 makes it clear, however, that Paul did not labor alone. He was assisted and supported in his apostolic ministry by the likes of Phoebe, a deacon and patron (vv. 1-2); Prisca and Aquila, coworkers and church hosts (vv. 3-5a; cf. 1 Cor. 16.19); and Andronicus and Junia, Paul's kin and fellow prisoners who were "prominent among the apostles" and believers in Christ before Paul (v. 7).[11] Paul also asks the Roman Christians to greet his coworker Urbanus (v. 9), even as he extends greetings to the Romans from his coworker Timothy (v. 21) and his (and the Corinthian church's) host Gaius (v. 23).[12]

Based upon the grace given him as an apostle, Paul enjoins the Romans in 12:3 "not to think of [themselves] more highly than [they] ought to think," but to think soberly and to live according "to the measure of faith God has assigned." He then likens Roman believers to the human body—they, though many with various functions, are "one body in Christ" and "members of one another" (12:4-5). Even as Paul was the beneficiary of divine grace and gifting, so, too, were they, receiving such *charisms* as prophecy, ministry, teaching, exhorting, giving, leading, and showing compassion (12:6-8). This sevenfold list illustrates the gifts that God gives the body for ministry. Far from being the exclusive preserve of Paul and his fellow workers, ministry is of, by, and for the body (see Ellis 1989). In Romans 16, Paul names a number of local leaders and workers in Rome, including Mary (v. 6), Tryphaena and Tryphosa (v. 12a), and Persis (v. 12b).

Were we to pause to consider the picture of leadership and ministry that emerges from the pages of Romans, it would not look too dissimilar to that which Meeks

---

9   Regarding "ethnic issues" in Romans, see Walters 1993. Cf. also Kaylor 1988. On the "weak" and the "strong," see esp. Barclay 1996.

10 For a study of the circumstances surrounding and the reasons for the writing of Romans, see Wedderburn 1988.

11 On Junia, see now esp. Epp 2005.

12 On the Roman believers mentioned in Romans 16, see esp. Lampe 2003: 153–83.

discovered with special reference to 1–2 Corinthians and Galatians. Although Paul did not found any of the house churches in Rome, he does not hesitate to appeal to his apostolic calling and commission in writing to them, nor does he avoid offering them theological and pastoral instruction. Additionally, as we have seen, there is ample evidence in Romans of both Pauline coworkers and local leaders, who along with members of the Roman churches, actively engaged in ministry. As with the churches of Paul, there was apparently a confluence of supralocal and local leadership.

Turning to "warrants for authority," Paul seeks to cultivate and inculcate "a common ethos" by reminding Roman believers of shared convictions and commitments, such as their being baptized into Christ Jesus' death (6:3), Christ's resurrection to eternal life (6:9), creation's current unredeemed state (8:22), God's working for good on behalf of believers (8:28), and the presumed proximity of the *parousia* (13:11). An extended *paraenetic* section also appears in Romans, even if it is more general than contextualized instruction (so Meeks 2002: 154; note, e.g., 12:9-21; 13:8-10).[13] Furthermore, Paul taps into Jewish wisdom tradition to instruct Roman Christians regarding governing authorities, arguably a "live issue" in Rome at the time (13:1-7; cf. 1:18-32).[14]

With respect to "specific warrants," we have seen that Paul speaks of his apostleship in conjunction with his call and commission to take the gospel to the nations (1:1, 5; 15:15-16). Additionally, Romans is saturated with scriptural quotation and interpretation[15] and may employ early Christian confessions (esp. 1:3-4). Furthermore, the Holy Spirit features in chapter 8 of the letter and is said to empower Paul to perform "signs and wonders" in conjunction with the proclamation of the gospel (15:19) as well as to indwell and enable believers to experience hope, love, righteousness, peace, and joy (5:5-6; 14:17). In addition, the Pauline dialectic of strength in weakness is especially pronounced in 8:31-39 and 15:1-7. In the latter passage Christ's sacrificial service becomes an example for the "strong" as they deal with the "weak." Living and dying with the crucified, risen Lord is to inform and transform their communal life (14:7-9). Regarding "rules," while aspects of Paul's ethical and ecclesial instructions to the Romans may be general and descriptive, the apostle's admonitions to the churches regarding their submitting to governing authorities (13:1, 5), paying taxes (13:6-7), and

---

13 Although some scholars side with Meeks in viewing Paul's instruction to Roman believers in the "ethical section" of the letter as general Pauline *paraenesis*, others, with whom I concur, maintain that the pastoral counsel Paul sets forth in Rom. 12:1–15:13 is at least partly occasional (so, e.g., Horrell 2003; 2005: 182–89). For the contours of this and other academic debates related to Romans, see Donfried, ed., 1991. For a study of Rom. 12:1–15:13 with a view to discovering whether and how "Jesus Tradition" informed Paul's ethics, see Thompson 1991.

14 On how a number of major theological interpreters have read Rom. 13:1-7 (and other debated passages in Romans) over the Christian centuries, see Reasoner 2005.

15 E.g., 3:10-18; 4:7-8; 9:13-14, 25-26, 29, 33; 10:18-21; 11:7-10, 26-27, 34-35; 15:9-12. See further Wagner 2002 and Watson 2004.

welcoming other believers regardless of dietary and calendric scruples (14:1–15:6) seem to be occasional and prescriptive.

Philippians

Although congregational conflict may not have been acute in Philippi when Paul composed Philippians, the letter indicates that there was some relational tension among Philippian believers, particularly between Euodia and Syntyche (see 4:2-3; cf. 2:1-4, 14 [note esp. Garland 1985]). In addition, the letter suggests that Paul was concerned about the possible presence and influence of (Jewish-Christian) interlopers, whom Paul regarded as an ever-present threat to the stability and unity of his assemblies (3:2; cf. 3:18-19 [see further, e.g., Williams 2002]). Moreover, the Philippians were experiencing some external opposition because of their commitment to the faith (1:27-30 [note Bloomquist 1993 and Geoffrion 1993]).

In writing to his "beloved" Philippians (1:7-8; 4:1), Paul does not employ the title "apostle."[16] Rather, he describes himself as a slave (1:1) and a prisoner (1:7, 13, 17) who partners with the Philippians in the gospel (1:5; 4:15) and partakes of grace with them (1:7). In the course of the letter, however, Paul expresses confidence in the church's ongoing obedience (to God? Paul? Both? [2:12; see, e.g., Bockmuehl 1998: 150–51]), and he enjoins them to imitate him (3:17; 4:9). Paul also underscores the significance of his physical presence with the assembly (1:24-26; 2:24).

Within the letter, Paul also makes mention of supralocal and local coworkers. In both the salutation and the letter body Paul refers to Timothy, in the latter instance as a "slave" and a "son" (1:1; 2:22). The loyal companion (*syzyge*) of 4:3, along with Clement and other unnamed coworkers of Paul, may also belong to the category of Paul's supralocal associates. On the other hand, Epaphroditus, who is favorably described by Paul in 2:25, was a member of, messenger from, and minister to the Philippian assembly. Euodia and Syntyche mentioned above were also local leaders and colaborers in the gospel, and it may be that they were numbered among the *episkopoi* and *diakonoi* (1:1).[17] Additionally, it is possible to read 2:14-16 as a Pauline admonition for the entire congregation to engage in mission and ministry (see Ware 2005: 251–70).

When considering "warrants for authority" in Philippians, Paul's call for the assembly to "have the habit of mind among [themselves] that [is] also in Christ Jesus" (2:5) looms large. That the Philippians would think and act in ways consonant with Jesus' self-emptying, self-humbling enslavement is Paul's central concern in the letter (so, too, Meeks 2002: 112). To the extent that he, Timothy,

---

16 In writing a commentary on Philippians, I have found the work of Holloway 2001 and Oakes 2001 to be particularly helpful.
17 On Phil. 1:1, see esp. Reumann 1993.

Epaphroditus, and others emulate Christ's kenotic pattern, they are worthy of imitation. The assembly's unity and generosity are not to be sabotaged by selfishness or petty rivalry; rather, with hearts and minds shaped by joyful prayer, wholesome meditation, and Christ-centered contentment, they are to await the transformation of their lowly bodies as they strive for the perfection that will be theirs on the day of Christ Jesus (3:20–4.20).

Philemon

Paul's 335-word letter to Philemon is an unexpected treasure trove for those seeking an understanding of governance in the Pauline churches. The storyline of Philemon is well known and need not detain us here, even if some of the letter's prehistory, not to mention its post-history, remains murky.[18] In writing to Philemon on behalf of Onesimus, the titles Paul dons are "prisoner" (vv. 1, 9, 10, 13) and "old man" (v. 9). Conspicuous is the absence of epithet "apostle," although Paul insists that he is "bold enough in Christ to command" Philemon (v. 8) and that he is confident that Philemon will obey, indeed exceed, his request (v. 21). Paul indicates that he does not desire to command or to compel Philemon (v. 14), but the letter makes it clear that he does desire to persuade him to embrace his view of things. In writing to Philemon, Paul displays many of the rhetorical skills and strategies that are at his disposal (see further Wilson 1992). For example, he affirms Philemon (v. 5); delays mention of Onesimus's name (v. 10); produces wordplays on Onesimus's name (vv. 11, 21); links Philemon's response to Onesimus as a response to himself (v. 17); reminds Philemon of his indebtedness to him (v. 19); asks Philemon to refresh his heart (v. 20; cf. vv. 7, 12); and requests that Philemon prepare a guest room for his hoped-for visit (v. 22).

Paul also seeks to place pressure upon Philemon, whom he regards as his "dear friend and coworker" (v. 1), by drawing other Pauline leaders and believers into the epistolary fray. Specifically, Paul mentions Timothy, "the brother" (v. 1); Apphia, "the sister"; Archippus, "our fellow soldier"; and "the church in [Philemon's] house" (v. 2). In addition, as Paul concludes the letter he extends greetings to Philemon from five of his coworkers: Epaphras, Mark, Aristarchus, Demas, and Luke (vv. 23-24).

Reading Philemon with the purposes of this investigation in mind brings the following issues to the fore. First, Paul assumes the "senior" role in his relationship with Philemon and anticipates that Philemon will do what he asks.[19] That being said, given that Paul is advocating on behalf of a slave, I find it difficult to reduce the letter to a "Pauline power play." Second, one infers from this letter that

---

18   For a recent treatment of Philemon replete with up-to-date bibliography, see Nicklas 2008.
19   Arguably, the precise nature of Paul's request would have been clearer to him than it has been for belated readers! See further esp. Barclay 1991.

Philemon (along with Apphia and Archippus?) is a leader of a (Colossian?) house church and that he, who like Onesimus became a believer through Paul, has contact with other Pauline coworkers. Lastly, whatever hierarchy is presumed within the letter, it is only made operative through compliance. As an aged prisoner Paul is in no physical position to force Onesimus, much less Philemon, to do anything against their wills. He is left to appeal to their common conversion to Christ, to their shared concern for fellow believers, and to their mutual convictions and commitments as "brothers."

Second Thessalonians

Second Thessalonians is another Pauline letter that may enable additional insight into governance in Paul's churches. While New Testament specialists continue to debate the letter's authenticity, few interpreters would deny that the work was composed to address concrete eschatological and ecclesial conflicts. The letter indicates that "Paul, Silvanus, and Timothy" (1:1) are writing to the Thessalonian church to offer believers encouragement in the face of external, non-Christian opposition (1:3-12); corrective instruction regarding the coming of Christ (2:1-16); and admonitions with respect to the *ataktoi* (3:6-15).

Beyond broad ecclesial and familial language, authoritative titles are conspicuously absent from the letter. This is not to suggest, however, that authoritative claims are not made. Appeals to oral and written traditions (2:15; 3:6) as well as to the model of Paul and his associates (3:7, 9) appear. Earnest pleas (2:2) and firm commands (3:4, 6, 10, 12, 14-15) are also present. Indeed, the last chapter of the letter may be fairly described as rather authoritarian in tone.

Scholars dispute what precipitated the eschatological alarm and the congregational trouble evinced in 2 Thessalonians 2–3 as well as the possible connection between the two problems (see Still 1999: 275–80). Second Thessalonians 2:2 seems to suggest that there were other "teachers," probably internal to the assembly, who had taken the eschatological baton from Paul and were running with it. In contradistinction to Paul, however, these apocalyptic enthusiasts were claiming that "the day of the Lord had come." The writer(s) of 2 Thessalonians counter this assertion by appealing to previous oral and written instruction (2:5, 15).

Appeals to *traditio* and *imitatio* recur in 2 Thess. 3:6-15, a passage that seeks to shame the *ataktoi* (i.e., work-shy, disorderly congregants).[20] Whatever the reasons(s) for and the nature of their (in)activity, our present interests are in the instructions set forth to counter their unwelcome influence. At the outset of this section, the author(s) enjoin the recipients to stay away from fellow believers who are unruly/lazy, iterating that such behavior was not in accord with the tradition

---

20 On the identity of the *ataktoi*, see, among others, Jewett 1986.

they had received from their founders and teachers. In addition to specific instructions, the Thessalonians were given an example to follow. Their missioners were neither loafers nor freeloaders; instead, they labored continuously so that they might not be an unnecessary burden upon the congregation (3:7-8; cf. 1 Thess. 2:9). Even though they had the authority (*exousia*) to be supported by the church, they relinquished this right for the benefit of the fellowship (3:9; cf. 1 Thess. 2:7; 1 Cor. 9:1-18; 2 Cor. 11:7-11; 12:14-15). At least in this regard, they "practiced what they preached." They turned their hands to keep the command they had previously given: "If anyone does not wish to work, neither let this one eat" (3:10).

Verse 11 indicates that "Paul" and his colleagues were being told that some (*tinas*) of the church were walking *ataktōs*; they were not working but working around (i.e., being busybodies). In response to this report, the writer(s) command and exhort these people in the Lord to work quietly and to eat their own bread (= earn their own keep, pay their own way) (3:12). Furthermore, all of the "brothers and sisters" are encouraged not to grow weary in well-doing, an exhortation that may have eschatological overtones (3:13; cf. Gal. 6:9).

The passage concludes with the congregation being told what to do relative to those who refuse to obey what is written in the letter (3:14). The author(s) tell(s) the assembly to do three things: (1) Take special note of such individuals. (2) Do not mingle or associate with them so that they might be shamed. (3) Do not regard these "deviants" as *echthroi* but as *adelphoi.*

4. CONCLUSION

As we draw this chapter to a close, it is worth pausing and asking how one might best describe governance in the Pauline churches based upon Paul's seven undisputed letters, with Colossians and 2 Thessalonians supplementing this composite picture. As we will see, the three binary pairings I have chosen to depict interaction and organization in the churches of Paul are not unrelated to the dialectical patterns that mark the apostle's thinking and writing.

Conflict and Community

Paul's ecclesial vision was one of unity (not uniformity) and maturity (not perfection) (see Horrell 2005: 116–21; Samra 2006). This pastoral passion is most obvious in 1 Corinthians and Philippians (cf. Romans 9–15), but Paul's conviction that Jew and Greek, slave and free, male and female are "one in Christ Jesus" (Gal. 3:28; cf. 1 Cor. 12:13; Col. 3:11) drives his apostolic mission and impacts both the composition and relations of his churches. Paul's hope that Christian congregations with whom he is in contact "might think the same thing with one another according to Christ Jesus" (Rom. 15:5; cf. Phil. 4:2) was frequently shattered into shards by congregational discord. Theological and moral troubles that threatened to stunt or short-circuit an assembly's growth in the gospel prompted Paul to respond, often swiftly and strongly.

Mutuality and Authority

It is, in fact, in times of conflict that Paul was most inclined "to flex his apostolic muscles." The Corinthian correspondence and Galatians are cases in point. Be that as it may, even in less confrontational letters (Romans, Philippians, 1 Thessalonians, and Philemon come to mind), Paul does not abdicate his apostolic call and role. He offers instructions and enjoins imitation with little to no hesitation or equivocation. He thinks it his spiritual business to consider and confront forces and factors affecting congregations that he founded or assisted.

If Paul proves (all too) willing to speak and to act, he does not do so alone. In addition to a capable cadre of mobile coworkers, he depends upon, even if he sometimes differs with, local leaders. Although Paul may have played the leading role among early Christians in a concerted effort to take the gospel to the nations, he had a supporting cast that he needed and appreciated. Ehrensperger captures the complex picture of power and authority among Pauline associates and assemblies well: "The power at work among leaders, between leaders and communities, and among communities oscillates between power-over, power-to and power-with, and frequently some or even all of these aspects are closely intertwined with each other" (2007: 179).

While not seeking to deny that Paul and his associates exercised power over various groups of Christ-followers, Ehrensperger contends—convincingly in my view—that the "transformative empowering dimension of power," as opposed to a domination or a command-obedience model, best characterizes the interaction between supralocal Pauline leaders and local Pauline churches. Paul and his fellow missioners related to churches they founded and/or directed "as 'weak' apostles, 'nursing fathers' and 'teaching mothers', models to imitate, and messengers who transmit God's call to response-ability" (Ehrensperger 2007: 179).

Structure and Spontaneity

If formal church offices and an ordained ministry post-date Paul, Paul's letters do not suggest wholly amorphous fellowships.[21] Not only did Paul and his

---

21 See Garland 2003 and the response by Still 2003a.

coworkers maintain contact with churches via visits and letters, but there were also local leaders, some of whom may well have been selected, trained, or affirmed by Paul as he sought to guide, guard, and minister to given congregations. Although some local leaders of Pauline churches may have also been patrons, the various "gift lists" in Paul's letters reveal that there was "local variation and considerable freedom for charismatic leadership" (Meeks 1983: 135). Furthermore, despite Paul's desire for at least some semblance of order when his churches assembled, it appears that Pauline worship gatherings were lively, participatory events where the saints welcomed the Spirit as well as unbelievers (cf. 1 Cor. 14:20-40).

Leaving Loose Ends Untied

Paul of Tarsus fathered and mothered churches of Christ-followers in the eastern Roman provinces in the second half of the first century. The literary legacy that this radical, atypical Jew bequeathed to posterity spawns questions and prompts examination of all sorts and sundry of matters. At the outset of the twenty-first century, queries and quandaries regarding (ecclesial) order and power remain (see esp. Sykes 2006). Many people, whether clergy or laity, fully devoted or decidedly disaffected, have turned to Paul's letters to explore issues of (church) structure and authority. In doing so, they have discovered paucity and ambiguity on one side and the other and Paul himself at the center.

Indeed, Paul has become a storm center. A number of contemporary readers and interpreters have found objectionable, if not offensive, Paul's spiritual claims and his superordinate status relative to his coworkers and converts. Those attempting a sympathetic reading of Paul and his letters, however, draw attention to a number of mitigating factors, not the least of which is the paradoxical nature of Paul's proclamation and self-presentation, wherein weakness outstrips and subverts power, and divine grace is declared to be sufficiently strong. Furthermore, in Paul's angle of theological and moral vision, any and all earthly power (his own included) is temporary and penultimate. The gospel not the apostle, God not church governance, will have ultimate sway at the end of the day.

Elsewhere, Meeks perceptively and poignantly notes: "At the center of Paul's concern is his labor to give birth . . . to a community that will be conformed to . . . that paradoxical story of life in death, of power in weakness, of joy in suffering, of judgment and waiting, of striving and receiving, a community in which 'Christ will be formed'" (2006: 137). I concur, and so would Paul, I figure. In addition, Paul would, I think, support this contention of Meeks: "[T]he victory of the Son of God is not that of the triumphalist church's dreams [and, we might add, of the pilloried apostle's schemes], but the victory that reveals the heart of the loving, inscrutable, ironic God" (2006: 140).

Were we to ask Paul to offer a statement on and a summary of the topic we have treated here, it might run something like this: "For [Christ] was crucified in weakness, but lives by the power of God. For we are weak in him, but we will live with him by the power of God toward you" (2 Cor. 13:4; cf. 4:7-12). "The paradox," Meeks remarks, "is that [Paul] is both weak and a charismatic" (1983: 183). For Paul and his churches, this enigmatic existence was expected to persist until the "perfect comes" and "the imperfect ceases to exist" (1 Cor. 13:9).

Chapter 6

RITUAL AND THE FIRST URBAN CHRISTIANS: BOUNDARY CROSSINGS OF LIFE AND DEATH

Louise J. Lawrence

Life becomes transparent against the background of death.
—*Peter Metcalf and Richard Huntington*, Celebrations of Death

In the twenty-five years since the publication of *The First Urban Christians*, analysis of "ritual" has undergone major methodological developments. There is today a discrete discipline of "ritual studies" that draws not only on the history of religion but also on cultural anthropology, archaeology, performance theory, and related fields.[1] Ritual is no longer viewed as a phenomenon that merely reflects a previously defined narrative, but rather as politically-charged, dynamic, and transformative. Catherine Bell's work in particular has proposed that ritual should be seen as "practice" which is endemic to a variety of spheres of life and conceptualized in relation to dynamics of power (Bell 1992, 1997).

In many ways Wayne Meeks was before his time in paying due acknowledgment to a "practice"-based reading of ritual. Drawing on J. L. Austin's speech act theory, he prioritized the question of action (what does this ritual *do*?) over the question of meaning (what does this ritual *represent*?). He was also sensitive to the gap that exists between "external observer" and "ritual actors" (1983: 142). He was aware that anachronism was a particular threat in relation to understanding the rituals of baptism and the Lord's Supper when over two thousand years of sacramental theology flowed between the exegete and Paul's communities.[2]

---

1 *The Journal of Ritual Studies* began in 1987. Most articles in the journal focus on contemporary ritual practice. Hal Taussig notes that "of 210 articles in the journal over the past 15 years, only 13 are about rituals in an [*sic*] historical past" (Taussig 2002).

2 Richard DeMaris's recently published work on ritual in the New Testament world likewise consciously sets out to avoid "interpretive frameworks that assume the referential or symbolic nature of rites" (2008: 8) He regards "rites as generative and creative—as having a life of their own—as opposed to how they are often regarded: derivative and ancillary" (p. 8). Practice-based approaches

Meeks's focus also challenged what Mark McVann has characterized as a deeply ingrained suspicion of ritual in Protestant circles, in part on account of its links in the popular imagination with "the magical and savage" so unpalatable to the modern disposition (McVann 1994: 7). Following other pioneering social-scientific interpreters, Meeks wanted to challenge the separation of body and soul, practice and theology, and to employ comparative perspectives to reimagine early Christians not as disembodied "theological heads" but as flesh and blood people living in specific social contexts (see Scroggs 1980: 166). As an anthropologist entering a "foreign field," Meeks thus set out to provide a Geertzian "thick description" of early Christian life and conscious action.

It is testament to the veracity of Meeks's ritual analysis that many of the points he made have now been accepted as received wisdom within the field.[3] To do full justice to the "history of effects" of chapter 5 in *The First Urban Christians* would therefore be well beyond the limits of this essay.[4] My aim is far more modest. First, I am going to focus on some of the discussion that has been generated around Meeks's categorizations of early Christian ritual into "major," "minor," and "unknown and controverted." Second, I am going to consider some key developments that were inspired in part by Meeks's work under the following headings: ethnography—thick descriptions of textual worlds; ritual and morality; ritual and the construction of social memory; and ritual and empire. Finally, I will offer some brief thoughts on the unifying symbolic factor of life and death as boundaries of early Christian ritualizing.[5]

1. FROM MAJOR TO MINOR: CATEGORIZING RITUAL

Meeks provides a classification of ritual into major, minor, and unknown/ controverted. The major rituals are, unsurprisingly, baptism, as a rite of initiation, and the Lord's Supper, as a rite of integration. Baptism is compared with Jewish immersion of proselytes and admissions into pagan mystery religions, which often demanded a ritual cleansing prior to initiation. In contrast, for the Christians, the immersion of the full body into water itself constituted the initiatory rite (p. 150). Meeks viewed the water bath as a "permanent threshold between the clean group and the dirty world" (p. 153), and adopting Arnold van Gennep's work, via Victor

---

take seriously the fact that participants within rituals can have their own particular take on the meanings of the actions in which they are involved.

3   Concurring with Meeks are MacDonald 1988 and Horrell 1996 to name just a sample.

4   The profound influence of his work is illustrated by the seventy-two entries on *The First Urban Christians* alone in the ATLA database.

5   My argument throughout this piece is informed by DeMaris's recently published book, *The New Testament in its Ritual World* (2008). It is a superb discussion of current ritual theory and is innovative in its application of these perspectives to the church in Corinth and Mark's Gospel.

Turner, Meeks classified baptism as a rite of passage. Each rite of passage for van Gennep involved first, a separation and isolation from the commonplace world of things; second, liminality—a space set apart; and, finally, reaggregation back into the world. Meeks, accordingly, interpreted the baptismal immersion as a taking off of the old self and "putting on instead Christ, the new human" (p. 151). Drawing out the Pauline association of baptism with dying and rising with Christ, Meeks interpreted baptismal practice as "symbolic death, rebirth as a child, [and] abolition of distinctions of role and status—all are typical of the transitional or liminal phase in initiations" (p. 157). Meeks also saw the androgynous "image of God" motif from Genesis as symbolic to the rite, for "baptism suggests a restoration of paradisiac motifs: the lost unity, the lost image, the lost glory" (p. 155).[6] Meeks was aware that the anti-structure of the liminal phase in fact marked more fundamentally the identity of the church than the reaggregation phase: "The *ekklēsia* itself, not just the initiates during the period of their induction, is supposed to be marked by sacredness, homogeneity, unity, love, equality, humility, and so on—as Turner would say, by *communitas*" (p. 157).

The Lord's Supper was also compared with other urban feasting and cultic practices, including festal meals common in voluntary associations. Casting the Lord's Supper as a rite of integration and solidarity, Meeks closely follows Gerd Theissen in showing how "Paul uses the symbolism of the Supper ritual not only to enhance the internal coherence, unity, and equality of the Christian group, but also to protect its boundaries . . ." (p. 160). The repetition of the words "do this in remembrance of me" heightens for Meeks the practice of the "cultic commemoration of Jesus" (p. 158) and the eschatological proclamation within the community of the "Lord's death until he comes" (1 Cor. 11:26).

Minor rituals are harder to classify. Within this category Meeks includes "coming together" for regular meetings. Certain ritualized actions characterized these gatherings of baptized members for "common meals in memory of Jesus." "By these gestures, formulas and patterns of speaking they discovered and expressed their identity as 'brothers and sisters in Christ,' 'the assembly of God,' 'the holy and elect,' 'the body of Christ,' and so on" (p. 142). The setting apart of specific times and places for such gatherings was itself ritualistic. Similarly Meeks names worship "in the *ekklēsia*" as another context marked by minor ritual actions. These include the singing of psalms and hymns that by rhythm, recitation, and emotion fostered cohesion and reiterated "statements and metaphors of fundamental beliefs." Similarly "teaching and admonition" played a ritualistic part in "the formation of the community's ethos" (p. 145). Prayer, likewise, can be cast in a ritualistic light; whether unprompted or habitual, coherent or charismatic, acclamation or doxology, it links the community into a "set apart" state. Even glossolalia is

---

6   He even proposes that the aggregation ceremony involved a miming of the enthronement "with Christ in heavenly places" as hinted at in Eph. 2:6.

seen as ritualistic: "It happened at predictable times, accompanied by distinctive bodily movements . . . It did what rituals do: it stimulated feelings of group solidarity . . . it increased the prestige of individuals, thus creating or underlining roles, and marked the occasion as one of solemnity . . ." (p. 149).

The unknown and controverted rituals comprise a much shorter section within Meeks's work (just over a page, pp. 162–63). Funeral rites are mentioned here, not least because of their profound significance in the urban contexts of the time. Meeks presumes that Christians buried their dead in ways comparable to their neighbors and thus deduces that a memorial meal in honor of the deceased, perhaps at the anniversary of the death, may well have featured in their rituals (p. 162). He also puts "baptism for the dead" within this category, though coming to no firm conclusions whatsoever about the possible practice this could have involved. Quite the contrary, he states: "What *are* they doing? The Corinthians presumably knew, but we do not, despite interesting speculations without end" (p. 162). He also mentions marriage within this category, particularly the remarriage of widows, but whether a specifically Christian rite of marriage was practiced is for Meeks an open question. Meeks finally considers rituals marking seasonal or annual celebrations. While he contends that Paul fiercely resisted syncretistic cults that marked "days and months, seasons and years," there could be evidence in 1 Cor. 5:6-8 and 16:8 that Paul celebrated both Passover (with a Christian gloss) and Pentecost, but yet again Meeks comes to no firm historical conclusions on this (p. 163).

For Meeks, in a broadly functionalist frame, major and minor ritual complexes within the Pauline communities fostered togetherness. Through gatherings, worship, washing, and feasting, the human imagination and social world were reorganized and renewed; the church as anti-structure occupied a "liminal" space where unity and love were cultivated among participants. Margaret MacDonald showed as much when she used Meeks's classification as a central theoretical plank in her sketch of the "community-building stage" of the Pauline churches (MacDonald 1988: 31–83) marked by group solidarity and upbuilding (*oikodomē*) (1988: 61–71). Ekkehard and Wolfgang Stegemann similarly concur that these rituals "reinforce in a prominent way the specific, somehow divinely ordained, cohesion of the Christ-confessing group which is defined metaphorically in the image of one body of many believers in Christ" (Stegemann and Stegemann 1999: 283).

Despite these positive adaptations, Meeks's schematic portrayal of ritual has not been without its critics. Stanley Stowers, aware of the potentially reductionist impulse in a sociological approach, criticized Meeks for turning everything into latent ritual and not conscious belief (Stowers 1985). However, with the development of a wider definition of ritual, broader than that which is specifically "holy" or "religious," the force of this criticism is somewhat tempered. John Pilch, for example, cautions interpreters not to limit ritual to the sacred; he cites challenge-riposte, a mode of interaction central to the honor and shame complex, as an example of wider ritualistic modes of human exchange (Pilch 1994: 39).

In his review of Meeks's work, Bruce Malina charges Meeks with lacking "conceptual specificity" as regards ritual. He wonders, given that Turner's definition of *communitas* is so central to Meeks's analysis, why all aspects of Christian practice that foster solidarity in a variety of contexts (teaching, worship, etc.) are not also classified as major rites (Malina 1985: 156). Richard DeMaris also questions Meeks's categorization of rituals, particularly the privileging of baptism and the Lord's Supper as "major" rituals and how these feature in the context of other so-called minor ritual activities. DeMaris is suspicious of Meeks's separation of the "baptism for the dead" from the "major" complex of baptism into an "unknown and controverted ritual" (2008: 60). He criticizes Meeks for not acknowledging that van Gennep also ties rites marking birth, marriage, and death together as "potent metaphors for one another" (p. 60). This, he concludes, firmly connects baptism with the dead, "that is the funerary, as not an unknown application of baptism but a logical extension of it" (p. 60). He also notes how funerary practices could be adapted to non-funerary situations, for example expulsions of members from communities where their departure was literally mourned.[7] DeMaris thus criticizes Meeks for artificially isolating baptism and the Lord's Supper from other ritual complexes. He also warns against too hastily assigning a function or meaning to these rituals without due consideration of whether the complex of themes they address are relevant elsewhere.

Malina picks up on the fact that in Meeks's adoption of van Gennep's rite of passage model, Meeks actually omits the final stage of reaggregation: "living as *ekklēsia*, 'in Christ,' is a transitional state that cannot be maintained for any substantial length of time. Thus, the problem of the delay of reaggregation, of the Messiah's coming, and the question of how members might still be *ekklēsia* when they left the 'gathering' remains" (Malina 1985: 349). A similar point has been made by DeMaris who also notes Meeks's problematic assigning of the church to the liminal stage of the rite of passage model. He raises the question: If the final aggregation stage is omitted, then how can baptism be called a rite of passage at all? He also contends that the sorts of groups that Turner had in mind as instances of those which embodied liminal status long-term were twentieth-century hippy groups which are very hard to draw on as comparative material for the church's relationship to the wider social world in the first century. Turner himself had stated that even the sacrament of baptism in the Roman Catholic Church was brief and simple when compared with the complex varieties he witnessed in tribal religions, a point similarly made by John Ashton in his

---

7   On mourning in non-death contexts see Saul Olyan's study, *Biblical Mourning: Ritual and Social Dimensions* (2004). He notes how mourning behavior can be found in crisis situations, for instance in military defeat or the destruction of a city (p. 106).

recent comparative study of Paul with shamanism. Ashton disconnects the early church and long-term liminal anti-structure on the grounds that "baptism, even where it involves total immersion, is clearly no more than a token gesture when placed against the lengthy rites of passage practiced in other societies" (Ashton 2000: 135, cited in DeMaris 2008: 20). With all this is mind DeMaris urges interpreters to avoid using the phrase "rite of passage" to denote baptism, and alternatively classifies it as a "boundary crossing ritual" (p. 20). One of the key points in this regard is the fact that boundary-crossing rites are again and again associated with situations of community or individual crisis. DeMaris helpfully reminds us that "it is easy to miss this aspect of baptism in the ancient church because the New Testament omits it" (p. 24). He suggests that the profound crisis that provided the social context of baptism was the breaking of natural family ties at conversion (p. 27). DeMaris views ritual as a "traditionalis-ing instrument" (p. 34), normalizing the extraordinary in situations of tension. Entering Christian community may to us seem straightforward, but in respect to natural kin relationships it was far from this. Baptism thus aided and masked the difficulties of this complex social adjustment (p. 34).

Moving away from the rights and wrongs of categorizing rituals as major, minor, and unknown/controverted, Jerome Neyrey (1990) has made much of a distinction between *ritual*, which he defines as involving status reversal or transformation, and *ceremony,* which he defines as confirming the existing status of a collective or individual. Accordingly, rituals are seen as irregular and often unpredictable events, while ceremonies occur regularly and predictably. With a focus on trans-formation, it is claimed that ritual focuses on present to future boundaries, whereas ceremonies with their confirmation of an existing state tend to focus more on past to present boundaries. Furthermore, rituals are presided over by professionals (doctors, school presidents, lawyers), whereas officials (father, mother, presidents, popes) tend to preside over ceremonies (though this particular distinction seems less than clear). Rituals in Pauline communities identified by Neyrey include bap-tism, excommunication, marriage, judgment, etc. Ceremonies include community shared meals (the Lord's Supper, etc.), which affirm the unity of congregation; the collection, which affirms the Jerusalem church's centrality; and the sending of letters, which affirms the status of Paul as founder or leader of the congregation. Neyrey concludes that for Paul most concentration is given to ceremonies rather than rituals as his writings tended to address "a crisis about the blurring of internal lines within a group or trespassing on the periphery of the group's boundaries" (Neyrey 1990: 79). In such situations the public rehearsal of the identity of the community is central to overcoming conflict and restoring order. Neyrey's exten-sion of ritual categories to activities like the writing and reading of letters helpfully reflects current ritual studies' interest in broadening the frameworks of ritual. One could perhaps add travel and rhetoric under a similarly ritualistic rubric. As for the concrete distinctions between ritual and ceremony that Neyrey proposes, as with all such distinctions, it is their heuristic value that ultimately counts. Emphasizing the respective transformative and confirmatory aspects of particular actions, the ritual/ceremony model seems helpful to some degree.

One important contribution of Meeks's work, then, was highlighting the centrality given to baptism and the Lord's Supper, though this, as DeMaris cautions, should not have been to the exclusion of establishing links between these and the rest of the ritual world of the early Christians. The debate about the applicability of the rite of passage model to the baptismal initiation rite also helpfully reminds us not to manipulate information into a predefined model. However, in this instance the picturing of the church as an anti-structure liminal community waiting for its final reaggregation at the parousia seems largely persuasive. When social conflict or breakdown occurs, many groups try to maintain the experience of *communitas* experienced within the liminal period. A ritual of status transformation may be envisaged indefinitely, thus leading to the "creation of a new kind of fundamental human community" in which *communitas* is "traditionalised" as normality (Draper 2000: 124). Perhaps a more damaging criticism of Meeks concerns the way he seems to suggest that all rituals ensure the solidarity and protection of group identity. In this respect Meeks is broadly functionalist: ritual helps to legitimate and sustain the community's worldview. He does not address internal group disputes to a great extent (conflict theory is not adopted), nor the fact that a purpose Paul envisaged for a practice may not be borne out in reality.[8]

2. SELECTED KEY DEVELOPMENTS

Ethnography—Thick Descriptions of Literary Worlds

Meeks characterizes himself as an ethnographer, an interpretive "describer of culture" (p. 6). While Meeks provides a "thick reading" of the ritual phenomena observed within the Pauline texts, he is also acutely aware of the gap that exists between interpreter and interpreted. He is alive to the fact that the context in which he works is not long-term fieldwork among Pauline communities but rather sifting through ancient texts left in their wake. Many others have since followed Meeks in providing "thick descriptions" of literary worlds (Bergant 1994; Elliott 1990; Robbins 1996; Lawrence 2003). Others, most notably the Context Group,[9] have developed the "comparative" nature of ethnography and employed insights from Mediterranean ethnography to undertake their readings of biblical worlds (see, e.g., Neyrey 1991; Malina and Rohrbaugh 1992; Malina 1996).

---

8 First Corinthians 1:14–15 seems, for instance, to reflect power controversies within the community. The logic employed in Paul's retort is centered on ritual: "I thank God that I baptized none of you except Crispus and Gaius, so that no one can say that you were baptized in my name."

9 On the development of this group see Esler 2004.

Meeks implicitly acknowledges the central importance of literary texts in bringing certain social ideologies into consciousness and challenging existing ones.[10] While the default position in the past may well have been to understand as primary the narrative or mythology lying behind a ritual (thus the death and resurrection of Christ lying behind baptism and the Lord's Supper etc.), Meeks considers "what it does" within the community as central to its understanding as well. In this respect he is at one with Roland Grimes, who wants to see ritual as a performance on its own terms. This should begin with the description of the ritual and the social context in which it was performed/embedded (Grimes 1990: 109–44). The fact that Meeks undertakes some data comparison with other relevant contemporary practices in urban contexts means he makes firm steps toward linking textual data with contextual material.

Building on Meeks's insights into the ways in which literary texts shape social worlds, DeMaris has recently adopted Christian Strecker's analysis of the different ways in which ritual and texts could interplay (DeMaris 2008: 6–7). Among these are the following: a text could prescribe particular pointers for executing a ritual (the words of institution at the Lord's Supper could stand as an example of this); a text could reveal the meaning or function of a ritual (as in the mythology of the dying and rising Christ in Romans 6); or a text could have been produced directly from ritual practice. DeMaris contends that 1 Corinthians is itself reflective of a ritual logic (p. 9), centering as it does on group purity, restoration, and maintenance through ritual action. We could also imagine that preexisting meal-customs, funerary practices, washing, etc. were only later linked fully with specific Christian narratives. Ritual logic may have therefore shaped a number of biblical texts. In short, Meeks's work paved the way for the relationship between social action and literary texts to be understood in more complex ways.

Ritual and Morality

Viewing ritual behavior as formative for Christian morality was an implied assumption in *The First Urban Christians* that was to be developed further by Meeks in his 1993 book, *The Origins of Christian Morality*. Meeks once again here sought to undertake an ethnographic description of Christian origins (p. ix), this time, though, with the assumption that most New Testament documents were preoccupied with the behavior of Christian converts and the maintenance and growth of Christian communities (p. 5). Taking a largely Aristotelian approach

---

10 Judith Perkins, for example, has shown how the image of suffering in early Christian narratives perhaps "worked not simply to represent a realistic situation as much as to prove a self-definition that marked the growth of Christianity as an institution . . . This new body of knowledge, around the suffering body, provided a basis of power and enabled the formation of new institutions incorporating this power" (Perkins 1995: 12).

(pp. 7–8), Meeks prefers the term morality (inculcated in practice) to ethics (seen as a higher-order philosophical pursuit). Ritual is regarded in this book as "paradigmatic practice" (p. 91) in which the functioning religious community is educated and formed in Christian morality. In this work Meeks was much more sensitive to the literary and social contexts in which particular rituals came into view: "it will be important to set their moral talk within the context of social forms" (p. 15). Baptism, for example, most frequently appeared in *"paraenetic* or hortatory contexts" (p. 92) in which writers wanted to foster particular modes of action within their readers. Eucharist, celebrated more frequently than baptism, was used to "recall the memory of sacred events" (p. 96). This is particularly true in the Corinthian church where, due to status differences and the persistence of pre-baptismal behavior, Paul asserts that it is not really the Lord's Supper that they eat (1 Cor. 11:20). Meeks thus sees ritual as providing "a dramatic structure within and on which a pattern of moral reasoning may be erected and an interpretive dialectic begun between ritual and common life experience" (p. 97). Exclusion from common meals is seen as a disciplinary sanction in which those "who persisted in unacceptable occupations or other activities [are] regarded as unholy" (p. 97). In many ways Meeks trod the path that other moral theorists have in picturing the church as "a community of moral discourse" and specifically linking conceptions of character with culture. David Horrell has recently drawn on Meeks in his study of Pauline ethics to establish the fact that ritual plays an important part in the "construction of a new form of corporate solidarity" with "egalitarian impulses" (Horrell 2005: 110, 130).[11] Meeks thus contends that moral formation in the earliest Christian communities was not achieved solely by telling stories, but rather by embodiment in ritual, liturgy, and practice (Meeks 1986). Once more we see his interest in "what rituals do" rather than merely "what they represent."

Ritual and the Construction of Social Memory

A key point related to the above emphasis on how ritual educates communities in "paradigmatic behavior" is also how ritual sustains or reconstructs social memory. Meeks recognized that rituals *"re-present[ed]* to [believers] . . . the passage from death to new life and *remind[ed]* them of the obligations undertaken under those solemn circumstances" (1993: 95, my italics). Alan Kirk has similarly

---

11   DeMaris, in his reading of 1 Corinthians 5, applies a ritual logic to claim that the chapter has less to do with morality and more to do with purity and holiness. He questions: "If Paul already turned to ritual matters in 5:2, how relevant are ethics or discipline to chapter 5? They appear to be secondary to ritual. Paul may well have been unhappy about Corinthian moral laxity or lack of discipline, but the primary disappointment in 5:2 is over their failure to carry out a rite" (DeMaris 2008: 84). However, his definition of morality seems too narrow; indeed, the casting of the debate in purity terms implies a moral component.

identified the "mnemonic effect of ritual" residing in material signs and gestures as well as "its incorporation of the kinetic, emotional and sensory capacities of the bodies of participants into the ritualised act of remembering" (Kirk 2005: 8–9). Georgia Keightley (2005) likewise asserts that Paul could give such a moving recollection of Jesus without probably ever meeting him primarily through the use of ritual. She argues that ritual "provides the community with its overarching view of reality" (p. 134); memory is enlivened and sustained in ritual settings and traditions. Barry Schwartz similarly argues that ritual "transforms as it institutionalises" (2005: 253). So, for example, ritual separated Christianity from Judaism by baptism supplanting circumcision as a rite of initiation and food laws being abrogated. Schwartz contends that "through ritual Jesus denied invidious social distinctions within Judaism. Through ritual Paul embraced the Gentile world and denied the privileged status of Judaism itself" (2005: 253).

Continuing the theme of ritual as a powerful aid to construct identity and social memory, David Sutton, in his ethnography of the Greek island of Kalymos, draws on Paul Connerton's distinction between "inscribed" memories promoted by written forms and "incorporated memories" promoted by habitual embodied experience (ritual). In early Christianity, ritual eating, being submerged in water, singing psalms or hymns, and praying, have profound sensory aspects.[12] Sutton perceives the link between sensory experience and memory in three main ways. First, senses aid people in empathizing with distant experiences or events. Second, material elements such as bread, wine, and water can evoke a variety of meanings in a variety of settings. Third, sensory experience and material elements can be used as "a cultural site," particularly in the restoration of social concord. Other ethnographic studies show, for example, that those who had experienced disintegration under colonial power often use food rituals to fuse past and present and restore social unity: "a domain of experience that is experienced as fragmented or deprived is revalued by simply marking it for ritual participation" (Sutton 2001: 76). In Frank Gorman's terms, ritual meaning is conveyed through "bodily performance, experience and gesture" (Gorman 1994: 22). Thus, the link between ritual, social memory, and community solidarity highlighted by Meeks is once again rehearsed.

Ritual and Empire

One of the major developments since the publication of *The First Urban Christians* has been the rise of reading nascent Christianity in relation to the Roman imperial world.[13] While literary texts are seen to resist and/or echo

---

12   On Sutton and 1 Corinthians see Lawrence 2005: 172–86.
13   See, for example, Elliott 1994; Horsley 1997a, 2000a, 2001; Horsley and Silberman 1997; Howard-Brook and Gwyther 1999; Carter 2001.

imperial mythologies and claims, the rituals promoted therein are also viewed as powerful tools in empire-building and empire-resistance. Ritual studies have revealed that ritual can generate hostility just as much as social cohesion, particularly in response to colonial powers. In one place a rite can confirm existing social relations, while in another place it can disrupt or subvert these. William Cavanaugh, in his celebrated work *Torture and Eucharist: Theology, Politics and the Body of Christ* (1998), illustrates just this. Writing about the Pinochet regime in Chile, he views torture as a "ritual activity" that aims to destroy social bodies by creating "mutually suspicious individuals." For Cavanaugh, torture was the "central rite in the liturgy in which the Chilean state manifested its power" (p. 22). What did this ritual do? It attempted to break down solidarity and promoted atomized individualization of the citizens (p. 15). It did not just constitute a "physical assault on bodies but the formation of a social imagination" (p. 12). Cavanaugh pictures the ritual of Eucharist as a powerful resistant site to the oppressive political regime. He writes: "A Eucharistic counter-politics is not otherworldly or sectarian, it cannot help but be deeply involved in the sufferings of the world, but it is in sharp discontinuity with the politics [of the governing state]" (p. 13). The Eucharist resisted the atomistic process by promoting solidarity and collectivism.

Similarly, in the first century, the main rituals of Christianity that promoted an egalitarian ethos gave powerful resistance to the hierarchical politics of Rome. Michael Northcott, for example, has pictured the Eucharist as an alternative to imperial Rome's injustices against the poor in its food economy. For him, Christian collective eating constituted an enacted "parable of a moral economy which recalls the idealised moral economy of the Torah" (2007: 251). In the Kingdom of God, the poor do not have their land taken from them to furnish the tables of the elite; instead, "they are welcomed to the messianic banquet alongside the rich, where they find not only a place but a voice in worship after breaking the bread" (Northcott 2007: 251).[14]

DeMaris finds a similar anti-imperial logic in his reading of the "the contested waters" of the Roman Empire and the Christian communities in Corinth. Cross-cultural studies over and again reveal the aqua-politics employed by ruling powers. Vernon Scarborough's ethnographic work in the Maya, for example, reveals that water projects were themselves used as rituals of power: "by locating tanks near the largest civic architecture—structures used in the public theatre— the Maya elite employed ritual acts derived from water use and availability" (Scarborough 1998: 137). Such projects ritualized the power of the ruling center

---

14   Northcott compares the imperial situation then to globalization and the rise of genetically modified crops now: "Profane eating, eating food offered to idols, has become the norm in twenty-first century and like earlier cults, this idolatry involves sacrifices—of the healthy rural communities and now the climate of the earth" (Northcott 2007: 257). Robert Song similarly reads the Eucharist in reference to genetically modified foods (Song 2006: 400).

and ideology through linking water with "everyday" rituals. By "reaching into the base structure of society, examining aspects of routine behaviour that reflect ordinary activity and exaggerating and formalizing ritual in a widely public context . . . the ordinary is made extraordinary" (Scarborough 1998: 146). Scarborough describes shamanistic rituals surrounding water that center on "the influence of mirrors and reflections on reservoirs" as powerful sites of "spirit" resistance to the ruling "political" elite. Similarly, in the first-century Mediterranean, Nicholas Purcell suggests that water management was seen to express Roman power, not just in the conquest of people but of the natural world (Purcell 1996). Thus, DeMaris probes the political context of the ritual of baptism in the Corinthian community and pictures this as a direct response to imperial projects that dominated water supplies and use within the city. Through water an alternative society was symbolically created, a society that challenged Roman hegemony. It was in effect a "symbolic inversion": "This response to the Roman way may have been signalled in simple but pointed ways, such as by the church's emphasis on baptism's once-ness, which contrasted starkly with the daily-ness of public bathing" (DeMaris 2008: 49). This symbolic inversion also provided a commentary on wider use of water within the area, a direct challenge to the ritualized and hegemonic control of water by Rome "expressed in the proliferation of baths, aqueducts, and nymphaea in Corinth and throughout the Mediterranean world" (DeMaris 2008: 50).

Thus, the Body of Christ ritually and symbolically constituted an alternative to the politics of Rome (see Martin 1995). Nonaggressive ripostes in the form of ritual illustrated the alternative superiority of the oppressed Christian group. Through ritual they made the "life of Jesus visible in mortal flesh" (2 Cor. 4:11). In worship and charismatic gifts the fledgling Christian communities declared a world where the Emperor was not in control of the human or natural world, and the power of the Spirit challenged the power of the state.

3. LIFE AND DEATH: BOUNDARIES OF EARLY CHRISTIAN RITUALIZING

Throughout this brief review of developments in the study of ritual since the publication of *The First Urban Christians*, the themes of life and death within the early Christian ritual world have appeared with marked regularity. The ritual complexes of baptism and the Lord's Supper embody and dramatize not only death and rebirth (Rom. 6:4), but also commemoration and proclamation of the "Lord's death until he comes" (1 Cor. 11:26). The Eucharist is accordingly often viewed as a mortuary or remembrance meal (see Smith 2003: 188–91). I want to suggest here that due to the ritualistic focus on death in early Christianity, actual physical death was given less attention.

We know that various issues surrounded the marking of the boundaries between life and death within Pauline communities. Richard Ascough in his study of

1 Thessalonians 4 reveals how funerary and mortuary practice featured prominently in voluntary associations of the time. Patrons would often bequeath resources so that a commemoration ceremony could be held on the anniversary of their death; the association would also guarantee a proper burial for members (Ascough 2004: 513). Paul's message of imminent judgment and deliverance may have struck some Thessalonians as a betrayal of their fellow members who had already died. Paul, however, assured them that "the dead members of the Christian association still belong to the community and will have a part in the anticipated return of their patron deity." He also reaffirms the association of the "deceased in the community of the living" (Ascough 2004: 530). In his recent review of research on this passage, Todd Still likewise demonstrates how many commentators take 1 Thess. 4:13 as a specific comparison between Christian and non-Christian mourning (the former live with the hope of Christ's return, the latter have no such reassurance). John Barclay (2003) and Abraham Malherbe (2000) have both recently argued that Paul's directives were strong in this respect: Paul wished "to make an absolute prohibition" (Malherbe 2000: 264) on grief for those in Christ. The new life in Christ represented a radical shift in thinking regarding mortality.

Similarly, in Corinth the practice of a vicarious "baptism for the dead" (1 Cor. 15:29) was developed. DeMaris notes comparative practices in the Greco-Roman world in which an "effigy replaced the corpse; a living club member took the place of the deceased, or some other substitution" occurred (DeMaris 2008: 62). Accordingly, baptism for the dead is seen among "the typical range of ritual variation in the Greco-Roman world" (p. 64; see also DeMaris 1995). In this respect the boundary that is crossed vicariously is between the isolated dead and the "living" (ancestral) Christian community. However, Paul likewise wishes to de-emphasize the community's concentration on the deceased.

Perhaps, if one of the main functions of ritual is to "traditionalize" or "normalize" situations of conflict or cataclysmic chaos,[15] then it should come as no surprise that a sect founded on the memory of a tortured crucifixion victim should embody various ritual responses to the cult founder's traumatic death, burial, and glorious resurrection, and accordingly relativize the impact of physical death.[16] Gerd Theissen, in his study of primitive Christian religion, accordingly views baptism and Eucharist respectively as a symbolic self-destruction and a symbolic ingesting of life-giving flesh, illustrating the anti-structure of the Christian cult (Theissen

---

15   Jonathan Parry in his article on "Death and Digestion" in North Indian mortuary rites claims that physical experiences of the world (such as eating) are used in ritual to "define and get a handle on other kinds of cultural reality" that are less concrete, for example death. He continues: "Natural processes provide Hindus with a language for talking about and for creating a representation of the way in which the cosmic and social order is maintained" (Parry 1985: 612).

16   Keith Bradley recognized that the link between belief in one God and the unity of the Pauline churches, also their close association with God through Jesus and the close relationships with one another, effects transformation of the complexities and contradictions seen in death and resurrection (Bradley 1983).

1999: 132–37). Many other cultures likewise "ritualize" mortality and accordingly de-emphasize the actual event of physical death.

Previously I cited DeMaris's position in categorizing baptism not as a rite of passage but rather, following van Gennep, as a boundary crossing ritual in which themes of life, death, and birth coalesce and become metaphors for one another. In this respect it is no accident that Turner famously saw that metaphors of liminality are often drawn from sexuality and fecundity.[17] DeMaris urges us to view all Christian "ritualizing" within the same complex of themes and not, as Meeks had done, artificially separate rituals into major, minor, etc. It is the intermingling of life and death and rebirth metaphors in boundary-crossing rites that I want to probe a little further here.

Since van Gennep's famous analysis, anthropologists have recognized the force of the imagery of death and rebirth within rituals of transformation whereby the symbolism of the body created, mutilated, and restored takes center stage. Peter Metcalf and Richard Huntington show that this "occurs regardless of the occasion; skulls and skeletons intrude incongruously at a harvest festival, whereas death rites are filled with the symbolism of rebirth" (1991: 30). It is no coincidence then that in 1 Corinthians 15 Paul links death and resurrection with powerful fertility and agricultural metaphors: "what you sow does not come alive unless it dies" (v. 36); "you do not sow the body that is to be, but a bare seed, perhaps of wheat or some other grain" (v. 37); "what is sown is perishable, what is raised is imperishable" (v. 42). Similarly, the experience of being submerged in water at baptism also symbolically links with death and rebirth images. Donald Tuzin (1977: 195–223) in his ethnographic analysis also attests to the link between death and rebirth, indeed he views the grave as a symbolic equivalent to the vagina and womb, and views birth waters as an apocalyptic image.

Rebirth is also a common cross-cultural image associated with the conferral of spiritual and charismatic capacities. Harvey Whitehouse, for example, identifies the use of metaphorical dismemberment in Melanesian initiation cults, often featuring terrifying practices. He notes that the single most dramatic effect of the embalming ritual is to kill the initiate. Through the loss of their vitality, they are seen to take on characteristics of transcendental beings. Their return is conceived as a way of "conceptualising and instituting a political order which is subject to

---

17   DeMaris accordingly contends that while baptism is more usually understood as an initiatory rite into the Christian community, it could also have functioned within the Corinthian worldview as a boundary-crossing rite from life to death. Inspired by the death imagery in Rom. 6:1-11, it is not hard to imagine the possible development of this thinking. Paul's answers in 1 Cor. 15:29 in response to so-called baptism for the dead accordingly state that not only is a passage to death protected but more importantly through Christ a passage to resurrection life is assured. As such "dying and rising with Christ to new life represents a reversal of the journey from life to death" (DeMaris 1995: 682). It is on this very point that Paul urges the Christians to rethink the meaning of their vicarious rite of baptism for the dead.

ancestral authority" (Whitehouse 1996: 705). Similar thematic complexes are observable in initiatory rites of shamans, in which death and dismemberment images are central. Graphically illustrating this point, Ioan M. Lewis reveals that "a man must die before he becomes a shaman" (1989: 63). Just as Christ had undergone awful mutilation and death at crucifixion, only to pass through the decisive rebirth in resurrection, so the Christian was likewise beckoned to death of self as a precursor to spiritual transformation: "He who raised Christ from the dead will give life to your mortal bodies also through his Spirit that dwells in you" (Rom. 8:11).

Meeks's emphasis on the ritualizing of "Christ devotion" (Hurtado 2003) in the Christian community and their singing, praying, speaking in tongues, etc., pays due attention to the community's charismatic identity. It is also on those occasions of *communitas* that the boundary of life and death is most clearly overcome, with new life in the Spirit being celebrated. Robert Lifton and Eric Olson in their cross-cultural study likewise reveal that moments of experiential transcendence can be gained in ritual celebrations and festivals, where routine is broken and singing, dancing, and the spirit of excess are promoted. They continue that experiential transcendence is an important part of the sense of immortality within communities, for "experiential transcendence involves entry into what has been called 'mythic time' in which the perception of death is minimized and the threat of extinction no longer foreboding; one feels alive in the continuous present in which ancient past and distant future are contained" (Lifton and Olson 2004: 38). One can imagine such gatherings corroborating the triumphant Christian cry that "death has been swallowed up in victory" (1 Cor. 15:54).

Lifton and Olson also suggest that experiential transcendence is linked to "a reordering of the dominant symbols and images by which one lives," and this in turn can lead to greater integrity and "more courageous moral actions" (Lifton and Olson 2004: 37). It is no accident that Meeks perceived the profound link between ritual and morality as central in early Christian formation. Accordingly, the individual body is cast as no longer one's own but rather "a temple of the Holy Spirit within you" (1 Cor. 6:19). Linked to this is DeMaris's point that the dying and rising metaphor constitutes "an expression of the believer's post-baptismal life in Christ" (De Maris 2008: 19). He cites 2 Cor. 6:8-9 to illustrate just this point: "We are treated as impostors, and yet are true; as unknown and yet are well known; as dying, and see—we are alive." In some respects this links in with Meeks's point that the *ekklēsia* is called to live a "liminal" existence in the world, while waiting for the return of Christ. Pagan converts to Christianity may well have compared the "putting on of Christ's death" with the ritual displays of a wax mask of a deceased honorable person in Roman society. This "imago" or "icon" of the deceased was frequently used to "stimulate pride in all Roman citizens and to inspire them to noble deeds" (Shelton 1998: 95).

Robert Hertz's work on those societies that do not see death as immediate but rather an ongoing process is also enlightening on this theme. Hertz traced the so-called intermediary period in Borneo where secondary burial is practiced.[18] He catalogs the end of the period as marked by a great feast where the remains of the dead are collected and deposited in another location. Hertz traced the correlation between the fate of the body and the fate of the soul; both initially are isolated from the world of the living, but at the feast when the dry bones are collected, the soul also is collected into the land of the ancestors, "marking the reestablishment of normal relations among survivors" (Hertz discussed in Metcalf and Huntington 1991: 34).[19] Building on this very theme Norman Petersen's 1986 article "Pauline Baptism and Secondary Burial" notes that "for Paul the baptismal burial of believers marks the beginning of a process that will be completed only when Christ returns, raises those who have died and transforms the bodies of all believers into glorious bodies like his own" (p. 218). Paul thus places physical death as one mere (relatively unimportant) stage within a process that will culminate in the "taking on of a new bodily form and a new social life in the kingdom of God" (p. 218). This "boundary crossing" process can be used symbolically for the identity of the entire church. The church temporarily hosts those who have "died" but are still awaiting "rebirth" in conformity to Christ's own form at the parousia. Petersen draws on work on Jewish double burial to substantiate his point that Paul's thought may have been informed by double burial. Although there is no specific evidence to prove this historically, what does seem plausible is the symbolic force of double burial in Pauline ethics and theology. Read against the backdrop of second burial, the logic of all ritualizing within the community is to begin the process in which the believer becomes a citizen in the kingdom of God (p. 225). Petersen sees Christ's parousia as the "symbolic corollary of a second burial." Similarly, the rotting of the organic flesh and blood is symbolic of the gradual "putting on of Christ" at the symbolic level (p. 226).

 The image of an individual whose remains after secondary burial are entrusted to the collective care of the community is a powerful metaphor for the members of the Christian community who have died to the world and look for the culmination of their "rebirth" and incorporation into the community of saints at Christ's return. Christian ritualizing did indeed cross boundaries of life and death at many points, not least because that was the central experience of Jesus Christ. The *ekklēsia* was called out from the world to embody different values from those

---

18 Secondary burial refers to that practice of a primary burial in one place, which allows decomposition, then a retrieval of the bones and a second internment. These actions are reflective of a worldview that views the person's journey from life to death as a process.

19 Hertz also forged a link between the decaying corpse and sacrifice. Objects need to be dismembered in this world to ensure safe passage to the other world. In a similar vein, Pardo, in his study of life, death, and social dynamics of inner Naples, similarly sees that death is a "public issue rather than a strictly private matter." Moreover, it is not seen as a once and for all event but rather a process: "Such transition concerns both the body and the soul and is effected through complex mortuary practices. This is based on the belief that the living can, by their rites, influence the position of the dead, who are, in turn, perceived as having power in life" (Pardo 1989: 103).

around them, but looked toward the glorious reaggregation into life with Christ. Paul said as much when he wrote: "while we live, we are always being given up to death for Jesus' sake, so that the life of Jesus may be made visible in mortal flesh" (2 Cor. 4:11).

4. CONCLUDING THOUGHTS

Meeks opens his chapter on ritual citing Edwin A. Judge's opinion that Christianity was not a religion, for it lacked "shrines, temples, cult statues, and sacrifices" and "staged no public festivals, dances, musical performances, pilgrimages" (p. 140). Meeks, of course, rejects this picture of a religionless sect and shows that ritual was absolutely central to Christian religion, constituting a kind of "grammar and syntax" (p. 141). He asserts that while the *idiōtes* stumbling into a Christian meeting might have thought them an odd crew, he nonetheless would have "recognized them as a cultic community of some kind" (p. 163).

No matter how we choose to classify these ritualized moments, Meeks has powerfully shown that their purpose was to sensuously dramatize and rhythmically instill the precarious boundary crossing between life and death that Christ himself had conquered. Embodying life and death threw into greater relief all other cultural values by which members of the earliest Christian congregations assessed their experiences. As the opening quote of this essay suggests, "Life becomes transparent against the background of death" (Metcalf and Huntington 1991: 25), and primary communal and formative knowledge is made known at that life/death frontier. Meeks recognized this most poignantly when he suggested that for the first urban Christians, "the life of the 'new human' [is] now to be manifested in the life of the congregations and, in God's future, in the world" (p. 161).

Chapter 7

PATTERNS OF BELIEF AND PATTERNS OF LIFE: CORRELATIONS IN *THE FIRST URBAN CHRISTIANS* AND SINCE

Dale B. Martin

Wayne Meeks's monumental book *The First Urban Christians* presented a social-historical account of the churches established by Paul as may be constructed from his letters, but the book did not stop at social history. The last chapter of the book, "Patterns of Belief and Patterns of Life," went further to address the extent to which we may relate the different religious beliefs of these early followers of Jesus and Paul to their social situations and experiences. Building on the idea that human beings live not only within particular social formations or structures but also within "worldviews," "plausibility structures," or "symbolic universes," the chapter asks whether we may relate the systems of Christian beliefs reflected in Paul's letters to imagined systems of social relations experienced by these early urban Christians.

Wishing to distance himself from earlier historiography sometimes associated with "vulgar Marxism"—the thesis that religious beliefs are rather simply produced "effects" of material "causes"—Meeks explicitly and quickly points out that he does not believe we can posit particular "social forms" that directly cause particular beliefs or behaviors. He prefers the term "correlation," indicating that he believes we may relate certain aspects of social experience or structure to certain beliefs or structures of religious symbols without positing a direct *causal* relationship in either direction. Thus, in parallel to Meeks's self-conscious "eclecticism" when it came to what sociological or anthropological methods, theories, or models he adopted (p. 6), so also he avoids "strong theoretical assumptions" about causation in the production of religious belief or behavior. His use of the notion of "correlation" signals his caution concerning theories of causation. Meeks also maintains that influence may flow in both directions: social experience may influence religious belief, and religious belief may influence social experiences or forms. "Religions both respond to and create needs" (p. 184). These caveats constitute Meeks's attempt to avoid historical reductionism or "vulgar Marxism."

Though some suggestions or allusions to correlations between the social and the symbolic occur throughout the book and are addressed explicitly throughout the last chapter, the clearest description of correlations occurs in the final pages of the book, where Meeks lists and briefly discusses four.

First, Meeks points to Paul's emphasis on the "one God," what we may call the "monotheism" of Pauline Christianity.[1] Paul's movement took its monotheism from Judaism, with little alteration other than accepting Jesus into some kind of divine role. The social correlation to this emphasis on the "one God," according to Meeks, was the emphasis in Pauline Christianity on "a network of local groups that wants to be a single 'assembly of God' in the whole world" (p. 190). Unlike most Jewish synagogues we know about, and unlike just about all Greek "voluntary associations," Paul and his followers went to impressive lengths to establish and maintain a strong network among the (possibly distinct) house churches within one city and those in other cities. The unity of the one God correlates with the attempted unity of the "body of Christ" over a vast area.

The second correlation centers on the emphasis in Paul's letters on God as "personal and active." In the symbol system of Pauline Christianity, God is neither an impersonal, mechanical force of nature—as we may imagine was the case for some ancient philosophers who thought of "nature" itself as a divine though sometimes rather impersonal force—nor a supremely powerful though distant figure, as many people may have imagined Zeus or even the Emperor. Meeks finds the social correlate to this belief in "the intimacy of the local household assembly," including a demand for a high level of commitment, intense interpersonal engagement, a fluid authority structure, and weak "internal boundaries" (p. 190). This last term is intended to express the observation that different individuals in Paul's groups could not necessarily expect that significant aspects of their "private lives" could remain only "their own business." Their sexual relations, their financial dealings, and their familial situations all come under the purview of the group

---

1   I use the term "monotheism" with due caution, realizing how difficult it may be to find in the ancient world what might pass as "true monotheism" according to modern ideas. What actually would count as "monotheism" is disputable even in the modern world. Muslims and Jews, for instance, may believe that Christian confessions in the divinity of Jesus and the Holy Spirit, along with the "person" of the Father, offend a commitment to true "monotheism," in spite of Christian insistence that the doctrine of the Trinity is able to maintain confessions of the three "persons" of God while also maintaining a commitment to "one God." In the ancient world, things were even more complex. The Dead Sea Scrolls, for instance, are full of comments about many gods or other figures that seem "divine" to modern eyes, and yet these Jews would certainly have thought of themselves as committed to belief in the "one God." Recent studies of ancient philosophy, especially in the late ancient period, show that a certain kind of "monotheism" could be maintained by "pagans" who also accepted the reality of many "gods" (Athanassiadi and Frede 1999). These different observations simply demonstrate that the very concept of "monotheism" is more complex than we might think at first blush.

and its concerns. The belief that God is both personal and active is matched by the close nature of the personal relations within the group and the intense demands the group makes on individual members.

Third, Meeks points to Pauline eschatology as constituting a particular world-view that relates to the social experiences of Pauline Christians. As Jewish apocalypticism, at least for its "believers," both explains and predicts social upheaval, indeed *cosmic* upheaval, so the Pauline churches are populated by persons who have experienced, and continue to experience, radical changes of "social place." They have gone through significant, perhaps even wrenching, changes in allegiances, from former commitments to different gods of their own culture to the "one God" of Israel. In fact, their senses of ethnicity must have been challenged and to some extent changed as Paul speaks of them as "no longer" Gentiles, but now at least in some way as people of the God of Israel themselves (see, e.g., 1 Cor. 5:1; 6:11; 10:1). Furthermore, they are now expected to be completely committed "to a new, tightly bonded, exclusive cultic community" (p. 190). The eschatology of the gospel of Paul thus causes radical change in the lives of these people, and it may also have functioned to "make sense" of their experiences of social change and disruption.

Fourth, the emphasis in Paul's message on loyalty to a "crucified Messiah" finds its correlation in the fact that Pauline churches are themselves sites of "social contradictions." As Meeks had shown earlier in the book, the groups contain persons of different social levels. Though a few may have held relatively more comfortable social positions than the truly destitute poor, most of them are "weak in terms of social power and status," and "they experience indifference or hostility from neighbors, yet they are exhilarated by experiences of power in their meetings . . ." (p. 191). Moreover, there is among these people a high incidence of "status inconsistency" or "social mobility." There are tensions between their roles outside the group (as masters or slaves, for instance) and the *communitas* of the group and its "charismatic" structures of role and authority. The contradictions contained and manifest by the centrality of the "crucified Messiah" find correlations in the social contradictions embodied within the group and in the personal contradictions experienced by the individuals (status inconsistency and some social mobility).

In at least these four ways, therefore, Meeks posits correlations between the symbolic structures (patterns of belief) of Pauline churches and the social structures and experiences of their members (patterns of life). Some members may have been drawn to allegiance to the groups because these symbolic patterns helped "make sense" of their "real life" experiences. Conversely, once they became members of the groups, individuals may have been influenced by the beliefs and their ramifications to alter their lives and behaviors. Thus, the causal influences may have gone either way or both ways. Thus the notion is not simply of causality, but of "correlation."

1. What, More Precisely, Is This "Correlation"?

Before examining similar scholarship since the publication of *The First Urban Christians*, it may be helpful to explore a bit more what precisely is involved in correlating patterns of belief with patterns of life. To some extent, we should admit that everyone who interprets a text at all does something like this. We never read texts with no assumptions at all about "social reality." In order to read, we must relate the symbolic world "created by the text," we may say (to use of course a metaphor, since the text is not really creating a world, even a symbolic one; we the readers are), to some kind of social reality. We normally imagine, even when we do not realize we are, some kind of social situation in which the words work and have meaning. In fact, we often know about *different* kinds of meanings. As Mikhail Bakhtin has taught us to recognize, every "utterance" partakes in fact of more than one "world." A particular word or phrase may live one life when we think of it occurring in, say, the world of legal discourse, and a different life in medical discourse ("Could you close for me?"). Language is always social, and the social is always multiple.

For example, when a New Testament scholar talks about Paul's texts referring to slaves, we all imagine some kind of social "reality" that corresponds to the symbols of the texts we take as referring to slaves. Recent scholarship has gone to some lengths to convince modern readers that the social realities of slavery in the Roman Empire were different from those we imagine in terms of modern, American slavery. The scholarship assumes a correlation between the symbols of slavery in ancient language and Paul's texts and some imagined social reality of ancient slavery. So *some* "correlation" between symbolic systems and social structures must be assumed as part of every interpretive activity, especially perhaps when we are attempting to bridge historical gaps we recognize as separating our world from theirs.

We need, therefore, a more robust and specific understanding of what we mean here by "correlation" between "patterns of belief" and "patterns of life." I think we can produce this more robust understanding by examining how studies influenced by Meeks's own work make such correlations. And here, I am in the rather embarrassing position of pointing to my own publications over the past twenty years as an exceptionally obvious example of such scholarship. Since I was a doctoral student of Meeks during the 1980s, beginning in fact in 1982 just before the publication of *The First Urban Christians*, it may come as no surprise that I have followed his example in my own attempts at social history of early Christianity. But even beyond that circumstance, I find myself a bit surprised, now looking back, at how extensively my work has attempted to establish "correlations" between systems of ideas and beliefs, on the one hand, and particular social forces and structures, on the other—even more so, I think, than most of Meeks's students. So though the practice may seem a bit self-centered, I shall use a few examples from my own work to illustrate more fully what we should look for when seeking to compare Meeks's use of "correlation" with scholarship since the publication of *The First Urban Christians.*

Though my first book, *Slavery as Salvation* (Martin 1990) argued for some correlations—between slave structures and theological metaphors, and between political structures and rhetoric, on the one hand, and Paul's self-portrayal and Christology, on the other—a more elaborate attempt to demonstrate correlations came in my second book, *The Corinthian Body* (Martin 1995). I argued that two different models of the human body and two different assumptions about health and disease existed in the Greco-Roman world. Philosophers and medical writers portrayed the healthy body as a balanced ecosystem and disease as the disruption of that balance. They therefore de-emphasized more popular notions that disease resulted from hostile forces attacking the body or from pollutants that invaded the body from particular or personal sources. The more "popular" notion, held in my view by all other persons in ancient society not under the influence of philosophers and their ideas, was that the human body was a precariously permeable entity and that at least many diseases (not all) were the result of attack or invasion caused by a superhuman being, such as a god or *daimōn*. These two different constructions of the body and disease, I argued, are matched by the social experiences of, on the one hand, upper-class persons, who were relatively comfortable in their worlds and able to a greater extent to control their own fates, and, on the other hand, lower-class persons, who occupied much more precarious social positions or relatively little power. I attempted to "map" each of the different "disagreements" reflected in 1 Corinthians onto this difference between "elite" and "popular" notions of the body and disease. The higher status members of the Corinthian church, I argued, were more likely to have been influenced by the philosophical and medical notions, whereas the lower status members, with less opportunity for exposure to elite, philosophical teachings, and Paul himself assumed notions of the body and disease of the "popular" type. These differences in social location and power correlated with differences in assumptions about the body, and those differences caused the conflict portrayed in the pages of 1 and 2 Corinthians.

In a later book, *Inventing Superstition from the Hippocratics to the Christians* (Martin 2004), I shifted my attention away from Paul and his churches and to a much broader scope of the entire ancient Greek and Roman worlds from classical Greece to Constantine. In *Inventing Superstition*, I reintroduced the notion of the balanced body and the disease etiologies sketched in *The Corinthian Body.* But I explained here what gave rise to the philosophers' innovative view that gods and *daimones* are benign and do not cause disease. I argued that a combination of new ideologies produced by and in the rise of democracies in Greek cities, along with new philosophical doctrines traceable at least to Socrates, led upper-class philosophers to insist that beings superior to human beings ontologically were also superior to them ethically. Therefore, it made no sense to believe that gods or *daimones* were hostile or intent on harming human beings at all. Nature was itself a benign entity that when in proper relation to itself constituted a state of balance. This caused a shift in notions of the body, now seen as balanced nature, with disease portrayed as disruption of that balance. I argued that significant changes in society and politics prompted by the rise of Greek democracies led to changes in the symbolic construction of the body, disease, and all of nature, including the gods as part of nature. The philosophers labeled the more popular notions—that gods and other intelligent beings cause disease or harm human beings—"superstition."

In the last sections of *Inventing Superstition* I further argued that these philosophical notions rejecting daimonic causation of disease eventually died out in late antiquity, even among most philosophers. And I argued that this change in beliefs was again the result of changes in politics. The late ancient Empire finally left behind political notions first created by the democracies and returned to a more hierarchical, monarchical ideology. As the political and social structures of the late ancient Empire changed so drastically from its earlier embodiment in Augustan propaganda, which had itself taken over many political ideas from the Greek democracies and the Roman Republic, the ideology of the body, disease, and nature, again including superhuman beings such as demons and angels, changed in corresponding ways. In my reckoning, it was not only that there was a "correlation" between structures of society and power and structures of belief. I argued in fact that shifts in those very social structures *brought about* changes in the ways people viewed nature, changes in their symbolic universe, in their fundamental beliefs about themselves, the gods, demons, the body, and disease.

I should point out how my own work, though building on and inspired by that of Meeks, differs from his and in some ways exceeds his more modest claims. First, my own work, especially on Paul's letters, has obviously been heavily influenced by Michel Foucault and Mikhail Bakhtin. Without going into detail, the emphasis of Foucault on "epistemes," referring to entire epistemological systems and their possibility only within particular historical societies and economies, has been important for me. Foucault's emphasis on power and discursive realms shows itself in my work. Indeed, the very rise of what has come to be called "discourse analysis," as an analysis of society, culture, and power, strongly influenced my work. Bakhtin's theories of the social locations and various possibilities for "utterances," the infinity of interpretation, and the analysis of linguistic events as always working differently in different "registers" influenced especially my first two books. I do not know if Meeks had read Foucault or Bakhtin when he wrote *The First Urban Christians*. If he did, he never spoke about them, as I recall, to us students. I was enthusiastically submerging myself in Foucault and Bakhtin— along with lots of other "theory"—when I was a graduate student in the mid-1980s, but not on the prompting of Meeks. It was just that every graduate student at Yale at the time, it seemed, was reading them.

Moreover, I would admit that whereas Meeks has always been wary of Marxism, I have found classical Marxist theory as well as many of the more recent forms of "Marxian" thought indispensable. I have been much more willing than Meeks to entertain the notion that certain belief systems may indeed be practically *produced* by certain social structures, modes of production, or political ideologies. Of course, as someone quite happy with post-structuralist and postmodernist notions (which would not describe Meeks), I do not believe that texts or societies or ideologies *themselves* actually do the producing. That must be done by human beings. But as long as I am allowed to use the terms as metaphorical "agents" that stand in for what I actually believe are complex procedures done by human beings, I have no problem imagining that social structures or economic modes of production produce ways of being in the world, ways of conceiving the world and ourselves. I believe, for instance, that modern individualism, especially in its form in the United States, is practically inconceivable apart from modern capitalism, and perhaps even "Fordism."[2] So, I would admit that my work differs from Meeks's, especially in his earlier work, in the influence on me of much contemporary "theory"—linguistic, post-structuralist, postmodernist, and feminist—and in my commitment to some basic Marxist themes.

I have no interest in this context in defending my publications, but merely in using them as one fairly clear example of work deriving from *The First Urban Christians*, especially in its attempt to correlate social and symbolic structures. I also want to use them here to illustrate what I am—and am not—referring to as "correlations" between "patterns of belief" and "patterns of life." First, I do not mean the finding simply of *connections* between particular details. The emphasis, rather, must be on "patterns." Indeed, I have long felt that though he would probably reject the label, Meeks's work, especially in *The First Urban Christians*, is a kind of structuralism. By taking over ideas from the sociology of knowledge and from the anthropology of Clifford Geertz and others, the book enters into a stream of twentieth-century sociology and anthropology much indebted to the linguistic structuralism of Ferdinand de Saussure and the cultural structuralism of Claude Lévi-Strauss. The very idea that both complex linguistic artifacts and complex social realities could and should be interpreted as "structures of meaning" is part of the broader, immensely important influence of twentieth-century structuralism.

Moreover, structuralism and the many kinds of scholarship influenced by it attempted to break out of the habit of keeping the analysis of different aspects of culture separate. It analyzed dietary practices and restrictions by comparing not

---

2   By "Fordism" here, I mean primarily the factory innovations of interchangeable parts and specialized, even atomized, roles assigned to workers; the practice of turning the producing worker also into the main consumer of his or her product, but only after the artifact has had its value altered by journeying through "the market"; and the creation (at least ideologically if not socially) of the "nuclear family" as the main unit of consumption.

just issues related to food or eating, but also issues of social space, notions of personal or ethnic identity, or other socially meaningful activity not explicitly thought of as related to food and eating. Structuralist-influenced work tends to construct two "systems" from two aspects of human activity normally assumed to be relatively discrete, and it relates the two systems to one another, to show, for instance, how "patron-client" *social structures* relate to "honor-shame" *value structures*. So, one of the things that makes Meeks's approach different from previous attempts (say, in the "history of religions school") is that (1) it attempts correlations between and among *structures* or *systems* and not between single details, and (2) it attempts correlations between systems of meaning derived from observing different aspects of social life not theretofore normally thought about together.

For example, the earlier "history of religions" movement in New Testament studies had tended to compare, say, Christian baptism with rituals involving cleansing or other water rituals in other ancient cults. It compared the early Christian Eucharist with "sacred meals or eating" in other "religions." Meeks's work was quite different from that of the "history of religions" in seeking correlations in parts of society that did not already look like "religion" to us. And it differed from previous searches for "parallels" to New Testament practices or beliefs by focusing not on particular details, but on *systems* of details, practices, or beliefs.

Another way Meeks's method differed from older approaches was his lack of interest in finding the "origins" of Christian practices or beliefs in Jewish or Hellenistic "sources." Yes, Meeks points out that Christian monotheism was taken over from Judaism, but that does little analytical "work" in Meeks's book. Rather, he is more interested in interpreting the "meaning" of, say, monotheism by analyzing its "function" in Paul's churches, both its theological *and its social* functions. When we look, therefore, for other scholarship that correlates symbolic with social structures—of belief *and* practice—we should keep in mind these aspects of Meeks's method: (1) we are looking not for mere connections, but for patterns or systems; (2) we are looking for studies that make correlations or connections between realms of society not normally connected or compared; and (3) we are looking not for "origins" to supply meaning but for "function."

2. SOME NOTABLE EXAMPLES AFTER *THE FIRST URBAN CHRISTIANS*

From the legions of studies that have been influenced by *The First Urban Christians* or written in response or critique of it, I have selected only a few to discuss. I offer here a rather simple taxonomy of such studies, grouping different works and authors in ways that are not particularly significant analytically but merely reflect a way I have myself categorized these studies in my head. First, I discuss a very few examples of studies that I take as basically doing the same kind of "correlation" work attempted by Meeks, though in some cases disagreeing with him or refining his ideas. Second, I point to the "Context Group" as an intentionally and socially formed grouping of scholars with some shared methodological ideas and goals. Third, I mention those I group together because of a shared commitment to liberation theology and progressive interpretation of the Bible, including feminist approaches.

One of my favorite studies that takes its lead from *The First Urban Christians* (along with Gerd Theissen's work) is an article by John M. G. Barclay (1992). One of the things that makes the article interesting is the way Barclay refined Meeks's analysis of the function of eschatology for Pauline churches. Barclay notes that Paul's apocalypticism seems to have worked differently in Thessalonica than in Corinth. Also, we sense that the Thessalonian converts experienced more hostility and alienation from their neighbors and social environment than at least a significant group of the Corinthians did. Barclay suggests a correlation between the function of the eschatology in the two different communities and their different social experiences that followed on their conversion to the new sect.

Upon their conversion, the Thessalonians apparently experienced hostility from their neighbors and some social alienation. That experience enabled a message of apocalyptic, with its positing of sharp boundaries between the Christians and "the world" around them, to "make sense" of their world, and also to reinforce their experience of alienation. The Corinthians, on the other hand, or at least a significant number of them, experienced no such negative reactions from most of their neighbors. They continued to enjoy fairly good relations with people outside the community. This explains why they seemed less taken with the strong boundary-maintaining aspects of Paul's apocalyptic message. For example, leaders of the Corinthian house groups seem disinclined to punish the man, mentioned in 1 Corinthians 5, for sleeping with his stepmother. Barclay suggests that they may not see the community as "a moral arbiter at all" (p. 60). According to Barclay, the harmonious relations the Corinthians enjoy with outsiders and their relative ease in their social communities explain two things: (1) their lack of a sense of the necessity of firm boundaries, and (2) their disinclination to think of the church as a place of rigid enforcement of moral norms. Barclay concludes his comparison of Corinth and Thessalonica by saying that we have here "an example of the mutual reinforcement of social experience and theological perspective. . . . The apocalyptic notes in Paul's theology which harmonized so well with the Thessalonians' experience simply failed to resonate with the Corinthians" (p. 71).

The language here is very much like that of Meeks, demurring from talking about "causation" from social reality to theological belief, but arguing for "mutual reinforcement" and "correlation." The innovation in Barclay's article, beyond Meeks's work, is its observation that eschatology may have worked in very different ways in two different Pauline churches, a refinement Meeks would certainly welcome.

Another study that both builds upon and extends the ideas of Meeks and Theissen is David Horrell's *The Social Ethos of the Corinthian Correspondence: Interests and Ideology from 1 Corinthians to 1 Clement* (1996). One thing that differentiates Horrell's study is its appropriation of the theories of Anthony Giddens, particularly Giddens's "structuration theory." This enables Horrell better to concentrate on how ideologies and other symbolic systems, including patterns of religious belief or the "ethos" of a person or group, may change over time, both reflecting and influencing social behavior and forms. Horrell thus supplements rather "synchronic" portraits from Meeks and Theissen by adding a "diachronic" component—and extending it to *1 Clement*.

Horrell's study also attempts to balance the "functionalist" accounts of Meeks and Theissen (functionalist accounts often see religion as supporting and reinforcing dominant social structures and hierarchies) with attention to the "conflict" that may arise between and within groups and conflicting uses of symbol systems and ideologies. Horrell, for example, argues (*contra* Theissen) that "love patriarchalism" was *not* the "ethos" advocated by Paul at Corinth, though it may correctly reflect the assumptions or ideology of the higher status Corinthians. Paul urges a more radical message of hierarchical disruption, both through his own example and the ways he manipulates Christian symbols and beliefs. Paul uses "central symbolic resources of his Christian faith . . . to undergird an ethos which builds community unity through the honouring of the weak and the self-giving and self-lowering of the socially strong" (p. 282). Paul opposed one symbolic order (which would support the "socially strong") with another (which would support the "socially weak").

Correlation between social position and "ethos" or religious belief is certainly here addressed. The "symbolic order of Pauline Christianity was reproduced over time, by those in positions of power," sometimes supporting or legitimating "the interests of dominant social groups and the hierarchical social order" (p. 282). Yet Paul resisted one symbolic order by means of another, leading to conflicts evident in the fragments of other letters contained now in 2 Corinthians. Horrell suggests that, by following the letters reconstructed chronologically, we may imagine how that conflict ended: "The clash between Paul and some of the more socially prominent members of the congregation does indeed come to a head and is resolved, to a degree at least, through the power of the majority [represented mainly by those of less social power], whose perspective Paul has sought to adopt and defend" (p. 283).

By the time we get to *1 Clement*, the strategy is reversed. "Clement" writes to the Corinthian church decades after Paul but attempts to mine Paul's Corinthian correspondence to address again the problem of division and conflict in the church. But unlike Paul's strategies, the author of *1 Clement* reinforces traditional social order. "Clement's theology, by contrast [with that of Paul's], offers a strong and profound undergirding to the established order, ecclesiastical, domestic and political. It provides a theological ideology which legitimates the *status quo*; preserving this order is, for Clement, the way to peace and harmony" (pp. 284–85). Horrell's book, therefore, builds on those by Meeks, Theissen, and others, but adds interesting aspects in its emphasis on *conflicts* among different social groups and symbolic orders and its extension of the analysis diachronically through several decades.[3]

It is not only in the works of those who to a great extent agree with Meeks that we can see attempts at correlations between beliefs and social structures. Justin Meggitt's *Paul, Poverty and Survival* (1998) severely criticizes the proposals of Theissen, Meeks, and others that the Pauline groups comprised persons of mixed status. Meggitt argues that all members of Paul's various churches, including Paul himself, "*shared fully in the bleak material existence that was the lot of the non-élite inhabitants of the Empire*" (p. 153; emphasis in the original). Meggitt insists that there was no significant difference in the status or economic situations of any early Christians. Meggitt therefore proposes, for all practical purposes, an economic egalitarian situation in Paul's churches. They even developed, according to Meggitt, a "new" economic survival strategy: "mutualism." They shared economic resources both within individual congregations and among different congregations, including the Jerusalem church. Meggitt therefore proposes a situation of economic equality within Paul's churches matched by an economic practice of "mutualism" or sharing of goods and resources.[4] "Mutualism" was an intentional economic strategy (see p. 158). It was "a significant form of economic relationship practised by the Pauline communities," intentionally and not "accidentally" (p. 163).

It is therefore not surprising that Meggitt believes that this social situation of equality, matched by an economic strategy of equality and mutualism, was also matched by "a similar, inter-community mutual ethic" (p. 161) and was expressed also in theological and particularly Christological language and beliefs (p. 173). Paul's "participationist, corporate, Christology," his "body imagery," Paul's "pneumatology," and the emphasis on *koinōnia* are all related, by Meggitt, to the economic strategy and ethic of mutualism. The "theological solidarity" ritually emphasized in baptism and the Eucharist, "expressions of the unity of the congregation," was also an expression of and contributor to mutualism.

---

3   Many other such studies, of course, could be cited. I think, for instance, also of MacDonald 1988 as valuable in its extension of focus beyond the churches of Paul himself to those represented in the deutero-Pauline Epistles of a later time (see also MacDonald 1990).

4   Though Meggitt does not often explicitly talk about the "egalitarianism" of Pauline Christianity, he does seem to assume it. For instance, he rejects "reciprocity" as a way to describe his notion of "mutualism" because "reciprocity" refers to all sorts of exchange that are not "equitable" (p. 158). "Mutualism" must therefore include "equality," or as Meggitt here puts it, perhaps, "horizontal reciprocity."

Thus, even though Meggitt is highly critical of the work of Meeks and proposes a very different economic and social situation along with a very different analysis of theological language, and even though Meggitt does not use the language of "correlation," his work falls within the basic interests of other scholars, following Meeks, who propose a correlation between patterns of life and patterns of belief.

Certainly many more such works could be mentioned, but my purpose is to be illustrative, not comprehensive. What I hope to illustrate with these examples is how some New Testament scholarship has remained relatively close to the concerns of Meeks's attempt to correlate patterns of belief with patterns of life and yet has extended, refined, or expanded Meeks's own observations. I turn now to cite some examples from a group of scholars who have often been quite critical of *The First Urban Christians*.

3. THE CONTEXT GROUP

"The Context Group" has been described and discussed elsewhere in this volume, so I shall forgo any lengthy account here (see esp. pp. 10–12 above). We should note, however, that although many of the members of the Context Group have sharply criticized the work of Meeks, when it comes to the existence of a "correlation" between belief systems and social systems, they are basically in agreement.

Actually, much of the work produced by members of the Context Group—just like most of the work produced by most New Testament scholars in general— seems not much concerned with establishing correlations between symbolic structures and social experiences, even when they may assume the existence of such correlations. In one collection of essays by members of the Context Group, for example, most of the authors use specific theories or models from the social sciences, but they do so in order to construct the social world and institutions of antiquity, with its own cultural realities and values, rather than establishing correlations between patterns of life and patterns of belief (Esler 1995). John Pilch, for instance, uses modern studies of "alternate states of consciousness" to explain ancient accounts of Jesus' "transfiguration." Duncan Derrett uses modern studies of the "evil eye" to suggest how the concept may have functioned in ancient Christianity. Several essays in the collection use social science to help us understand how early Christian groups were formed or maintained.

Other studies produced by members of the Context Group, however, do propose correlations between social experience and religious beliefs. In his *An Ideology of Revolt: John's Christology in Social-Science Perspective*, Jerome Neyrey (1988) argues that the Johannine community went through three stages of development, discernible in different parts or layers of the Gospel and letters. Moreover, each "stage" developed its own particular kind of Christology. Different presentations of Jesus in Johannine literature correlate with different social relationships experienced by the community. This interest in correlations arises again in Neyrey's later book, *Paul, in Other Words* (1990). To cite just one such example from the book, Neyrey interprets Paul's concerns about purity and impurity as reflecting a conception of the world as requiring firm boundaries. The concern for order and classification (everything in its place; the need to maintain purity and to control pollution) reflects an "experience of hostility and conflict" in society, at least as experienced by Paul (p. 221). Thus, in spite of Neyrey's disagreements with Meeks's methods (and he does so disagree), he shares with Meeks the belief that we may legitimately look for correlations between Paul's theology and social world.

Many more such examples from the Context Group could be given, but they would only further illustrate my point: members of the Context Group, though often highly critical of *The First Urban Christians*, share with Meeks an interest in sketching correlations between patterns of belief and patterns of life.[5] Their work has taken those ideas in several different directions from those explicitly addressed by Meeks.

4. LIBERATION THEOLOGY AND SOCIAL CONTEXTS

Though not produced by an actual "group" of scholars working together intentionally, as is the case with the Context Group, other studies may be grouped together because of their commitment to analyzing early Christianity with interests in politics and ideology. Many scholars of such studies have been influenced by Marxist theories, or at least progressive commitments, and in many cases liberation theology in particular. Though they do not all come to the same conclusions about the political or ideological significance of early Christian texts, they all foreground such questions. I include here also those produced from a feminist perspective.

Richard Horsley has not only written many such works himself, but has also taken a lead in organizing conferences, founding sections within scholarly societies, and editing collections of essays on the politics of early Christianity and its texts. One of his most important earlier works is *Sociology and the Jesus Movement* (1994), first published in 1989 and reissued in a second edition in 1994. Horsley mined the canonical Gospels to construct a picture of the early Jesus movement as a movement of protest against the central authorities of Jerusalem, the priesthood, and Rome, along with Rome's "retainers," such as the Pharisees.

---

5   An excellent example is the fine book by Philip Esler (1994). Through studies of several different texts and topics of the New Testament (including some comparison with the community suggested by the Dead Sea Scrolls), Esler insists that there is a "pervasive relation" (he does not use the word "correlation" here) "between the religious affirmations of the early Christian communities and the social realities which affected them" (p. ix).

Jesus' followers later saw him as an anti-establishment prophet killed by the authorities for challenging their power, and this Christology also reflected their own social situation (see, e.g., p. 122). Horsley compares the Jesus movement with other Palestinian groups and in each case relates their social situation to their beliefs and practices (pp. 137–38). The reaction of the Jews represented by the Dead Sea Scrolls against the Temple and its custodians, for instance, was one of withdrawal. But their own social connections to priests and priestly families made their reaction different from that of the Jesus movement. What differentiated the Jesus movement, on another side, from those popular "messianic" movements that actually took up arms was that Jesus inspired a "social revolution" rather than a military one. Also, the differences between the Jesus movement and the later Zealots, who arose during the war with Rome, can be related to different social situations—such as, for one thing, the war itself. Thus, Horsley relates social situation to belief structures and religious practices for different movements of the time.

The same approach may be observed in a collection of essays by different scholars on *Paul and Politics*, edited by Horsley (2000a). These essays arose out of the first four years of the Paul and Politics Group of the Society of Biblical Literature. Some use postcolonial studies, with tropes such as "center and periphery" or dominant and subaltern positions. In his own essay, "Rhetoric and Empire—and 1 Corinthians," Horsley argues that the social situation of Paul is one of a colonized subject with a peripheral view of the world. Paul opposes Roman imperial ideology, including its way of relating the self to the divine, with a Jewish apocalypticism that embraces and emphasizes the "lowly social status" of Paul and most of his converts. This opposition of apocalyptic to Roman ideology also helps explain conflicts related to worldview and values in the Corinthian church (see esp. pp. 88–91). In many of the works published by Horsley and his coworkers, the beliefs and practices of early Christians are related to their social positions as subalterns resisting Roman dominance and Empire.[6]

Some of the earliest works highlighting the ideology and political significance of early Christianity were feminist studies. I include explicit attention to this scholarship because, while we might not immediately think of such studies as related to our topic of "correlation," they certainly do practice it: almost all of them take as their starting point the observation that women in the ancient world did not necessarily experience their society and world in the same way men did. Simply by the *social fact* that they were women rather than men, they likely had different social experiences, and therefore quite likely different beliefs or assumptions about both the world and religious realities in it. Since *gender* was everywhere in the ancient world, even when *women* were not, certainly the

---

6   Other books important early on for this approach include Horsley 1997a and Elliott 1994.

social fact that one was a woman would affect one's experience of the world, perhaps even producing a different "symbolic universe."

The many works by Elisabeth Schüssler Fiorenza are perhaps the most often cited. Her most famous book, *In Memory of Her* (1994), first published in 1983, emphasized the necessity of "a feminist model of historical reconstruction" to reeducate the modern, androcentric imagination so as to imagine the realities and experiences of women in the Jesus movement and early Christian communities. She went so far as to suggest that women may have been able to construct more egalitarian spaces for themselves, that house churches may have "provided equal opportunities for women," and that women may have enjoyed more equality, and even at times more power, than patriarchal historiography or official ecclesiastical institutions have acknowledged. Thus, her book has often been interpreted as positing a more egalitarian "stage" in the early history of Christianity.[7]

Antoinette Clark Wire (1990) took a somewhat different rhetorical tack in her book *The Corinthian Women Prophets: A Reconstruction Through Paul's Rhetoric.* Wire reads Paul's rhetoric against the grain, one may say, of his own attempts to control and contain the activities of women in the church. Wire thus constructs, from Paul's rhetoric, what we may imagine as the (counter?) theology of the women prophets in the Corinthian church. When we stop to think about it, this constitutes itself a strong attempt to correlate social position with religious belief.

To round out this very brief mention of some feminist studies of early Christianity, I would also like to mention the more recent book by Jorunn Økland, *Women in Their Place: Paul and the Corinthian Discourse of Gender and Sanctuary Space* (2004), precisely because it offers a more complex study than most in its attempt to correlate the symbolic with the social. Both the social and the symbolic are acknowledged, but Økland points out not only the places where they may "match" but also where they do not "match." For example, in ancient Greek culture, "private" space is often coded as "female" and "public" space as "male." Thus, ideologically, at least in upper-class Greek culture, women are expected to remain in private and hidden space. When they venture outside the private space of their homes, they are often expected to cover themselves. Yet Økland shows, as some other studies have done, that this was true more ideologically than as the social reality experienced by the vast majority of women in ancient Greek societies.

To take another example, there existed both household space and sacred space, again at least symbolically and often socially as well. Yet Paul, according to Økland, attempts by his instructions in 1 Corinthians to turn the household space, where early churches were certainly physically gathered, into a "sacred space."

---

7   I believe this is still a fair reading of the book published in 1983, but see Schüssler Fiorenza's comments on this sort of reading of the book in the edition published in 1994 (see, e.g., pp. xxii–xxv).

And he does so precisely in order to alter the behavior of women in the churches. By turning the household church into sacred space, Paul masculinizes the space and thus limits certain behaviors for female church members.

Women in Their Place works with correlations between the social and the symbolic, between social experiences of women and Paul and the ideological ways Paul attempts to define the social by means of the symbolic. But it shows how complex and variable the relations between the social and the symbolic may be—and how they may be intentionally manipulated and redefined. For all these studies, in any case, their authors, even when not explicitly acknowledging it, are attempting to discern correlations between patterns of life and patterns of belief.

5. CRITIQUES

Of course, the proposition of correlations we find in Meeks and other scholars has not escaped criticism. Though I have no desire to enter into lengthy debates, which would take us far into theory, methodology, and even philosophy, I will mention some particular criticisms that have been voiced over the past twenty-five years.[8]

One of the most commonly encountered objections is that this sort of social study of religious belief is "reductionistic," meaning that the accounting of religious beliefs in the terms of social structures or forces "reduces" those beliefs to "nothing more" than social products, thereby necessarily rendering the beliefs not "true" in the sense in which they are held by the believers. The charge is that the social-scientific account "reduces" the religious beliefs to "nothing more" than an epiphenomenal expression of social or political realities.

In this fullest sense of the charge of "reductionism," I believe Meeks is completely innocent of the crime. Meeks went out of his way to make it clear that noting a social correlation for a religious belief does not in itself say anything at all about the "truth" of the belief—nor does it claim to capture completely every possible "meaning" of the belief. To cite another scholar, Philip Esler explicitly insists that one should not take his work to imply "that the faith of the early church was solely the product of its social context or had no transcendental referent" (1994: 10). To believe that positing a social correlation for a religious belief in itself "reduces" that belief to *nothing more* than the social facts is, in my view, to hold a simplistic notion of both religious belief and the multiple functions of "truth." At the very least, the criticism does not do justice to the stated purposes of many of the scholars so criticized.

Bengt Holmberg raised what I consider a rather curious objection to the constructions of correlations by Theissen and Meeks. He notes that "the symbols

---

8   Two of the most trenchant critiques of *The First Urban Christians* have come from Stanley Kent Stowers (1985) and Bengt Holmberg (1990).

are our only or most important means of information about the social situation"
(1990: 136). If we use those very symbols in an attempt to reconstruct a social
situation, for which we have no other information than the symbols themselves
(i.e., the texts), we are practicing circular reasoning. He concludes that "judgments
about such correlations are necessarily tentative and uncertain, simply because of
the complex and multidimensional character of texts" (p. 137). Holmberg even
goes so far as to say that "we must state that nothing can be known" about the
social situation (p. 136).

This criticism, to my mind, seems to forget that we are, after all, here engaged
in interpretation. Holmberg seems to be working with a model of historiography
dependent on a rather naïve kind of "scientism": that we need more than just
texts; we need real "data" to which we may hold up our admittedly "tentative"
interpretations for testing purposes. Meeks saw his practices, though, not as
"science" but as interpretation. All interpretations of texts—or anything else
for that matter—are necessarily circular: the "hermeneutical circle," after all. If
we could never legitimately imagine a social context for a text, we would not
be able to read texts at all.

Another criticism suggested by Holmberg and Stanley Stowers as well is that
many modern constructions of either social positions or belief systems of ancient
persons would not be recognized by those ancient persons themselves as what
they think they believe. The systems suggested by the modern scholar are seen as
something like foreign products rather imperialistically imposed on the "native"
actor.

This critique also seems to me not convincing. In fact, it seems something like
a confusion of the old "emic/etic" debate: whether an account is better if it is
constructed from the "native's point of view" (emic) or from the point of view of
the researcher using "nonindigenous" concepts (etic). In my view, however, it is
simply not valid to imply that an account, in order to be "correct," "true," or
"adequate" for the purposes of the observer, must be recognized by the actor
or believer as correct, true, or adequate. Many native speakers of a language may
not understand or even recognize a grammatical analysis of statements they make
in their own language. They may know nothing about grammar—even of their
own language. But that should not stop a grammarian from offering a "true" grammatical account of their speech. Sociological accounts of religious beliefs and
practices need not be recognized or accepted by the religious persons themselves
in order for them to be "true" *sociologically speaking*. And an analysis of a religious statement may be grammatically or sociologically true even if it is *theologically* false (by the standards of the "believers" themselves). What counts as true
or false varies according to the discourse in which the statement occurs.

These and other criticisms may continue to be mounted against scholarship
that attempts to discern or construct correlations between symbolic and social
systems. They need not stop the practice. As long as we realize that we are still,

after all, basically just interpreting texts, we can live with the known uncertainties and vagaries of interpretation.

Whether one is persuaded by such critiques of Meeks's method or results, we can all admit that *The First Urban Christians* provoked or inspired new and significant work in studies of Paul and early Christianity more broadly. One of the topics that continues to engage scholars are the problems and possibilities of relating patterns of belief among early Christians to patterns of their lives as we imagine them to have been.

Chapter 8

TAKING STOCK AND MOVING ON

Wayne A. Meeks

In 1975, as I began a sabbatical year, I set out to explore what seemed a very simple question: What sort of groups were those *ekklēsiai* to which Paul wrote his letters? Calling them "churches," as we were wont to do, invited us to think in all sorts of anachronisms: there were no churches in the cities of Rome's eastern provinces. So if an outsider, one of those *idiōtai* or *apistoi*, were to happen into one of their noisy meetings (as Paul imagines, 1 Cor. 14:23), what would he have called it? Were there groups or movements common in the larger society with which a native speaker would naturally compare these gatherings of new believers in the Christ? And would we learn something from such a comparison? On the other hand, if a modern social scientist could be transported, by some time-machine magic, into the first century, what theoretical tools and models would she bring along in an attempt to understand what those people were doing?

Armed with those simple questions, I plunged into regions of libraries where New Testament scholars were seldom seen. In midyear, I emerged long enough, on an extended detour between New Haven and London, to visit archaeological sites in Turkey. In London a seminar at University College, through the kindness of Mary Douglas, continued my education in modern ethnographic theory, even as I immersed myself in the unparalleled collections of the Warburg Institute and the British Library. At the end of the year I discarded all my drafts for the simple article I had hoped to write. The issues were far more complicated than I had imagined. The only visible product I could show from my year's leave was the outline for a new project. Seven years later it appeared at last as *The First Urban Christians: The Social World of the Apostle Paul.*

I am grateful to Todd Still and David Horrell for having chosen that publication as a kind of surveyor's stake to mark an era in Pauline studies—not just for the honor, though they and the other members of the team they assembled have been very generous toward my work, nor for stirring this bit of nostalgia on my part. Rather, the enormous labor invested in this volume by the editors and all the contributors has produced an exceptional gift to all who want to think more clearly and honestly about the formative period of the Christian movement, to learn about the past and to learn from the past. As we try to do that, thinking about ourselves thinking about the past can occasionally be useful. A look back in order to look forward: that is the purpose of histories of research. The foregoing seven chapters of this volume together constitute a model of such a history—comprehensive in their purview, accurate in reporting, incisive in analysis, generous in assessment of disputatious positions but candid in criticism, inventive in discovering the evidence unexplored and the questions unasked, forward-looking in their focus on the next steps to be taken. My largest reason for gratitude to the contributors is this: they have done such a good job of describing twenty-five years of social-scientific study of Pauline Christianity that I, with a great sigh of relief, am spared any need to attempt that.[1]

1. The Matter of Method

All of the essays above touch in important ways on questions of method, but these questions receive special emphasis from the symmetry between the opening chapter by David Horrell and the concluding one by Dale Martin, both of which focus on general questions of interpretive strategy. Horrell takes up the complaint, most forcefully advanced by Bruce Malina and some other members of the Context Group, that those of us who aim to do mere social history are not *scientific*, and therefore not worth reading. It will surprise no one that I agree entirely with Horrell's critique of that position, and I need add nothing to his admirably clear analysis. It may be useful, however, to underscore some of the underlying issues that seem to me central to this debate.

In retrospect it is clear that what we were trying to correct, when a number of us began in the 1960s and 1970s to explore "the social world of early Christianity," was a persistent idealist bias in biblical scholarship. In our immediate environment, it was the generalizations of the biblical theology movement in its various forms from which we sought to free ourselves by a new collection and constructive recategorization of such historical evidence as was available. More generally, though, the question we were pressing had to do with the appropriate relation between induction and deduction. To put it crudely, when theory and facts conflict, which trumps? The long history of Western science, before the extended Copernican revolution of modernity, privileged deduction as the reliable means to distinguish truth from mere opinion. What made modern science modern was its elevation of induction. Theory still had its role to play, but it was no longer imperial; theory could be humbled and corrected by observation. When theory generated hypotheses that were not confirmed by data, then theory must yield.

---

1 Anyone wishing to pursue the history of this period further may be interested in my "Reflections on an Era" and "Afterword" in Meeks 2002a, xi–xxviii, 254–61; my "Preface to the Second Edition" of Meeks 2003: ix–xi; my Introduction to Schütz 2007: xii–xxiv; and, from a different perspective, Meeks 2002b.

In former times, *scientia* amounted to the disciplined deduction of the facts from general principles learned from the ancients and received by authoritative tradition. The reigning model for discerning the truth of a hypothesis, as Galileo learned to his dismay, was the judicial detection of heresy. In the discourse of modern science accusations of heresy, while not unheard of, are generally regarded as not the way we do things.

Our theories and our models are our constructions, whether they are cast in theological language or in the language of experimental or observational science. In the search for truth, they are tools, nothing more, to be prized and carefully honed so long as they work, but remade or discarded when they do not. And, especially in the social sciences, all theories are partial. A Grand Unified Theory of human behavior is not on the horizon. Hence, I have explicitly adopted a practical eclecticism, which, as Horrell shows by his examples, is the normal practice of sociologists and anthropologists. This is not to say, of course, that when their conclusions or mine lack logical coherence, the inconcinnity is not fair game for critics. One of the principal uses of theory, apart from its primary function in generating hypotheses that can be tested, is to help us to think our way toward rational coherence. That is not the same thing, however, as denouncing results that deviate from some theory deemed orthodox. Enforcing school orthodoxy is a poor substitute for trying to discover the actual roots of error by looking again at the facts we think we know.

To be sure, it does not help that those facts, too, are constructs. The Nietzschean recognition that every fact bears an ineluctable substratum of interpretation is now a leitmotif of contemporary philosophy of science. The freshman physics student, repeating one of the classic experiments of the past, after patiently noting down the measurable quantities, asks, "What is it I am measuring?" Exactly the right question, the very locus of the genius that long ago conceived this experiment. How much harder it is to answer that question in the social sciences. The vaunted objectivity promised by modernist science, source of the "physics envy" that John Gaddis finds in so many scientific historians, is an illusion, if we mean it in an absolute sense (Gaddis 2002: 89). Facts are not picked up like pebbles. They are won, wrested out of the maze of phenomena, invented. To find a fact, we need not only sharp eyes but also tough-minded imagination. Nevertheless, this more chastened understanding of scientific method is reason only for humility—not for retreating into the safety of deductive truth claims. The construction of a fact is different from the construction of a theory. There is a stubbornness to facts, in which the historian, like the scientist, should rejoice. Those theories and the models derived from them which are most helpful in advancing us toward a fuller understanding of the past are those that are open to being falsified by data.

There follows one further rule of thumb: the most valuable facts we discover are those which we wish were otherwise. No field of inquiry is immune from wishful thinking, but the study of religion is perhaps more at risk than most from the desire to see what ought to have been rather than what inconveniently was.

That risk seems to affect more or less equally those who passionately believe and those who passionately despise.

For students of ancient Christianity, the temptation to find what we wish for is especially acute when we try to discover correlations between "patterns of belief and patterns of life." It is a temptation I fell into more than once in the final chapter of my book, and I am grateful to Dale Martin for not pointing out all those sins. When I wrote of "correlations," of course, I was paraphrasing Max Weber's key notion of *Wahlverwandtschaften*, which Talcott Parsons translated as "elective affinities." The "elective" was important to me precisely because, as Martin points out, I wished to avoid the implication that social structures *cause* structures of belief (or the reverse, for that matter), in either a Durkheimian or a Marxist fashion. When we talk about society doing this or that, we are talking about the generalized vector that results when people severally make choices. Hence, I welcome Martin's postmodernist observation that any sentence in which a social pattern is represented as an agent is to be taken as metaphorical. Convenient as the metaphor often may be, societies do not in fact *do* things. But it is also true (and this is the main point of Martin's appeal to Foucault and especially to Bakhtin) that choices in a particular society at a particular historical moment are limited by that society's structures. Because language itself is socially constructed, some things that are obvious to us were literally unthinkable in another time and culture. When we try to understand another culture—or subculture—we involve ourselves in a series of dialectical moves: between distance and empathy, between the unique and the general, between theory and observation, between the way the others conceived of their world (as well as we can imagine it) and the way we must try to make sense of that world within *our* socially constructed world.

The epistemological issues are obviously of daunting complexity. In moments when they seem overwhelming, I recall my first year of graduate school, also a time when "methodology" was on every student's mind. On one occasion several of us, gathered in the living room of Nils Dahl, asked him where he stood on the current debate. "Well," he said, "thinking about methodology is like cleaning your glasses. You need to do it from time to time, but the point, after all, is then to put the glasses on and look through them." He had written, more formally, "Nevertheless, it must be said that the really burning questions cannot be answered in principle but only through constant new encounter with the material" (Dahl 1991: 29). It is very encouraging that each of the contributors to this volume has brought to the discussion some fresh encounter with the primary evidence.

2. READING THE CITY

Basic to any attempt to understand the social relations of a city's population is knowledge of its physical shape and environment. The ancient geographers knew that. They also knew many details about the cities of their day which we, too, would like to know, but which were so obvious that no one bothered to write them down for us. The material remains of those cities are therefore of fundamental importance if we are to gain an accurate impression of the conditions of life there, both in order to correct the omissions from the literary sources and to correct the élite bias implicit in their point of view. Fortunately the twentieth century brought a transformation of archaeological practice, shifting gradually from a search for imposing and beautiful monuments, often with a view to bringing them home as trophies for the sponsoring institutions, to an emphasis on discovering how people actually lived. The rising interest in social history profited from these more systematic and comprehensive fashions of archaeology and also reinforced them. Peter Oakes has shown, by his publications elsewhere and by his survey of recent work in Chapter 2 above, what a wealth of pertinent and constantly increasing data is now available to students of ancient Christianity. I am tempted to call it an *embarras de richesses*, for if so much new information had been available when I began writing *The First Urban Christians*, I suspect I might never have finished it.

Oakes also offers help in sorting out the data, by suggesting two different kinds of models for organizing the comparisons that illuminate each particular city. The first, which he has used in earlier publications, employs ideal types—a Weberian concept notably adopted by Moses Finley and more recently by a number of other ancient historians. The other, the key to Oakes's contribution here, begins with a comprehensive view of a single city. His choice of Pompeii is, as he says, a bit counterintuitive, but it proves, because of the extent and detail of Pompeii's modern exploration, to be a very serviceable template against which to measure the three Pauline cities Oakes treats here. The advantage of this kind of comparison, as I see it, is that it immediately confronts us with facts on the ground rather than a theoretical construct. Moreover, it allows us to think historically about the development of particular places, in a much more specific way than generalized studies of "urbanization." Oakes's brief remarks about Philippi, Thessalonica, and Corinth show how productive this approach can be; I hope we may look forward to seeing more expansive analyses from him.

One thing that the excavations of Pompeii have brought to light is the complexity of living space: both the variety and mixture of private dwellings and the further mixing of domestic and commercial buildings. Anyone acquainted with the large and still growing literature about the so-called house church will see that many of our assumptions about size, composition, visibility, and relationships of those household-based meetings will have to be reconsidered, as David Horrell, Bruce Longenecker, and Edward Adams have also pointed out here and elsewhere.

3. MAKING SENSE OF STATUS

I have been perplexed that so many readers have taken my chapter on the mixed and confusing indicators of social level in the Pauline groups to be an attempt to explain at a stroke the "success" of early Christianity. The questions I raised at the end of the book were not merely rhetorical. I genuinely thought it worth asking whether there might be some explanatory power to the "correlations" I saw between, on the one hand, the mixed social structure implied by Paul's letters and the mixed status attributable to those very few individuals about whom we have enough information to make an informed guess and, on the other hand, some of the more paradoxical patterns of belief that Paul emphasizes. I still think the questions worth asking, and I still do not know the answers. The debate that has ensued tends to confirm my conviction that such questions are important. That the debate has not come to rest is hardly surprising, given the scarcity of pertinent data as well as the difficulty of finding the appropriate theoretical tools for sorting out questions of status in any society, particularly one so different from our own. Nevertheless, the debate (including even those contributions that I find wrong-headed) has moved us toward a more nuanced understanding of the issues, and Bruce Longenecker has given us a masterly summary of the matter and pointers for moving forward.

The fundamental point is that status is never a single thing. The indicators of status are multiple: economic ability, family, ethnicity, gender, education, and so on. And what exactly they indicate varies with the observer. Whatever one may make of what seemed "a new consensus" a quarter-century ago, we cannot return to the oversimplifications about the social catchment of the Pauline groups that reigned more or less from Celsus to Deissmann. Longenecker's chart of economic indicators takes that complexity into account—improving on Friesen's taxonomy in several particulars—and permits a valuable revision of the economic prosopography of the Pauline groups insofar as we know anything about individuals in them. Two other facets of Longenecker's sketch are especially important. The first is his attention to the ways Paul constructs the audience to which he addresses his epistolary admonitions. The consistency of the results with the prosopographic clues is significant, and Longenecker's insistence on the importance of Paul's rhetorical constructions is more generally relevant. "Attributed status" is not necessarily the same as "objective status" as the sociologists remind us, and we must always consider the rhetorical situation when we attempt to move from Paul's representation of his audience to a description of the way that audience might have appeared to themselves or to others. That problem is related to the second aspect of Longenecker's essay that I want to emphasize: his recognition of the importance of reference groups for a social analysis of early Christian groups and their development. There is a considerable body of sociological literature about the functioning of reference groups. If we think of our identity as formed in large measure by the ways we learn to perform certain roles given us by our society, to act out in our own life stories some culturally common narratives, then our reference groups are those audiences that we imagine approving or disapproving our performances. It is a common experience that sometimes we are caught between different evaluations by different groups that are important to us—and the importance of different groups changes over time. Reference group theory potentially can thus offer special insights into the process that we call "conversion," and it has not been exploited for the study of ancient Christianity as fully as it might.[2]

4. INVENTING THE *EKKLĒSIA*

In Chapter 4 above, Edward Adams brings me back to the question that started me off on this curious journey nearly four decades ago: was there in ancient society or is there in modern sociological theory any one model that would explain exactly what those little groups *were* that gathered in Prisca's or Stephanas's or Chloe's house, those people who sat and listened to the letters from Paul? The answer I came to was "No." Frustrating, but not uninformative, as Adams agrees. Adams prescinds here from the complicated second half of the question, about useful modern models. That question is discussed at some length by Horrell, and touched on at several points by other contributors, as I mentioned above. There is good reason for Adams to concentrate on the ancient social formations with which the Pauline groups can be compared—that discussion has been vigorous, as he points out. In passing, I simply note that sociological theory of sects, of social movements, and of small group formation has by no means stood still since the writing of *The First Urban Christians*. Some of the newer developments have been exploited by the scholars whose work has been summarized here, but much more remains to be done. The burgeoning field of urban sociology is also emerging as a potential source of important insights for our inquiries.[3]

On the other question, the extent to which the Pauline groups exhibited features they shared with other familiar social formations in their environment, the debate has been quite lively indeed. On the whole it has been illuminating, and Adams is both an excellent guide and a fair critic. Of the many helpful observations he has gleaned from a wideranging survey, I will single out only a couple.

First, he emphasizes research into the nature of the voluntary association, which recently has enjoyed more attention than at any time since the fundamental investigations by Waltzing and Poland in an earlier generation. Publication of large bodies of well-edited inscriptions from some of the sites we are interested in has provided a much larger base of information for this purpose. The number of public inscriptions that are in some way related to the activity of local clubs is impressive testimony to the importance of these associations in the life of the cities.

This point is clearly illustrated by the corpus of inscriptions from Ephesus, which gives us a substantial basis for evaluating the role in that city's life, over a

---

2 I have written briefly on the topic. See, beside the references Longenecker cites, Meeks 1990.
3 For example, see the detailed observational analyses of life in multiethnic communities by Yale sociologist Elijah Anderson (e.g., Anderson 1990, 1999, 2004).

period of several centuries, of several different kinds of voluntary organization (Wankel 1979–84). Let me give two examples of things we can learn from this collection. First, a revealing anomaly. Numerous inscriptions show that craft and professional groups are very prominent in the public benefactions and concomitant quest for public honors. Yet the great inscription of 104 CE, detailing an endowment by a certain Salutaris for annual processions and cash gifts that, as Guy Rogers has argued persuasively, were intended to educate the aristocratic youth of the city in its hierarchy of honor, ignores the role of the trade associations altogether. We see here a classic case of "status dissonance." The status and honor that the craft and trade clubs ascribe to themselves are quite different from the way people like Salutaris, Roman knight and Ephesian citizen, perceive them. The dimensions of status and influence that enable them to place their monuments alongside the great and wealthy on the streets of Ephesus are counterbalanced by others—birth, family, occupation—that could never be overcome in the eyes of a Salutaris (Rogers 1991).

My second example leads to a correction of something I said earlier. Among the professional guilds, the athletes and the Dionysiac artisans are importantly connected with public festivals—games and theater respectively. They are particularly interesting for our purposes because they are not strictly local in character. The *technitai* of Ephesus honor a certain Alcibiades, for example, who has also been honored by the Dionysian artisans of Rome, to whom a copy of the decree is to be conveyed. Indeed, groups "from the whole world (*apo tēs oikoumenēs*)" honor this man. This evidence requires that, as Ascough has urged, I modify my earlier suggestion that Christians and Jews were unique among urban organizations in the Roman cities in translocal sensibilities and practices. Yet I cannot go as far as Ascough would like, for the "ecumenical" connections of the Ephesian artisans are rather different from the practical networking undertaken by Paul and his coworkers.

As we seek parallels between the Pauline *ekklēsiai* and other voluntary associations, I would continue to stress the associations of immigrants. As we have learned more and more about the variable organization of the Jewish diaspora communities and the various degrees and fashions of their adaptation to the social and cultural context of the cities, it is important to keep in mind that those adaptations were variants of a pattern being used by many other groups of resident aliens. To a very large degree, then, two of the four models I proposed in 1983, and which Adams reviews here, can be considered together: the synagogue as a special case of the immigrant association. I have gone so far as to call the Pauline community, at least as Paul and his fellow workers conceived it, an association of "artificial immigrants" (Meeks 2001).

The other part of Adams's survey that I would particularly emphasize is his review of work on the nature of the Greco-Roman household. As I noted above, in connection with observations by Horrell and Longenecker, we have been learning a great deal more about the variety of physical housing arrangements available in the cities of our concern as well as about the variety of domestic relationships that flourished in them. This is an exciting field, where the cooperation among archaeologists, Roman social historians and art historians, and specialists in ancient Christianity promises important new insights.

Taking all this into account, I find little reason to revise my general conclusion, which Adams quotes at the end of his essay. And I enthusiastically endorse his recommendation that we give up the search for a single ancient model with which to compare "Pauline Christianity" in favor of many detailed studies of "particular aspect[s] of group organisation or . . . of group practice."

5. Empowering, Leading, and Managing

Among the Presbyterians who guided my upbringing and my first theological formation, the Pauline text most beloved, as I remember, was "Let all things be done decently and in order" (1 Cor. 14:40, KJV). When I attended my first presbytery meeting, however, I discovered that there was a considerable range of opinion as to exactly what was proper order and what were the limits of decency. So it had been from the beginning—else Paul would not have had to admonish the unruly Corinthian brethren in this way. No wonder, given the outlandish beliefs and strange behavior that, from the point of view of any proper Roman, characterized the meetings of those who worshipped a crucified outlaw. Not surprising, too, when we consider how fierce the debates have been when people have tried to describe precisely what Paul's own standards were. It is entirely appropriate, thus, that Todd Still sums up his review of recent work on the structures of organization and authority in the Pauline communities by a series of "dialectical patterns." The rhetoric of Paul's letters is almost everywhere dialectical (his detractors speak less kindly of self-contradictions), and scholarly discussion of this issue hardly less so.

I believe my decision to focus on the points of conflict, insofar as we could discern them from the letters, in order to begin trying to sketch an anatomy of power structures and decision-making in the Pauline congregations, has been pretty well vindicated in the years since 1983. Still's review of the subsequent literature demonstrates the usefulness of that starting point, notwithstanding the need for correcting many particular points and the impossibility of reaching consensus on some of the most important of them. However, Still's call to look with equal care at those letters in which a local conflict is *not* the obvious occasion for the writing is also timely, and his necessarily brief assessment of the evidence to be gleaned from Romans, Philippians, Philemon, and 2 Thessalonians makes us wish for more.

For example, Still's attention to the people named in Romans 16 raises a number of questions that could be pursued with profit. What exactly does Paul's naming of just these persons—both people who have been associated with him in his eastern mission and people he knows or knows of in Rome—do for his rhetorical purpose in the letter as a whole? In particular, what does his associating himself with these persons and groups tell us about the kind of authority he is implicitly claiming by writing the letter? How does this epistolary move relate to the diatribal and protreptic characteristics of the letter?

To stay with Romans, I would add another text to Still's list of passages that offer insights into the ways Paul attempts to assert authority. The *paraenetic* section (chs. 12–15) reworks and adapts elements from the letters to Galatia and Corinth. Comparing the earlier responses to specific situations with the more general admonitions here provides us with an exceptional opportunity to glimpse a process of working out effective forms of persuasion. Here we see Paul learning from particular local conflicts some lessons that he now seeks to apply in a quite different situation. That ought to provide a number of insights into the way he thought he might persuade people he had not met to do things they ought to do—or, to put it another way, ways in which he sought to let one church learn from the experiences of others about appropriate patterns of "decency and order" in the *new* order established by "the gospel."

And what are we to say about those critics who, having looked closely at the exercise of power in the Pauline wing of the early Jesus movement, abhor what they see? They, too, are hardly a new phenomenon. We owe a great deal to the critics of Paul in his own day, who provoked those crises that have left the traces in the record that we have been analyzing. However, it is true, as Still points out, that the number of detractors within the guild of Pauline scholars itself has notably increased in the past few years. With Still I find little cause for optimism that the "interpretive impasse" he finds among those scholars or between them and those who look more kindly upon Paul's leadership style will be resolved anytime soon. I confess to being somewhat bemused at the shock with which some have discovered that Paul seeks to "manipulate" the audience of his letters in order to obtain desired behavior. One person's persuasion, of course, is another's manipulation, but I would have supposed that the principal purpose of ancient deliberative rhetoric was precisely to persuade people to feel, think, or do something toward which they were otherwise not inclined. The study of Paul's episto-lary style in the past quarter-century has shown that Paul was well acquainted with those persuasive or manipulative ploys, and that he was quite good at using them. In at least one respect I find that discovery salutary: we find once again that Paul was human, all too human, and that he was very much a person of his time and place. That should be shocking only to people who have belatedly taken off the rosy spectacles of biblicism. Surely it is only a hangover from the liberal/fundamentalist controversies of a century ago that we somehow still imagine that for an ethic to be informed by the Bible means that its tenets must be found *in* the Bible. To imagine that, if Paul's notions of power do not measure up to our postcolonial, postfeminist, postliberationist, postcapitalist standards, then we have no way to legitimate those standards is, I find, a very confused way of thinking. But at least to discover that Paul does not (and never could) fit those norms is at least a step toward unmasking the projection of our own judgments onto the texts. Such unmasking is perhaps the most important service that historical inquiry can still perform for those who are theologically inclined.

In this connection, Todd Still's survey of recent studies of Pauline governance underscores the importance and continued relevance of the position that John Schütz argued so forcefully more than three decades ago. The great mistake of most modern interpreters of Paul as well as of classic sociology of religion, Schütz showed, was the confusion of "legitimacy" with "authority." Authority is primarily an interpretation of power, and what Paul offers is a very special hermeneutics of power. That is an insight that still needs to be pondered as we try to sort out the divergent views of early Christian power structures in recent scholarship (Schütz 2007).

6. REHEARSING LIFE

Of all the aspects of the Pauline groups that I tried to analyze in 1983, none has enjoyed more intense or more fruitful attention in subsequent scholarship than the study of ritual. Louise Lawrence's rich and supple review of that scholarship is very welcome indeed. It leaves me with little need to comment, beyond underlining a few of the varied sides of the discussion that she has outlined. Though, not surprisingly, many areas remain controversial, it is gratifying to see how much has been learned about ritual process in a great variety of contexts, demonstrating ritual's quite diverse range of potential functions in society. In retrospect, my analysis appears inhibited in a number of particulars by the limits of ritual theory I was able to assimilate three decades ago, especially in my dependence on the work of Van Gennep and Turner. Very much of the ethnographic literature about ritual in an earlier generation was based on field work in relatively coherent and stable societies. I struggled to adapt the resultant theory in order to talk about the peculiar uses of ritual by a cult that was betwixt and between: in some ways mirroring the commonsense worldview of the society in which it was embedded, in other ways implicitly or intentionally countercultural.

There has been perhaps too much fuss about my distinction between the "major" rituals of baptism and Eucharist and the other "minor" rituals. The distinction carried no theoretical weight; it was only a classification of convenience. There were the two ritual complexes that we heard quite a lot about from the New Testament and other early Christian literature, and the others about which we heard only occasionally or which we could only surmise. This distinction was not intended to suggest *isolation* of the ones from the others. It is the case that baptism and the Lord's Supper do more work in Paul's epistolary arguments than any other ritual, and it appears likely that they did more work (but not necessarily always the same work as Paul hoped for!) in the communities themselves. But there should be no argument that, alongside any analysis of their individual functionalities, the interrelations among different rituals and between ritual behavior in the strict sense and behavior that is prima facie more spontaneous need careful thought.

Not only that, but new methodological studies of ritual, with their emphasis on performance, also put us into a better position to reconsider the perennial question, how the formative practices of the early Christian groups were related to common rituals of both civic and cultic life (insofar as one can make that distinction) in the world around them. The ways in which the History of Religions school addressed that question a century ago, focusing on diffusion, "borrowing," and "influence," have been superseded. At the same time, recent inquiries have emphasized the performative features of very many aspects of life in a Roman city that were not what we would call "religious."[4]

Indeed, ritual does not need "religion." When I tried to persuade Edwin Judge that the Pauline groups were religious, in passages Lawrence summarizes above, by emphasizing their ritual behavior, both my argument and his depended on a tacit assumption that everybody knew what religion was and was not. Of course we both knew that there were no words in Latin or Greek with which to say "a religion" in our sense of the phrase. Nevertheless, we assumed, as did most scholars, that religion was a more or less universal category in all human societies. We are now beginning to recognize that it is instead a modern, Western concept. Both our commonsense understanding of religion and our learned, scientific models of what religion is and how it works are cultural constructs, the product of centuries of social, political, and economic transformations and theoretical reflections on them. As we absorb the implications of that process, we will have to reconceive very many of the questions we have been asking about the formative years of the Christian movement.[5]

7. WHO NEEDS HISTORY?

I went to graduate school, just under a half century ago, because I wanted to learn how to do New Testament theology. The way to do that, I already vaguely understood, was by becoming a historian of early Christianity, and that lesson was constantly reinforced in the stressed but happy years of study that followed. My fellow students and I were socialized to believe that, if we could do really good history, we would have accomplished what was required of us. In the years since,

4 An example of the usefulness of such insights in exploring early Christian texts, in this instance the Apocalypse, is Frilingos 2004.
5 Many developments both in philosophy and in the social sciences have combined to make the notion of religion problematic. In our own field of work Jonathan Z. Smith has served as a catalyst for much of the discussion. See, e.g., Smith 1982, 1998. For a critical exploration of some consequences for studies of Paul, including Paul's ritual concerns, see Nongbri 2008.

we have learned how very difficult that task was. We have also experienced some disillusionment about historiography's potential to answer the really important questions. Of course it is not only New Testament scholars and other historians of ancient Christianity who have learned that lesson, yet the lesson has been complicated in our case by special issues. Our field is haunted by a set of expectations rather different from those of other fields of history. We cannot read the letters of Paul in the same way we read the letters of Cicero or Seneca, no matter how hard some of us may try to do so. The fact that Paul's letters, for nearly two millennia, have been part of the Bible exercises some constraints upon even the most avowedly secular of their interpreters. And the great majority of the readers of these letters are not secular, but have specifically theological (or perhaps anti-theological) interests in them. Those readers want to learn something more than historians generally are expected to provide: what to believe, how to live, what is ultimately true. How it came about that scholars of the New Testament thought to answer such questions as those *by doing history* is itself a long and complicated and decidedly modern story. In our time that story has arrived at an unexpected peripeteia, expressed in a widespread loss of confidence. Many of us, confronted with the questions that we historical critics so confidently presumed to answer a generation ago, want to say, "No, thank you." Nevertheless, the shadow of the earlier, often misdirected, self-confidence lies over all we do. This leaves us with two large questions.

First, if we could get the history exactly right, would it help us to be better at the task of being Christian—or, more important, of being human?

Second, since we cannot get the history exactly right—because historiography like all science must constantly correct itself, fated to produce only probabilities, never certainty—of what use is it? Does the effort, never completed, help us in any tangible way?

To come anywhere near answering these questions would require another book at least as large as this one, to be produced by a conversation among searchers of even more diverse interests and training. I want only to insist that the questions are important enough that all of us who labor in these fields ought to ask them of ourselves with some regularity. It will be obvious to most readers that my own answers to them, however tentative and unformed, are affirmative. Consequently, I imagine these metaquestions to be interwoven with others which can still be put to us by those squabbling groups of converts to Messiah Jesus, gathered by that assertive, elusive, protean apostle, groups whose shape and identity we struggle to divine from the obscure clues of the ancient texts and contexts.

BIBLIOGRAPHY

Aasgaard, Reidar (2004), *'My Beloved Brothers and Sisters!' Christian Siblingship in Paul* (JSNTSup 265/ECC; London/New York: T&T Clark).

Abrahamsen, Valerie (1995), *Women and Worship at Philippi: Diana/Artemis and Other Cults in the Early Christian Era* (Portland, ME: Astarte Shell Press).

Adams, Edward (2000), *Constructing the World: A Study in Paul's Cosmological Language* (SNTW; Edinburgh: T&T Clark).

Adams, Edward and David G. Horrell, eds. (2004), *Christianity at Corinth: The Quest for the Pauline Church* (Louisville, KY: Westminster John Knox).

Alexander, Loveday C. A. (1994), "Paul and the Hellenistic Schools: The Evidence of Galen," in Troels Engberg-Pedersen, ed., *Paul in His Hellenistic Context* (SNTW; Edinburgh: T&T Clark), 60–83.

Alexander, Loveday C. A. (2001), "*IPSE DIXIT*: Citation of Authority in Paul and in the Jewish and Hellenistic Schools," in Troels Engberg-Pedersen, ed., *Paul Beyond the Judaism/Hellenism Divide* (Louisville, KY: Westminster John Knox), 103–27.

Alföldy, Geza (1985), *The Social History of Rome* (Totowa, NJ: Barnes & Noble).

Anderson, Elijah (1990), *Streetwise: Race, Class, and Change in an Urban Community* (Chicago: University of Chicago Press).

Anderson, Elijah (1999), *Code of the Street: Decency, Violence, and the Moral Life of the Inner City* (New York: W. W. Norton & Co.).

Anderson, Elijah (2004), "The Cosmopolitan Canopy," *Annals of the American Academy of Political and Social Science* 595: 14–31.

Ascough, Richard S. (1998), *What Are They Saying about the Formation of the Pauline Churches?* (New York/Mahwah, NJ: Paulist Press).

Ascough, Richard S. (2000), "The Thessalonian Christian Community as a Professional Voluntary Association," *JBL* 119: 311–28.

Ascough, Richard S. (2003), *Paul's Macedonian Associations: The Social Context of Philippians and 1 Thessalonians* (WUNT 2.161; Tübingen: Mohr Siebeck).

Ascough, Richard S. (2004), "A Question of Death: Paul's Community-Building Language in 1 Thessalonians 4:13–18," *JBL* 123: 509–30.

Ashton, John (2000), *The Religion of Paul the Apostle* (New Haven/London: Yale University Press).

Athanassiadi, Polymnia and Michael Frede, eds. (1999), *Pagan Monotheism in Late Antiquity* (Oxford: Clarendon).

Bakirtzis, Charalambos and Helmut Koester, eds. (1998), *Philippi at the Time of Paul and after His Death* (Harrisburg, PA: Trinity Press International).

Balch, David L. (2004), "Rich Pompeiian Houses, Shops for Rent, and the Huge Apartment Building in Herculaneum as Typical Spaces for Pauline House Churches," *JSNT* 27: 27–47.

Balch, David (2008), *Roman Domestic Art and Early House Churches* (WUNT 228; Tübingen: Mohr Siebeck).

Banks, Robert (1994), *Paul's Idea of Community: The Early House Churches in Their Cultural Setting* (rev. ed.; Peabody, MA: Hendrickson).

Barclay, John M. G. (1988), *Obeying the Truth: A Study of Paul's Ethics in Galatians* (SNTW; Edinburgh: T&T Clark).

Barclay, John M. G. (1991), "Paul, Philemon and the Dilemma of Christian Slave-Ownership," *NTS* 37: 161–86.

Barclay, John M. G. (1992), "Thessalonica and Corinth: Social Contrasts in Pauline Christianity," *JSNT* 47: 49–74.

Barclay, John M. G. (1996), "'Do We Undermine the Law?' A Study of Romans 14.1–15.6," in James D. G. Dunn, ed., *Paul and the Mosaic Law* (Tübingen: Mohr Siebeck), 287–308.

Barclay, John M. G. (2003), "'That you may not grieve, like the rest who have no hope' (1 Thess 4:13): Death and Early Christian Identity," in Morna D. Hooker, ed., *Not in Word Alone: The First Epistle to the Thessalonians* (Rome: Benedictina Publishing), 131–53.

Barton, Stephen C. (1986), "Paul's Sense of Place: An Anthropological Approach to Community Formation in Corinth," *NTS* 32: 225–46.

Barton, Stephen C. (1993), "Early Christianity and the Sociology of the Sect?" in Francis Watson, ed., *The Open Text: New Directions For Biblical Studies?* (London: SCM), 140–62.

Barton, Stephen C. (1994), *Discipleship and Family Ties in Mark and Matthew* (SNTSMS 80; Cambridge: Cambridge University Press).

Barton, Stephen C. (1998), "Can We Identify the Gospel Audiences?" in Bauckham, ed., 173–94.

Bauckham, Richard J., ed. (1998), *The Gospels for All Christians: Rethinking the Gospel Audiences* (Grand Rapids: Eerdmans; Edinburgh: T&T Clark).

Becker, Jürgen (1993), "Paul and His Churches," in Jürgen Becker, ed., *Christian Beginnings* (Louisville, KY: Westminster/John Knox Press), 132–210.

Bell, Catherine (1992), *Ritual Theory, Ritual Practice* (Oxford/New York: Oxford University Press).

Bell, Catherine (1997), *Ritual: Perspectives and Dimensions* (Oxford/New York: Oxford University Press).

Bergant, Dianne (1994), "An Anthropological Approach to Biblical Interpretation: The Passsover Supper in Exodus 12:1-20 as a Case Study," *Semeia* 67: 43–62.

Berger, Peter L. and Thomas Luckmann (1966), *The Social Construction of Reality* (Garden City, NY: Doubleday).

Berry, Joanne, ed. (1998), *Unpeeling Pompeii: Studies in Region I of Pompeii* (Soprintendenza Archeologica di Pompei; Milan: Electa).

Best, Ernest (1986), "Paul's Apostolic Authority—?" *JSNT* 27: 3–25.

Best, Ernest (1988), *Paul and His Converts* (Edinburgh: T&T Clark).

Bhabha, Homi K. (1994), *The Location of Culture* (London/New York: Routledge).

Binder, Donald D. (1999), *Into the Temple Courts: The Place of the Synagogues in the Second Temple Period* (SBLDS 169; Atlanta: Society of Biblical Literature).

Blasi, Anthony J. (1991), *Making Charisma: The Social Construction of Paul's Public Image* (New Brunswick/London: Transaction Publishers).

Blasi, Anthony J., Jean Duhaime, and Paul-André Turcotte, eds. (2002), *Handbook of Early Christianity: Social Science Approaches* (Walnut Creek, CA: Alta Mira).

Bloomquist, L. Gregory (1993), *The Function of Suffering in Philippians* (JSNTSup 78; Sheffield: JSOT Press).

Blue, Bradley B. (1994), "Acts and the House Church," in David W. J. Gill and Conrad Gempf, eds., *The Book of Acts in its Graeco-Roman Setting* (The Book of Acts in its First Century Setting, vol. 2; Grand Rapids: Eerdmans), 119–222.

Bockmuehl, Markus N. A. (1998), *The Epistle to the Philippians* (BNTC 11; Peabody, MA: Hendrickson).

Bookidis, Nancy (2005), "Religion in Corinth: 146 B.C.E. to 100 C.E.," in Schowalter and Friesen, eds., 141–64.

Bormann, Lukas (1995), *Philippi: Stadt und Christengemeinde zur Zeit des Paulus* (NovTSup 78; Leiden: Brill).

Bradley, Keith R. (1983), "Review of *The First Urban Christians: The Social World of the Apostle Paul* by W. A. Meeks," *The American Historical Review* 88: 1253–54.

Branick, Vincent (1989), *The House Church in the Writings of Paul* (Wilmington, DE: Michael Glazier).

Bruce, Steve (2002), *God is Dead: Secularization in the West* (Oxford: Blackwell).

Burke, Trevor J. (2003), *Family Matters: A Socio-Historical Study of Kinship Metaphors in 1 Thessalonians* (JSNTSup 247; London/New York: T&T Clark).

Burtchaell, James T. (1992), *From Synagogue to Church: Public Services and Offices in the Earliest Christian Communities* (Cambridge: Cambridge University Press).

Campbell, R. Alistair (1994), *The Elders: Seniority within Earliest Christianity* (SNTW; Edinburgh: T&T Clark).

Carlson, Richard P. (1993), "The Role of Baptism in Paul's Thought," *Int* 47: 255–66.

Carson, D. A., Peter T. O'Brien, and Mark A. Seifrid, eds. (2001, 2004), *Justification and Variegated Nomism* (2 vols.; WUNT 2.140; Tübingen: Mohr Siebeck).

Carson, Marion (2004–05), "'For Now We Live': A Study of Paul's Pastoral Leadership in 1 Thessalonians," *Themelios* 30: 23–41.

Carter, Warren (2001), *Matthew and Empire* (Harrisburg, PN: Trinity Press International).

Carter, Warren (2004), "Going All the Way? Honoring the Emperor and Sacrificing Wives and Slaves in 1 Peter 2.13–3.6," in Amy-Jill Levine and Maria Mayo Robbins, eds., *A Feminist Companion to the Catholic Epistles* (London/New York: T&T Clark), 14–33.

Cartledge, Paul (1994), "The Greeks and Anthropology," *Anthropology Today* 10: 3–6.

Castelli, Elizabeth A. (1991), *Imitating Paul: A Discourse of Power* (Louisville, KY: Westminster/John Knox).

Catto, Stephen K. (2007), *Reconstructing the First-Century Synagogue: A Critical Analysis of Current Research* (LNTS 363; London: T&T Clark).

Chow, John K. (1992), *Patronage and Power: A Study of Social Networks in Corinth* (JSNTSup 75; Sheffield: JSOT Press).

Clarke, Andrew D. (1993), *Secular and Christian Leadership in Corinth: A Socio-Historical and Exegetical Study of 1 Corinthians 1-6* (AGJU 18; Leiden: Brill).

Clarke, Andrew D. (2000), *Serve the Community of the Church: Christians as Leaders and Ministers* (Grand Rapids/Cambridge: Eerdmans).

Clarke, Andrew D. (2008), *A Pauline Theology of Church Leadership* (LNTS 362; London/ New York: T&T Clark).

Clarke, John R. (1991), *The Houses of Roman Italy, 100 BC–AD 250: Ritual, Space, and Decoration* (Berkeley: University of California Press).

Clarke, John R. (2003), *Art in the Lives of Ordinary Romans: Visual Representation and Non-Elite Viewers in Italy, 100 BC–AD 315* (Berkeley: University of California Press).

Coleman, John (1999), "The Bible and Sociology," *Sociology of Religion* 60: 125–48.

Collart, Paul (1937), *Philippes, Ville de Macédoine: depuis ses origines jusqu'à la fin de l'époque romaine* (Travaux et Mémoires; Fascicule V; Paris: Ecole Française d' Athènes).

Collart, Paul and Pierre Ducrey (1975), *Philippes I: les reliefs rupestres* (BCHSup II; Paris: de Boccard).

Collins, John N. (1990), *Diakonia: Re-Interpreting the Ancient Sources* (Oxford/New York: Oxford University Press).

Crossley, James G. (2006), *The Spread of Earliest Christianity, c. 26 CE–50 CE: A Secular Approach* (Louisville, KY: Westminster John Knox).

Crossley, James G. (2008), *Jesus in an Age of Terror: Scholarly Projects for a New American Century* (London: Equinox).

Dahl, Nils A. (1991), "The Crucified Messiah," in Donald H. Juel, ed., *Jesus the Christ: The Historical Origins of Christological Doctrine* (Minneapolis: Fortress), 27–47.

Davie, Grace (1994), *Religion in Britain since 1945: Believing without Belonging* (Oxford: Blackwell).

Davie, Grace (2000), *Religion in Modern Europe: A Memory Mutates* (Oxford: Oxford University Press).

De Vos, Craig S. (1999), *Church and Community Conflicts: The Relationships of the Thessalonian, Corinthian, and Philippian Churches with their Wider Civic Communities* (SBLDS 168; Atlanta: Scholars Press).

Deissmann, G. Adolf (1910), *Light from the Ancient East: The New Testament Illustrated by Recently Discovered Texts of the Graeco-Roman World* (London: Hodder & Stoughton).

DeMaris, Richard E. (1995), "Corinthian Religion and Baptism for the Dead (1 Corinthians 15:29): Insights from Archaeology and Anthropology," *JBL* 114: 661–82.

DeMaris, Richard E. (2008), *The New Testament in its Ritual World* (London/New York: Routledge).

Dobbins, John J. and Pedar W. Foss, eds. (2007), *The World of Pompeii* (London/New York: Routledge).

Donfried, Karl P. (1985), "The Cults of Thessalonica and the Thessalonian Correspondence," *NTS* 31: 336–56.

Donfried, Karl P., ed. (1991), *The Romans Debate* (rev. and exp. ed.; Peabody, MA: Hendrickson).

Draper, Jonathan A. (2000), "Ritual Process and Ritual Symbol in Didache 7–10," *VC* 54: 121–58.

Dunn, James D. G. (1983), "The New Perspective on Paul," *BJRL* 65: 95–122 (repr. in James D. G. Dunn, *Jesus, Paul and the Law* [London: SPCK, 1990], 183–214).

Ehrensperger, Kathy (2007), *Paul and the Dynamics of Power: Communication and Interaction in the Early-Christ Movement* (LNTS 325; London/New York: T&T Clark).

Elliott, John H. (1985), "Review of W. Meeks, *The First Urban Christians*," *RelSRev* 11: 329–35.

Elliott, John H. (1986), "Social-Scientific Criticism of the New Testament: More on Methods and Models," *Semeia* 35: 1–33.

Elliott, John H. (1990), *A Home for the Homeless: A Social-Scientific Criticism of 1 Peter, Its Situation and Strategy* (with a new introduction; Minneapolis: Fortress Press).

Elliott, John H. (1993), *What is Social-Scientific Criticism?* (UK title: *Social-Scientific Criticism of the New Testament*) (Minneapolis: Fortress; London: SPCK).

Elliott, Neil (1994), *Liberating Paul: The Justice of God and the Politics of the Apostle* (Maryknoll, NY: Orbis).

Elliott, Neil (1997), "Romans 13:1-7 in the Context of Imperial Propaganda," in Horsley, ed., *Paul and Empire*, 184–204.

Ellis, E. Earle (1989), *Pauline Theology: Ministry and Society* (Grand Rapids: Eerdmans).

Ellis, Simon P. (2000), *Roman Housing* (London: Duckworth).

Engels, Donald (1990), *Roman Corinth: An Alternative Model for the Classical City* (Chicago: University of Chicago Press).

Epp, Eldon J. (2005), *Junia: The First Woman Apostle* (Minneapolis: Fortress).

Esler, Philip F. (1987), *Community and Gospel in Luke-Acts: The Social and Political Motivations of Lucan Theology* (SNTSMS 57; Cambridge: Cambridge University Press).

Esler, Philip F. (1994), *The First Christians in their Social Worlds: Social-Scientific Approaches to New Testament Interpretation* (London/New York: Routledge).

Esler, Philip F. (1995a), "Introduction: Models, Context and Kerygma in New Testament Interpretation," in Philip F. Esler, ed., *Modelling Early Christianity: Social-Scientific Studies of the New Testament in its Context* (London/New York: Routledge), 1–20.

Esler, Philip F., ed. (1995b), *Modelling Early Christianity: Social-Scientific Studies of the New Testament in its Context* (London/New York: Routledge).

Esler, Philip F. (1998a), *Galatians* (New Testament Readings; London/New York: Routledge).

Esler, Philip F. (1998b), "Review of D. G. Horrell, *The Social Ethos of the Corinthian Correspondence*," *JTS* 49: 253–60.

Esler, Philip F. (2000), "Models in New Testament Interpretation: A Reply to David Horrell," *JSNT* 78: 107–13.

Esler, Philip F. (2003), *Conflict and Identity in Romans* (Minneapolis: Fortress).

Esler, Philip F. (2004), "The Context Group Project: An Autobiographical Account," in Louise J. Lawrence and Mario I. Aguilar, eds., *Anthropology and Biblical Studies: Avenues of Approach* (Leiden: Deo), 46–61.

Finley, Moses I. (1975), *The Ancient Economy* (London: Chatto & Windus).

Finley, Moses I. (1985), *The Ancient Economy* (2nd ed.; London: Hogarth).

Fotopoulos, John (2003), *Food Offered to Idols in Roman Corinth: A Social-Rhetorical Reconsideration of 1 Corinthians 8:1–11:1* (WUNT 2.151; Tübingen: Mohr Siebeck).

Friesen, Steven J. (2004), "Poverty in Pauline Studies: Beyond the So-Called New Consensus," *JSNT* 26: 323–61.

Friesen, Steven (2006), "Injustice or God's Will: Explanations of Poverty in Proto-Christian Communities," in Richard A. Horsley, ed., *Christian Origins* (A People's History of Christianity, vol. 1; Minneapolis: Fortress), 240–60.

Friesen, Steven (2008), "Injustice or God's Will: Early Christian Explanations of Poverty," in Susan R. Holmen, ed., *Wealth and Poverty in Early Church and Society* (Grand Rapids: Baker Academic), 17–36.

Frilingos, Chris A. (2004), *Spectacles of Empire: Monsters, Martyrs, and the Book of Revelation* (Divinations: Rereading Late Ancient Religion; Philadelphia: University of Pennsylvania Press).

Gaddis, John Lewis (2002), *The Landscape of History: How Historians Map the Past* (New York: Oxford University Press).

Gager, John G. (1975), *Kingdom and Community: The Social World of Early Christianity* (Englewood Cliffs: Prentice-Hall).

Gager, John G. (1982), "Shall We Marry our Enemies," *Int* 36: 256–65.

Gandhi, Leela (1998), *Postcolonial Theory: A Critical Introduction* (Edinburgh: Edinburgh University Press).

Garland, David E. (1985), "The Composition and Unity of Philippians: Some Neglected Literary Factors," *NovT* 27: 141–73.

Garland, David E. (2003), "The Absence of an Ordained Ministry in the Churches of Paul," in William H. Brackney, ed., *Baptists and Ordination* (Macon, GA: National Association of Baptist Professors of Religion), 25–37.

Garrett, Susan (1992), "Sociology of Early Christianity," in David N. Freedman, ed., *Anchor Bible Dictionary* (vol. 6; New York: Doubleday), 89–99.

Gaventa, Beverly Roberts (2003), *Acts* (ANTC; Nashville: Abingdon).

Gaventa, Beverly Roberts (2007), *Our Mother Saint Paul* (Louisville, KY/London: Westminster John Knox).

Geertman, Herman (1998), "The Layout of the City and its History: The Dutch Project," in Berry, ed., 16–25.

Gehring, Roger W. (2004), *House Church and Mission: The Importance of Household Structures in Early Christianity* (Peabody, MA: Hendrickson).

Gellner, Ernest (2006), *Nations and Nationalism* (2nd ed.; Oxford: Blackwell).

Geoffrion, Timothy C. (1993), *The Rhetorical Purpose and the Political and Military Character of Philippians: A Call to Stand Firm* (Lewiston, NY: Edwin Mellen).

Glad, Clarence E. (1995), *Paul and Philodemus: Adaptability in Epicurean and Early Christian Psychagogy* (NovTSup 81; Leiden: Brill).

Gottwald, Norman K. and Richard A. Horsley, eds. (1993), *The Bible and Liberation: Political and Social Hermeneutics* (Maryknoll, NY: Orbis; London: SPCK).

Harland, Philip A. (2003), *Associations, Synagogues, and Congregations: Claiming a Place in Ancient Mediterranean Society* (Minneapolis: Fortress).

Harrington, Daniel J. (1980), "Sociological Concepts and the Early Church: A Decade of Research," *TS* 41: 181–90.

Hays, Richard B. (1989), *Echoes of Scripture in the Letters of Paul* (New Haven/London: Yale University Press).

Hays, Richard B. (2002), *The Faith of Jesus Christ: The Narrative Substructure of Galatians 3:1–4:11* (2nd ed.; Grand Rapids/Cambridge: Eerdmans).

Hellerman, Joseph H. (2005), *Reconstructing Honor in Roman Philippi: Carmen Christi as Cursus Pudorum* (SNTSMS 132; Cambridge: Cambridge University Press).

Hendrix, Holland (1984), "Thessalonicans Honor Rome" (PhD diss., Harvard University).

Hochschild, Ralph (1999), *Socialgeschichtliche Exegese. Entwicklung, Geschichte und Methodik einer neutestamentlichen Forschungsrichtung* (NTOA 42; Freiburg, Schweiz: Universitätsverlag; Göttingen: Vandenhoeck & Ruprecht).

Holloway, Paul A. (2001), *Consolation in Philippians: Philosophical Sources and Rhetorical Strategy* (SNTSMS 112; Cambridge: Cambridge University Press).

Holmberg, Bengt (1978), *Paul and Power: The Structure of Authority in the Primitive Church as Reflected in the Pauline Epistles* (Philadelphia: Fortress).

Holmberg, Bengt (1990), *Sociology and the New Testament* (Minneapolis: Fortress).

Hopkins, Keith (1965), "Elite Mobility in the Roman Empire," *Past and Present* 32: 12–26.

Horrell, David G. (1996), *The Social Ethos of the Corinthian Correspondence: Interests and Ideology from 1 Corinthians to 1 Clement* (SNTW; Edinburgh: T&T Clark).

Horrell, David G. (1997), "Leadership Patterns and the Development of Ideology in Early Christianity," *Sociology of Religion* 58: 323–41.

Horrell, David G., ed. (1999a), *Social-Scientific Approaches to New Testament Interpretation* (Edinburgh: T&T Clark).

Horrell, David G. (1999b), "Social-Scientific Interpretation of the New Testament: Retrospect and Prospect," in David G. Horrell, ed., *Social-Scientific Approaches to New Testament Interpretation* (Edinburgh: T&T Clark), 3–27.

Horrell, David G. (2000), "Models and Methods in Social-Scientific Interpretation: A Response to Philip Esler," *JSNT* 78: 83–105.

Horrell, David G. (2002), "Social Sciences Studying Formative Christian Phenomena: A Creative Movement," in Anthony J. Blasi, Jean Duhaime, and Paul-André Turcotte, eds., *Handbook of Early Christianity: Social Science Approaches* (Walnut Creek, CA: Alta Mira Press), 3–28.

Horrell, David G. (2003), "The Peaceable, Tolerant Community and the Legitimate Role of the State," *RevExp* 100: 81–99.

Horrell, David G. (2004), "Domestic Space and Christian Meetings at Corinth: Imagining New Contexts and the Buildings East of the Theatre," *NTS* 50: 349–69.

Horrell, David G. (2005), *Solidarity and Difference: A Contemporary Reading of Paul's Ethics* (London/New York: T&T Clark).

Horrell, David G. (2007), "Between Conformity and Resistance: Beyond the Balch-Elliott Debate Towards a Postcolonial Reading of 1 Peter," in Robert L. Webb and Betsy Bauman-Martin, eds., *Reading 1 Peter with New Eyes: Methodological Reassessments of the Letter of First Peter* (LNTS 364; London/New York: T&T Clark), 111–43.

Horrell, David G. (2008), "Pauline Churches or Early Christian Churches? Unity, Disagreement, and the Eucharist," in Anatoly Alexeev et al., eds., *Einheit der Kirche im Neuen Testament* (WUNT 218; Tübingen: Mohr Siebeck), 185–203.

Horrell, David G. (2009), "Aliens and Strangers? The Socio-Economic Location of the Addresses of 1 Peter," in Longenecker and Liebengood, eds., 176–202.

Horsley, Richard A. (1993), *Jesus and the Spiral of Violence: Popular Jewish Resistance in Roman Palestine* (Minneapolis: Fortress).

Horsley, Richard A. (1994), *Sociology and the Jesus Movement* (2nd ed.; New York: Crossroad).

Horsley, Richard A., ed. (1997a), *Paul and Empire: Religion and Power in Roman Imperial Society* (Harrisburg, PA: Trinity Press International).

Horsley, Richard A. (1997b), "Building an Alternative Society: Introduction," in Horsley, ed., *Paul and Empire*, 206–14.

Horsley, Richard A. (1997c), "1 Corinthians: A Case Study of Paul's Assembly as an Alternative Society," in Horsley, ed., *Paul and Empire*, 242–52.

Horsley, Richard A., ed. (2000a), *Paul and Politics: Ekklesia, Israel, Imperium, Interpretation: Essays in Honor of Krister Stendahl* (Harrisburg, PA: Trinity Press International).

Horsley, Richard A. (2000b), "Rhetoric and Empire—and 1 Corinthians," in Horsley, ed., *Paul and Politics*, 72–102.

Horsley, Richard (2001), *Jesus and Empire: The Kingdom of God and the New World Disorder* (Minneapolis: Fortress Press).

Horsley, Richard A., ed. (2004a), *Hidden Transcripts and the Arts of Resistance: Applying the Work of James C. Scott to Jesus and Paul* (SemeiaSt 48; Atlanta: SBL).

Horsley, Richard A., ed. (2004b), *Paul and the Roman Imperial Order* (Harrisburg, PA: Trinity Press International).

Horsley, Richard A. (2005), "Paul's Assembly in Corinth: An Alternative Society," in Daniel N. Schowalter and Steven J. Friesen, eds., *Urban Religion in Roman Corinth: Interdisciplinary Approaches* (HTS 53; Harvard: Harvard University Press).

Horsley, Richard A. and Neil A. Silberman (1997), *The Message and the Kingdom: How Jesus and Paul Ignited a Revolution and Transformed the Ancient World* (New York: Grossett).

Howard-Brook, Wes and Anthony Gwyther (1999), *Unveiling Empire: Reading Revelation Then and Now* (Maryknoll: Orbis Books).

Hurtado, Larry W. (2003), *Lord Jesus Christ: Devotion to Jesus in Earliest Christianity* (Grand Rapids: Eerdmans).

Jewett, Robert (1986), *The Thessalonian Correspondence: Pauline Rhetoric and Millenarian Piety* (FFNT; Philadelphia: Fortress).

Jewett, Robert (2007), *Romans* (Hermeneia; Minneapolis: Fortress).

Johnson, Terry and Chris Dandeker (1990), "Patronage: Relation and System," in Wallace-Hadrill, ed., 219–42.

Jongman, Willem M. (2007), "The Loss of Innocence: Pompeian Economy and Society between Past and Present," in Dobbins and Foss, eds., 499–517.

Judge, Edwin A. (1960a), "The Early Christians as a Scholastic Community," *JRH* 111: 4–15.

Judge, Edwin A. (1960b), *The Social Pattern of Early Christian Groups in the First Century: Some Prolegomena to the Study of the New Testament Ideas of Social Obligation* (London: Tyndale).

Judge, Edwin A. (2008), *Social Perspectives on Christians in the First Century: Pivotal Essays* (ed. David M. Scholer; Peabody, MA: Hendrickson).

Kaylor, R. David (1988), *Paul's Covenant Community: Jew and Gentile in Romans* (Atlanta: John Knox).

Keightley, Georgia (2005), "Christian Collective Memory and Paul's Knowledge of Jesus," in Alan Kirk and Tom Thatcher, eds., *Memory, Tradition and Texts: Uses of the Past in Early Christianity* (Atlanta: Society of Biblical Literature), 129–50.

Kirk, Alan (2005), "Social and Cultural Memory," in Alan Kirk and Tom Thatcher, eds., *Memory, Tradition and Texts: Uses of the Past in Early Christianity* (Atlanta: Society of Biblical Literature), 1–23.

Kittredge, Cynthia Briggs (1998), *Community and Authority: The Rhetoric of Obedience in the Pauline Tradition* (HTS 45; Harrisburg, PN: Trinity Press International).

Klauck, Hans-Josef (1981), *Hausgemeinde und Hauskirche im frühen Christentum* (SBS 103; Stuttgart: Katholische Bibelwerk).

Kloppenborg, John S. (1993a), "Edwin Hatch, Churches and Collegia," in Bradley H. McLean, ed., *Origins and Methods: Towards a New Understanding of Judaism and Christianity: Essays in Honour of John C. Hurd* (JSNTSup 86; Sheffield: JSOT Press), 212–38.

Kloppenborg, John S. (1993b), *"Philadelphia, Theodidaktos* and the Dioscuri: Rhetorical Engagement in 1 Thessalonians 4.9-12," *NTS* 39: 265–89.

Kloppenborg, John S. (1996a), "Collegia and Thiasoi: Issues in Function, Taxonomy and Membership," in Kloppenborg and Wilson, eds., 16–30.

Kloppenborg, John S. (1996b), "Egalitarianism in the Myth and Rhetoric of Pauline Churches," in Elizabeth A. Castelli and Hal Taussig, eds., *Reimagining Christian Origins: A Colloquium Honoring Burton L. Mack* (Valley Forge, PN: Trinity Press International), 247–63.

Kloppenborg, John S. and Stephen G. Wilson, eds. (1996), *Voluntary Associations in the Graeco-Roman World* (London/New York: Routledge).

Koukouli-Chrysanthaki, Chaido (1998), "Colonia Iulia Augusta Philippensis," in Bakirtzis and Koester, eds., 5–35.

Lampe, Peter (2003), *From Paul to Valentinus: Christians at Rome in the First Two Centuries* (trans. Michael Steinhauser; ed. Marshall D. Johnson; Minneapolis: Fortress).

Laurence, Ray (2006), *Roman Pompeii: Space and Society* (2nd ed.; London/New York: Routledge).

Laurence, Ray and Andrew Wallace-Hadrill, eds. (1997), *Domestic Space in the Roman World: Pompeii and Beyond* (JRASup 22; Portsmouth, RI: Journal of Roman Archaeology).

Lawrence, Louise J. (2003), *An Ethnography of the Gospel of Matthew* (WUNT 2.165; Tübingen: Mohr Siebeck).

Lawrence, Louise J. (2005), *Reading with Anthropology: Exhibiting New Testament Religion* (Carlisle: Paternoster).

Lazarides, D. (1973), Φίλιπποι—Ρωμαική αποικία (Ancient Greek Cities 20; Athens).

Lewis, Ioan M. (1989), *Ecstatic Religion: A Study of Shamanism and Spirit Possession* (London/New York: Routledge).

Lifton, Robert J. and Eric Olson (2004), "Symbolic Immortality," in Antonius Robben, ed., *Death, Mourning and Burial: A Cross-Cultural Reader* (Oxford: Blackwell), 32–39.

Ling, Roger (2005), *Pompeii: History, Life and Afterlife* (Stroud: Tempus).

Longenecker, Bruce W. (2003), *The Lost Letters of Pergamum: A Story from the New Testament World* (Grand Rapids: Baker Academic).

Longenecker, Bruce W. (2007), "Good News to the Poor: Jesus, Paul and Jerusalem," in Todd D. Still, ed., *Jesus and Paul Reconnected* (Grand Rapids: Eerdmans), 37–66.

Longenecker, Bruce W. (2009), "Exposing the Economic Middle: A Revised Economy Scale for the Study of Early Urban Christianity," *JSNT* 31: 243–78.

Longenecker, Bruce W. (forthcoming a), "Dating the Origin of Paul's Collection for the Saints in Judaea: The Corinthian Contribution," in Stylianos Papadopoulos et al., eds., *Saint Paul and Corinth: 1950 Years since the Writing of the Epistles to the Corinthians.*

Longenecker, Bruce W. (forthcoming b), *Remember the Poor: Paul, Poverty and the Greco-Roman World* (Grand Rapids/Cambridge: Eerdmans).

Longenecker, Bruce W. and Kelly Liebengood, eds. (2009) *Engaging Economics: New Testament Scenarios and Early Christian Reception* (Grand Rapids/Cambridge: Eerdmans).

Longenecker, Richard N. (2002), "Paul's Vision of the Church and Community Formation in His Major Missionary Letters," in Richard N. Longenecker, ed., *Community*

Formation in the Early Church and in the Church Today (Peabody, MA: Hendrickson), 72–104.

Lopez, Davina C. (2008), *Apostle to the Conquered: Reimagining Paul's Mission* (Paul in Critical Contexts; Minneapolis, Fortress).

MacDonald, Margaret Y. (1988), *The Pauline Churches: A Socio-Historical Study of Institutionalization in the Pauline and Deutero-Pauline Writings* (SNTSMS 60; Cambridge: Cambridge University Press).

MacDonald, Margaret Y. (1990), "Women Holy in Body and Spirit: The Social Setting of 1 Corinthians 7," *NTS* 36: 161–81.

MacMullen, Ramsay (1974), *Roman Social Relations: 50 BC to AD 284* (New Haven/ London: Yale University Press).

McCready, W. O. (1996), "*Ekklesia* and Voluntary Associations," in Kloppenborg and Wilson, eds., 59–73.

McLean, Bradley H. (1993), "The Agrippinilla Inscription: Religious Associations and Early Church Formation," in Bradley H. McLean, ed., *Origins and Methods: Towards a New Understanding of Judaism and Christianity: Essays in Honour of John C. Hurd* (JSNTSup 86; Sheffield: JSOT Press), 239–70.

McVann, Mark (1994), "Introduction," *Semeia* 67: 7–12.

Maier, Harry O. (1991), *The Social Setting of the Ministry as Reflected in the Writings of Hermas, Clement and Ignatius* (Dissertations SR 1; Ontario: Wilfred Laurier University Press).

Malherbe, Abraham (1977), *Social Aspects of Early Christianity* (Philadelphia: Fortress).

Malherbe, Abraham (2000), *The Letters to the Thessalonians: A New Translation with Introduction and Commentary* (AB 32; New York: Doubleday).

Malina, Bruce J. (1981), *The New Testament World: Insights from Cultural Anthropology* (Atlanta: John Knox; London: SCM).

Malina, Bruce J. (1982), "Social Sciences and Biblical Interpretation," *Int* 36: 229–42.

Malina, Bruce J. (1985), "Review of W. Meeks, *The First Urban Christians*," *JBL* 104: 346–49.

Malina, Bruce J. (1996a), *The Social World of Jesus and the Gospels* (London/New York: Routledge).

Malina, Bruce J. (1996b), "Understanding New Testament Persons," in Richard L. Rohrbaugh, ed., *The Social Sciences and New Testament Interpretation* (Peabody, MA: Hendrickson), 41–61.

Malina, Bruce J. (2001), *The New Testament World: Insights from Cultural Anthropology* (3rd ed. rev. and exp.; Louisville, KY: Westminster John Knox).

Malina, Bruce J. (2002), "Social-Scientific Methods in Historical Jesus Research," in Wolfgang Stegemann, Bruce J. Malina, and Gerd Theissen, eds., *The Social Setting of Jesus and the Gospels* (Minneapolis: Fortress), 3–26.

Malina, Bruce J. and John J. Pilch (2006), *Social-Science Commentary on the Letters of Paul* (Minneapolis: Fortress).

Malina, Bruce J. and Richard L. Rohrbaugh (1992), *A Social-Scientific Commentary on the Synoptic Gospels* (Minneapolis: Fortress).

Marchal, Joseph A. (2006), *Hierarchy, Unity, and Imitation: A Feminist Rhetorical Analysis of Power Dynamics in Paul's Letter to the Philippians* (SBLAB 24; Atlanta: Society of Biblical Literature).

Marchal, Joseph A. (2008), *The Politics of Heaven: Women, Gender, and Empire in the Study of Paul* (Paul in Critical Contexts; Minneapolis, Fortress).

Martin, Dale B. (1990), *Slavery as Salvation: The Metaphor of Slavery in Pauline Christianity* (New Haven/London: Yale University Press).

Martin, Dale B. (1993), "Social-Scientific Criticism," in Steven L. McKenzie and Stephen R. Haynes, eds., *To Each its Own Meaning: An Introduction to Biblical Criticisms and Their Application* (Louisville, KY: Westminster John Knox Press; London: Geoffrey Chapman), 103–19.

Martin, Dale B. (1995), *The Corinthian Body* (New Haven/London: Yale University Press).

Martin, Dale B. (2004), *Inventing Superstition from the Hippocratics to the Christians* (Cambridge: Harvard University Press).

Mason, Steve (1996), "*PHILOSOPHAI*: Graeco-Roman, Judean and Christian," in Kloppenborg and Wilson, eds., 31–58.

Meeks, Wayne A. (1972), "The Man from Heaven in Johannine Sectarianism," *JBL* 91: 44–71.

Meeks, Wayne A. (1983), *The First Urban Christians: The Social World of the Apostle Paul* (New Haven/London: Yale University Press).

Meeks, Wayne A. (1986), *The Moral World of the First Christians* (New Haven/London: Yale University Press).

Meeks, Wayne A. (1990), "The Circle of Reference in Pauline Morality," in David L. Balch, Everett Ferguson, and Wayne A. Meeks, eds., *Greeks, Romans, and Christians: Essays in Honor of Abraham J. Malherbe* (Minneapolis: Fortress), 305–17.

Meeks, Wayne A. (1993), *The Origins of Christian Morality: The First Two Centuries* (New Haven/London: Yale University Press).

Meeks, Wayne A. (2001), "Corinthian Christians as Artificial Aliens," in Troels Engberg-Pedersen, ed., *Paul Beyond the Judaism/Hellenism Divide* (Louisville, KY: Westminster John Knox), 129–38.

Meeks, Wayne A. (2002a), *In Search of the Early Christians: Selected Essays* (ed. Allen R. Hilton and H. Gregory Snyder; New Haven/London: Yale University Press).

Meeks, Wayne A. (2002b), "The Irony of Grace," in Darren C. Marks, ed., *Shaping a Theological Mind: Theological Context and Methodology* (Aldershot: Ashgate).

Meeks, Wayne A. (2003), *The First Urban Christians: The Social World of the Apostle Paul* (2nd ed.; New Haven/London: Yale University Press).

Meeks, Wayne A. (2006), *Christ Is the Question* (Louisville, KY: Westminster John Knox).

Meeks, Wayne A. and Robert L. Wilken (1978), *Jews and Christians in Antioch in the First Four Centuries of the Common Era* (SBLSBS 13; Missoula, MT: Scholars).

Meeks, Wayne A. and John T. Fitzgerald, eds. (2007), *The Writings of St. Paul* (2nd ed.; New York/London: W. W. Norton & Co.).

Meggitt, Justin J. (1996), "The Social Status of Erastus (Rom. 16:23)," *NovT* 38: 218–23.

Meggitt, Justin J. (1998a), "Review of Bruce Malina, *The Social World of Jesus and the Gospels*," *JTS* 49: 215–19.

Meggitt, Justin J. (1998b), *Paul, Poverty and Survival* (SNTW; Edinburgh: T&T Clark).

Metcalf, Peter (1981), "Meaning and Materialism: The Ritual Economy of Death," *Man* 16: 563–78.

Metcalf, Peter and Richard Huntington (1991), *Celebrations of Death: The Anthropology of Mortuary Ritual* (Cambridge: Cambridge University Press).

Minear, Paul S. (1960), *Images of the Church in the New Testament* (Philadelphia: Westminster).

Moore, David Chioni (1994), "Anthropology is Dead, Long Live Anthro(a)pology: Poststructuralism, Literary Studies, and Anthropology's 'Nervous Present,'" *Journal of Anthropological Research* 50: 345–65.

Moore, Stephen D. (1994), *Poststructuralism and the New Testament: Derrida and Foucault at the Foot of the Cross* (Minneapolis: Fortress).

Moore, Stephen D. (2006), *Empire and Apocalypse: Postcolonialism and the New Testament* (Sheffield: Sheffield Phoenix Press).

Morris, Ian (1991), "The Early Polis as City and State," in Rich and Wallace-Hadrill, eds., 24–57.

Moxnes, Halvor (1988), *The Economy of the Kingdom: Social Conflict and Economic Relations in Luke's Gospel* (Philadelphia: Fortress).

Murphy-O'Connor, Jerome (2002), *St. Paul's Corinth: Texts and Archaeology* (3rd ed. rev. and exp.; Collegeville, MN: Liturgical Press).

Neyrey, Jerome H. (1988), *An Ideology of Revolt: John's Christology in Social-Science Perspective* (Philadelphia: Fortress).

Neyrey, Jerome H. (1990), *Paul in Other Words: A Cultural Reading of His Letters* (Louisville, KY: Westminster John Knox).

Neyrey, Jerome H. (1995), "The Foot Washing in John 13:6-11: Transformation Ritual or Ceremony?" in L. Michael White and O. Larry Yarbrough, eds., *The Social World of the First Christian: Essays in Honor of Wayne Meeks* (Minneapolis: Fortress), 198–213.

Nicklas, Tobias (2008), "The Letter to Philemon: A Discussion with J. Albert Harrill," in Stanley E. Porter, ed., *Paul's World* (Pauline Studies 4; Boston/Leiden: Brill), 201–20.

Nongbri, Brent (2008), "Paul Without Religion: The Creation of a Category and the Search for an Apostle Beyond the New Perspective" (Ph.D. diss.,Yale University).

Northcott, Michael S. (2007), *A Moral Climate: The Ethics of Global Warming* (London: Darton, Longman and Todd).

Oakes, Peter (2001), *Philippians: From People to Letter* (SNTSMS 110; Cambridge: Cambridge University Press).

Oakes, Peter (forthcoming a), *Reading Romans in Pompeii: Paul's Letter at Ground Level* (London: SPCK; Minneapolis: Fortress).

Oakes, Peter (forthcoming b), "Urban Structure and Patronage: Christ Followers in Corinth" in Dietmar Neufeld and Richard E. DeMaris, eds., *The Social World of the New Testament* (London/New York: Routledge).

O'Day, Gail (1990), "Jeremiah 9:22-23 and 1 Corinthians 1:26-31: A Study in Intertextuality," *JBL* 109: 259–67.

Økland, Jorunn (2004), *Women in Their Place: Paul and the Corinthian Discourse of Gender and Sanctuary Space* (JSNTSup 269; London: T&T Clark).

Olyan, Saul (2004), *Biblical Mourning: Ritual and Social Dimensions* (Oxford: Oxford University Press).

Osiek, Carolyn (1989), "The New Handmaid: The Bible and the Social Sciences," *TS* 50: 260–78.

Osiek, Carolyn and David L. Balch (1997), *Families in the New Testament World: Households and House Churches* (Louisville, KY: Westminster John Knox).

Osiek, Carolyn and Margaret Y. MacDonald with Janet H. Tulloch (2006), *A Woman's Place: House Churches in Earliest Christianity* (Minneapolis: Fortress).

Papazoglou, Fanoula (1988), *Les Villes de Macédoine à l'époque Romaine* (BCHSup 16; Paris: De Boccard).

Pardo, Italo (1989), "Life, Death and Ambiguity in the Social Dynamics of Inner Naples," *Man* 24: 103–23.

Park, M. Sydney (2007), *Submission within the Godhead and the Church in the Epistle to the Philippians: An Exegetical and Theological Examination of the Concept of Submission in Philippians 2 and 3* (LNTS 361; London/New York: T&T Clark).

Parry, Jonathan (1985), "Death and Digestion: The Symbolism of Food and Eating in North Indian Mortuary Rites," *Man* 20: 612–30.

Patterson, John R. (2006), *Landscapes and Cities: Rural Settlement and Civic Transformation in Early Imperial Italy* (Oxford: Oxford University Press).

Perkins, Judith (1995), *The Suffering Self: Pain and Narrative Representation in the Early Christian Era* (London/New York: Routledge).

Perry, Jonathan S. (2006), *The Roman Collegia: The Modern Evolution of an Ancient Concept* (Leiden/Boston: Brill).

Petersen, Norman R. (1985), *Rediscovering Paul: Philemon and the Sociology of Paul's Narrative World* (Philadelphia: Fortress).

Petersen, Norman R. (1986), "Pauline Baptism and Secondary Burial," *HTR* 79: 217–26.

Pilch, John (1994), "Response to F. H. Gorman: Ritual Studies and Biblical Studies," *Semeia* 67: 37–42.

Pilhofer, Peter (1995), *Philippi I: Die erste christliche Gemeinde Europas* (WUNT 87; Tübingen: Mohr Siebeck).

Pilhofer, Peter (2000), *Philippi II: Katalog der Inschriften von Philippi* (WUNT 119; Tübingen: Mohr Siebeck).

Pleket, H. W. (1985), "Review of Wayne Meeks, *The First Urban Christians,*" *VC* 39: 192–96.

Polaski, Sandra Hack (1999), *Paul and the Discourse of Power* (Biblical Seminar 62/ GCT 8; Sheffield: Sheffield Academic).

Portefaix, Lilian (1988), *Sisters Rejoice: Paul's Letter to the Philippians & Luke-Acts as Seen by First Century Philippian Women* (ConBNT 20; Uppsala/Stockholm: Almqvist & Wiksell International).

Reumann, John (1993), "Church Office in Paul, Especially in Philippians," in Bradley H. McLean, ed., *Origins and Method: Towards a New Understanding of Judaism and Christianity* (JSNTSup 86; Sheffield: JSOT Press), 82–91.

Rich, John and Andrew Wallace-Hadrill, eds. (1991), *City and Country in the Ancient World* (London/New York: Routledge).

Richardson, Peter (1996), "Early Synagogues as Collegia in the Diaspora and Palestine," in Kloppenborg and Wilson, eds., 90–109.

Richardson, Peter (2004), *Building Jewish in the Roman East* (Waco, TX: Baylor University Press).

Riesner, Rainer (1994), *Die Frühzeit des Apostels Paulus* (WUNT 71; Tübingen: Mohr Siebeck).

Robben, Antonius, ed. (2004), *Death, Mourning and Burial: A Cross-Cultural Reader* (Oxford: Blackwell).

Robbins, Vernon K. (1996a), *The Tapestry of Early Christian Discourse: Rhetoric, Society and Ideology* (London/New York: Routledge).

Robbins, Vernon K. (1996b), *Exploring the Texture of Texts: A Guide to Socio-Rhetorical Interpretations* (Valley Forge, PA: Trinity Press International).

Rogers, Guy M. (1991), *The Sacred Identity of Ephesos: Foundation Myths of a Roman City* (London/New York: Routledge).

Rohrbaugh, Richard L. (1984), "Methodological Considerations in the Debate over the Social Class Status of Early Christians," *JAAR* 52: 519–46.

Rohrbaugh, Richard L., ed. (1996), *The Social Sciences and New Testament Interpretation* (Peabody, MA: Hendrickson).

Romano, David Gilman (2005), "Urban and Rural Planning in Roman Corinth," in Schowalter and Friesen, eds., 25–59.

Rubel, Paula and Abraham Rosman (1994), "The Past and the Future of Anthropology," *Journal of Anthropological Research* 50: 335–43.

Runesson, Anders (1999), "The Oldest Original Synagogue Building in the Diaspora: A Response to L. Michael White," *HTR* 92: 409–33.

Runesson, Anders (2001), *The Origins of the Synagogue: A Socio-Historical Study* (ConBNT 37; Stockholm: Almqvist & Wiksell).

Runesson, Anders (2002), "A Monumental Synagogue from the First Century: The Case of Ostia," *JSJ* 33: 171–220.

Runesson, Anders, Donald D. Binder, and Birger Olsson (2008), *The Ancient Synagogue from its Origins to 200 C.E.: A Source Book* (AGJU 72; Leiden/Boston: Brill).

Samra, James George (2006), *Being Confirmed to Christ in Community: A Study of Maturity, Maturation and the Local Church in the Undisputed Epistles of Paul* (LNTS 320; London/New York: T&T Clark).

Sande, Siri (1999), "Huskirker og tituluskirker—salmer i heimen eller i badet?" *Kirke og Kultur* 104: 5–16.

Sanders, E. P. (1977), *Paul and Palestinian Judaism* (Philadelphia: Fortress).

Scarborough, Vernon, L. (1998), "Ecology and Ritual: Water Management and the Maya," *Latin American Antiquity* 9: 135–59.

Schleich, T. (1982), "Missionsgeschichte und Sozialstruktur des vorkonstantinischen Christentums," *Geschichte in Wissenschaft und Unterricht* 33: 269–96.

Schmeller, Thomas (1995), *Hierarchie und Egalität: Eine sozial-geschichtliche Untersuchung paulinischer Gemeinden und griechisch-römischer Vereine* (SBS 162; Stuttgart: Katholisches Bibelwerk).

Schottroff, Luise (1985),"'Nicht viele Mächtige': Annäherungen an eine Soziologie des Urchristentums, " *BK* 1: 2–8.

Schottroff, Willi and Wolfgang Stegemann, eds. (1984), *God of the Lowly: Socio-Historical Interpretation of the Bible* (Maryknoll, NY: Orbis).

Schowalter, Daniel and Steven J. Friesen, eds. (2005), *Urban Religion in Roman Corinth: Interdisciplinary Approaches* (Cambridge: Harvard University Press).

Schüssler Fiorenza, Elisabeth (1983), *In Memory of Her: A Feminist Reconstruction of Christian Origins* (New York: Crossroad).

Schüssler Fiorenza, Elisabeth (1984), *Bread Not Stone: The Challenge of Feminist Biblical Interpretation* (Boston: Beacon).

Schüssler Fiorenza, Elisabeth (1992), *But She Said: Feminist Practices of Biblical Interpretation* (Boston: Beacon).

Schüssler Fiorenza, Elisabeth (1994), *In Memory of Her: A Feminist Theological Reconstruction of Christian Origins* (10th anniversary ed.; New York: Crossroad).

Schüssler Fiorenza, Elisabeth (1998), *Sharing Her Word: Feminist Biblical Interpretation in Context* (Edinburgh: T&T Clark).

Schütz, John H. (1975), *Paul and the Anatomy of Apostolic Authority* (SNTSMS 26; Cambridge: Cambridge University Press).

Schütz, John H. (2007), *Paul and the Anatomy of Apostolic Authority* (2nd ed.; New Testament Library; Louisville, KY/London: Westminster John Knox).

Scott, James C. (1990), *Domination and the Arts of Resistance: Hidden Transcripts* (New Haven/London: Yale University Press).

Scroggs, Robin (1975), "The Earliest Christian Communities as Sectarian Movement," in Jacob Neusner, ed., *Christianity, Judaism and Other Greco-Roman Cults. Studies for Morton Smith at Sixty. Part Two: Early Christianity* (Leiden: Brill), 1–23.

Scroggs, Robin (1980), "The Sociological Interpretation of the New Testament: The Present State of Research," *NTS* 26: 164–79.

Sève, Michel (1989, 1990), *Recherches sur les Places Publiques dans le Monde Grec du Premier au Septième Siècle de Notre Ère: L'Exemple de Philippes* (Microfiche; Lille: Lille-Thèses).

Shaw, Graham (1983), *The Cost of Authority: Manipulation and Freedom in the New Testament* (Philadelphia: Fortress).

Shelton, Jo-Ann (1998), *As the Romans Did* (Oxford: Oxford University Press).

Smith, Dennis (2003), *From Symposium to Eucharist: The Banquet in the Early Christian World* (Minneapolis: Fortress).

Smith, James A. (2006), *Marks of an Apostle: Deconstruction, Philippians, and Problematizing Pauline Theology* (SemeiaSt 53; Leiden/Boston: Brill).

Smith, Jonathan Z. (1982), *Imagining Religion: From Babylon to Jonestown* (Chicago Studies in the History of Judaism; Chicago/ London: University of Chicago Press).

Smith, Jonathan Z. (1998), "Religion, Religions, Religious," in Mark C. Taylor, ed., *Critical Terms for Religious Studies* (Chicago: University of Chicago Press), 269–84.

Snyder, Graydon F. (2003), *Ante Pacem: Archaeological Evidence of Church Life Before Constantine* (Macon, GA: Mercer University Press).

Song, Robert (2006), "Sharing Communion: Hunger, Food and Genetically Modified Foods," in Stanley Hauerwas and Samuel Wells, eds., *The Blackwell Companion to Christian Ethics* (Oxford: Blackwell), 388–400.

South, James T. (1992), *Disciplinary Practices in Pauline Texts* (Lewiston, NY: Edwin Mellen).

Spawforth, A. J. S. (1996), "Roman Corinth: The Formation of a Colonial Elite," in A. D. Rizakis, ed., *Roman Onomastics in the Greek East: Social and Political Aspects* (Μελετήματα 21; Athens: Research Center for Greek and Roman Antiquity; Paris: de Boccard), 167–82.

Stegemann, Ekkehard W. and Wolfgang Stegemann (1999), *The Jesus Movement: A Social History of its First Century* (Edinburgh: T&T Clark).

Stepp, Perry L. (2005), *Leadership Succession in the World of the Pauline Circle* (NT Monographs 5; Sheffield: Sheffield Phoenix Press).

Stowers, Stanley K. (1985), "The Social Sciences and the Study of Early Christianity," in William S. Green, ed., *Approaches to Ancient Judaism Vol. 5: Studies in Judaism and its Greco-Roman Context* (Atlanta: Scholars), 149–81.

Stowers, Stanley K. (2001), "Does Pauline Christianity Resemble a Hellenistic Philosophy?" in Troels Engberg-Pedersen, ed., *Paul Beyond the Judaism/Hellenism Divide* (Louisville, KY: Westminster John Knox), 81–102.

Still, Todd D. (1999), *Conflict at Thessalonica: A Pauline Church and its Neighbours* (JSNTSup 183; Sheffield: Sheffield Academic Press).

Still, Todd D. (2003a), "Historical Anachronism and Ministerial Ordination: A Response to David E. Garland," in William H. Brackney, ed., *Baptists and Ordination* (Macon, GA: National Association of Baptist Professors of Religion), 38–44.

Still, Todd D. (2003b), "Paul: An Appealing and/or Appalling Apostle," *ExpT* 114: 111–18.

Still, Todd D. (2005), "Philemon among the Letters of Paul: Theological and Canonical Considerations," *ResQ* 47: 133–42.

Still, Todd D. (2007), "Interpretive Ambiguities and Scholarly Proclivities: A Treatment of Three Texts from 1 Thessalonians 4 as a Test Case," *CBR* 5: 207–19.

Still, Todd D. (2008), "An Overview of Recent Scholarly Literature on Philippians," *ExpT* 119: 422–28.

Sugirtharajah, R. S. (2002), *Postcolonial Criticism and Biblical Interpretation* (Oxford: Oxford University Press).

Sutton, David E. (2001), *Remembrance of Repasts: An Anthropology of Food and Memory* (Oxford/New York: Berg).

Sykes, Stephen (2006), *Power and Christian Theology* (London/New York: Continuum).

Taussig, Hal (2002), "Promise and Problems in the Application of Ritual Studies to Greco-Roman Meals," accessed online July 2008 at http://www.philipharland.com/meals/2002%20Taussig%20Paper.pdf.

Taylor, Nicholas (1992), *Paul, Antioch and Jerusalem: A Study in Relationships and Authority in Earliest Christianity* (JSNTSup 66; Sheffield: JSOT Press).

Theissen, Gerd (1979 [3rd ed., 1988]), *Studien zur Soziologie des Urchristentums* (WUNT 19; Tübingen: Mohr Siebeck).

Theissen, Gerd (1982), *The Social Setting of Pauline Christianity* (trans. John H. Schütz; Edinburgh: T&T Clark).

Theissen, Gerd (1985), "Review of W. Meeks, *The First Urban Christians*," *JR* 65: 111–13.

Theissen, Gerd (1987), *Psychological Aspects of Pauline Theology* (Edinburgh: T&T Clark).

Theissen, Gerd (1993), *Social Reality and the Early Christians: Theology, Ethics, and the World of the New Testament* (Edinburgh: T&T Clark).

Theissen, Gerd (1999), *A Theory of Primitive Christian Religion* (London: SCM).

Thiselton, Anthony C. (2000), *The First Epistle to the Corinthians* (NIGTC; Grand Rapids: Eerdmans).

Thompson, Michael (1991), *Clothed with Christ: The Example and Teaching of Jesus in Romans 12.1–15.13* (JSNTSup 59; Sheffield: JSOT Press).

Thompson, Michael (1998), "The Holy Internet: Communication between Churches in the First Christian Generation," in Bauckham, ed., 49–70.

Tuzin, Donald (1977), "Reflections on Being in Arapesh Water Symbolism," *Ethos* 5: 195–223.

Veyne, Paul (1990), *Bread and Circuses: Historical Sociology and Political Pluralism* (London: Penguin).

Vial, Theodore M. (1999), "Opposites Attract: The Body and Cognition in a Debate over Baptism," *Numen* 46: 121–45.

vom Brocke, Christoph (2001), *Thessaloniki—Stadt des Kassader und Gemeinde des Paulus* (WUNT 2.125; Tübingen: Mohr Siebeck).

Wagner, J. Ross (2002), *Heralds of the Good News: Isaiah and Paul in Concert in the Letter to the Romans* (Leiden/Boston: Brill).

Wallace-Hadrill, Andrew, ed. (1990), *Patronage in Ancient Society* (London: Routledge).

Wallace-Hadrill, Andrew (1991), "Elites and Trade in the Roman Town," in Rich and Wallace-Hadrill, eds., 241–72.

Wallace-Hadrill, Andrew (1994), *Houses and Society in Pompeii and Herculaneum* (Princeton: Princeton University Press).

Wallace-Hadrill, Andrew (1998), "Region I, Insula 9: The British Project" (first part of article), in Berry, ed., 49, 52–56, 60–62.

Walters, James C. (1993), *Ethnic Issues in Paul's Letter to the Romans: Changing Self-Definitions in Earliest Roman Christianity* (Valley Forge, PN: Trinity Press International).

Walters, James C. (2005), "Civic Identity in Roman Corinth and its Impact on Early Christians," in Schowalter and Friesen, eds., 397–417.

Wankel, Hermann, ed. (1979–84), *Die Inschriften von Ephesos* (Inschriften griechischer Städte aus Kleinasien; vols. 11–17; Bonn: Habelt).

Ware, James P. (2005), *The Mission of the Church in Paul's Letter to the Philippians in Light of the Context of Ancient Judaism* (NovTSup 120; Leiden/Boston: Brill).

Watson, Francis (2004), *Paul and the Hermeneutics of Faith* (London/New York: T&T Clark).

Wedderburn, Alexander, J. M. (1988), *The Reasons for Romans* (SNTW; Edinburgh: T&T Clark).

Weima, Jeffrey A. D. and Stanley E. Porter (1998), *An Annotated Bibliography of 1 and 2 Thessalonians* (NTTS 26; Leiden/Boston/Köln: Brill).

Weissenrieder, Annette, Friederike Wendt, and Petra von Gemünden, eds. (2005), *Picturing the New Testament: Studies in Ancient Visual Images* (WUNT 2.193; Tübingen: Mohr Siebeck).

White, L. Michael (1990), *The Social Origins of Christian Architecture, Vol. 1: Building God's House in the Roman World: Architectural Adaptation among Pagans, Jews, and Christians* (HTS 42; Valley Forge, PA: Trinity Press International).

White, L. Michael (1997), *The Social Origins of Christian Architecture, Vol. 2: Texts and Monuments of the Christian Domus Ecclesiae in its Environment* (HTS 42; Valley Forge, PA: Trinity Press International).

White, L. Michael (1999), "Reading the Ostia Synagogue: A Reply to A. Runesson," *HTR* 92: 435–64.

Whitehouse, Harvey (1996), "Rites of Terror: Emotion, Metaphor and Memory in Melanesian Initiation Cults," *Journal of the Royal Anthropological Institute* 2: 703–15.

Williams, Charles K., II and Nancy Bookidis, eds. (2003), *Corinth: The Centenary, 1896–1996* (Corinth XX; Princeton: ASCS).

Williams, Demetrius K. (2002), *Enemies of the Cross of Christ: The Terminology of the Cross and Conflict in Philippians* (JSNTSup 223; London: Sheffield Academic Press).

Wilson, Andrew (1992), "The Pragmatics of Politeness and Pauline Epistolography: A Case Study of the Letter of Philemon," *JSNT* 48: 107–19.

Wilson, Brian (1970), *Religious Sects* (London: Weidenfield and Nicholson).

Wilson, Stephen G. (1996), "Voluntary Associations," in Kloppenborg and Wilson, eds., 1–15.

Wilson, Stephen G. (2004), *Leaving the Fold: Apostates and Defectors in Antiquity* (Minneapolis: Fortress).

Winter, Bruce (1994), *Seek the Welfare of the City: Christians as Benefactors and Citizens* (Grand Rapids: Eerdmans).

Winter, Bruce W. (2001), *After Paul Left Corinth: The Influence of Secular Ethics and Social Change* (Grand Rapids: Eerdmans).

Witherington, Ben (1995), *Conflict and Community in Corinth: A Socio-Rhetorical Commentary on 1 and 2 Corinthians* (Grand Rapids: Eerdmans).

Wire, Antoinette Clark (1990), *The Corinthian Women Prophets: A Reconstruction Through Paul's Rhetoric* (Minneapolis: Fortress).

Woolf, Greg (2006), "Writing Poverty in Rome," in Margaret Atkins and Robin Osbourne, eds., *Poverty in the Roman World* (Cambridge: Cambridge University Press), 83–99.

Wuellner, W. H. (1973), "The Sociological Implications of I Corinthians 1:26-28 Reconsidered," in Elizabeth A. Livingstone, ed., *Studia Evangelica* VI (TU 112; Berlin: Akademie Verlag), 666–72.

Zanker, Paul (1998), *Pompeii: Public and Private Life* (trans. D. L. Schneider; Cambridge: Harvard University Press).

INDEX OF BIBLICAL AND ANCIENT REFERENCES

INDEX OF MODERN AUTHORS

Spawforth, A. 34
Staab, K. 36n.1
Stegemann, E. 102
Stegemann, W. 18, 102
Stepp, P. 88
Still, T. 3, 31, 87, 89nn.6 and 8, 94, 96n.21, 111, 134, 142–3
Stowers, S. 4, 73nn.20 and 21, 74, 102, 131n.8, 132
Strecker, C. 106
Sugirtharajah, R. S. 19
Sutton, D. 14, 15, 108
Sykes, S. 97

Taussig, H. 99n.1
Taylor, N. 80
Theissen, G. 1, 6–8, 12, 39, 43, 66n.8, 88, 101, 111, 125, 126, 131
Thiselton, A. 49n.26
Thompson, E. P. 19
Thompson, M. 71n.16, 91n.13
Turner, V. 7, 101, 103, 112
Tuzin, D. 112

Van Gennep, A. 100, 103, 112
Veyne, P. 43
Vom Brocke, C. 31, 32
Von Campenhausen, H. 88

Wagner, J. R. 91n.15
Wallace-Hadrill, A. 23n.1, 27, 28, 66, 67n.9, 68
Walters, J. 34, 90n.9
Wankel, H. 141
Ware, J. 92
Watson, F. 91n.15
Weber, M. 88, 137
Wedderburn, A. J. 90n.10
Weima, J. A. 89n.8
Weissenrieder, A. 19
Wendt, F. 19
White, L. M. 63n.4, 64, 68, 71, 72n.19, 77n.28
Whitehouse, H. 112
Wilken, R. 21
Williams, C. 32
Williams, D. 92
Wilson, A. 93
Wilson, B. 88
Wilson, S. 56, 68, 87
Winter, B. 8, 33
Wire, A. C. 130
Witherington, B. 9
Woolf, G. 43
Wuellner, W. H. 39

Zanker, P. 25

INDEX OF SUBJECTS